Planting Your Family Tree Online

How to Create Your Own
Family History
Web Site

Cyndi Howells
Creator of Cyndi's List

Amy Johnson Crow, CG
Series Editor

Rutledge Hill Press®
Nashville, Tennessee

A Division of Thomas Nelson, Inc.
www.ThomasNelson.com

Published by Rutledge Hill Press, a Division of Thomas Nelson, Inc., P.O. Box 141000, Nashville, Tennessee 37214.

All Web site addresses in this book were verified prior to printing.

The following items mentioned in this book are registered trademarks or service marks:

Active Server Pages, ActiveX, Adobe Acrobat Reader, Adobe Illustrator, Adobe Photoshop, Adobe Photoshop Elements, AlltheWeb, AltaVista, Amazon.com, America Online, Ancestral File, Ancestral Quest, Ancestry, Ancestry.com, Ancestry Family Tree, Angelfire, AOL, Apple, Arachnophilia, ASP, Atomz, AT&T Worldnet, AutoScripter, BBEdit, Bobby, Bravenet, Brother's Keeper, Church of Jesus Christ of Latter-day Saints, Coffee Cup, CuteFTP, CyberSpyder, Cyndi's List, CyndisList.com, Dreamweaver, Earthlink, Eastman's Online Genealogy Newsletter, Family History Center, Family History Library, Family Origins, FamilySearch, FamilySearch.org, Family Tree Maker, Fetch, Fortune City, FreeFind, FrontPage, FTP Explorer, GED2GO, GED2HTML, GED2Web, GED2WWW, GED4WEB, GEDClean32, GEDCOM, GedHTree, GEDLiving, Gedpage, GeDStrip, GENDEX, Genealogical Publishing Company, Genealogy.com, Genealogy Home Page, Genealogy Site Builder, Generations, GeneWeb, GeoCities, Google, HotDog, IGI, International Society of Family History Writers and Editors, Inc., Internet Explorer, Iomega, Java, JavaScript, Kinship Archivist, Legacy, LinkAlarm, Linux, Macintosh, Macromedia Flash, Macromedia HomeSite, The Master Genealogist, Microsoft, MISSING LINKS: A Magazine for Genealogists, Mozilla, MSN, MyFamily.com, National Genealogical Society, NetLingo, Netscape Navigator, Network Solutions, NoteTab, Opera, Oxy-gen, PAF, Paint Shop Pro, Pedigree Resource File, PerlGed, Personal Ancestral File, phpGedView, PicoSearch, PKZip, QuickTime, RealPlayer, Register.com, Relatives, Res Privata, Reunion, RootsMagic, RootsView, RootsWeb, RootsWeb.com, Second Site, Shockwave, Sparrowhawk, Stuffit, TextPipe Pro, Tripod, uFTi, UncleGED, Unix, UpFront with NGS, U.S. Copyright Office, USGenWeb, Verisign, Visual Basic, Windows, Windows Media Player, WinZip, WS_FTP, XReplace-32, Yahoo!, Zip Disk, ZipIt.

Library of Congress Cataloging-in-Publication Data

Howells, Cyndi.
    Planting your family tree online : how to create your own family history web site / Cyndi Howells.
      p. cm. — (National Genealogical Society guides)
    Includes indexes.
    ISBN 1-4016-0022-0 (pbk.)
    1. Web sites. 2. Genealogy—Computer network resources. I. Title. II. Series.
CS21.H76 2003
929'.1'028567—dc22   2003020410

Printed in the United States of America

03 04 05 06 07 — 5 4 3 2 1

To those in my family who came before me and paved the way, no matter how difficult the path, so that my life . . . would be

Contents

Acknowledgments

CREATING AND MAINTAINING WEB SITES, ALONG WITH A PROJECT TO WRITE A BOOK about that process, are not endeavors I could have done alone. Throughout the years, the constructive criticism I have received from visitors to my own Web site has served me well and given me the ability to see my site as others see it. Without this useful input, my site wouldn't work as well as it does today. For this book, several people helped me with technical details, proofreading, and feedback, generously sharing their time and giving me invaluable advice. My thanks go to Sam Behling, Ann Fleming, Pam Porter, Bob Velke, and the editorial team for all their help. And while I was focusing on the book, my house and Web site would have fallen apart if it weren't for Krista McCauley and Michele Ingle, both of whom I am exceedingly lucky to have in my life. Of course, none of this would be possible without the unlimited help, support, and faith of my husband, Mark.

INTRODUCTION

Who Should Read This Book?

WHETHER YOU HAVE BEEN A FAMILY HISTORIAN FOR A FEW MONTHS OR for several years, odds are that you have thought about publishing the results of your research. You may have thought of writing the definitive book about your own family. Or of printing a set of charts and forms for each of your cousins. You may even have thought of trying your hand at creating a photo album or scrapbook filled with family anecdotes and photos.

Have you given any thought to publishing on the Web?

We genealogists begin our family history adventure for a variety of reasons. A death in the family prompts some of us to start asking questions about our ancestors. Others of us set off down the family history trail after we attend a family event—a wedding, reunion, or holiday gathering. We enthusiastically interview the elderly members of our family, recording every detail and fact they can recall about our ancestors. We contact long-lost cousins and network with others on the Internet, gathering everything we can find about our family. We invest in genealogy software and begin the process of entering thousands of names, dates, and places into our own personal genealogy database. Many of us also start playing with snazzy new techno-toys like scanners and digital cameras.

Next, we reflect, slowing down to take stock of what we know—and what we don't know. We read books, attend seminars, and join our local genealogical society in an effort to learn everything we can about family history research. We begin to organize our files, to put order to the chaotic bits of data and family memorabilia that we have collected along the way. As we look to the past, we think about the future and recognize the need to preserve the family records and treasures we are working so hard to collect, our family letters, diaries, Bibles, and photographs. We set some research goals and consider more thoughtfully *why* we pursue these genealogical mysteries. That's when we realize we are hooked—genealogy has become our life.

Are you at the point that you want to share what you know with your cousins? Do you want to publish your research for other family members to treasure long after you're gone? If so, you should read this book.

Planting Your Family Tree Online is designed to take you step by step through the process of creating your own genealogy Web site. Each chapter in the book leads you logically through a new aspect of your family history Web site project. Each chapter can also stand on its own as a reference for key concepts as you continue to work on your Web site. So even if you already have a genealogy Web site, this book can help you develop and maintain your site. If you follow the steps outlined throughout this book, you will have a wonderful Web site that honors the memory of your ancestors. In these pages you'll discover all the terrific ways that having a family history Web site enhances your research and brings your family members (both living and dead) closer to you.

The subtitle for this book could have been "All the Things Cyndi Learned the Hard Way." As I show you how to plan, create, and personalize your family history site, I share with you all the dos and don'ts I've learned from my experiences creating and maintaining Cyndi's List, my own comprehensive genealogy Web site. As Webmaster of Cyndi's List, I review the thousands of genealogy sites that are linked from my index. In these pages, I tell you about the successes and failures I see every day so you'll know what to emulate—and what to avoid at all costs. You'll learn how to make your site easy to use, index, reference, and maintain.

The Webmaster's job is not over once the site is created. Your online family tree must be nurtured. You'll find out how to select a Web hosting service, a place for you to plant your family history Web site. You'll learn how to test your site and look at it with a critical eye—and how to tell the world about it. And you'll find plenty of ideas for the care and feeding of your Web site over the long term.

In this book, I focus on all the tools and resources you need to present your family's history in an easy-to-use, reliable format that works for everyone online. I give you some basic tips for using HTML (Hyper Text Markup Language), the language of the World Wide Web that is used to display Web pages within a browser, and I help you with the HTML you must use in order to produce a high-quality family history Web site. The technical details of how to write HTML and other topics are beyond the scope of this book, but throughout the book, I point you to a wealth of online resources to help you in the process of creating your site.

As you read these chapters, you will learn about genealogy software as it pertains to creating genealogy Web pages. Software products are constantly being introduced and updated, so rather than engaging in the impossible task of teaching you to use every genealogy software program on the market, I instead supply you with the information you need to locate help elsewhere for using genealogy software to generate Web sites. You'll also find helpful computer tips and advice about scanning photographs and using photo-editing software to prepare your photos and digitized documents for the Web. Of course, computers, scanners, and photo-editing software packages differ, so you should refer to your user manuals for details on how to make the most of your own setup.

I have endeavored to keep the content of this book straightforward so that it is accessible to readers with all levels of computer experience. But there may be terms and phrases that are new to you. Throughout the book, you will find sidebars with examples, helpful hints, and definitions of terms. At the end of the book, an extensive glossary of terms and phrases provides you with a quick reference as you go about building your own Web pages.

In addition, this book is loaded with URLs to Web sites that give you everything you need to create a beautiful family tree online. The drawback of printing Web site addresses is that they can become outdated the second the ink hits the paper. Web site URLs change daily. As you use the book, you may find that some URLs no longer work. I have provided a solution for you online with Web pages that correspond to the features in this book:

Planting Your Family Tree Online
How To Create Your Own Family History Web Site
www.CyndisList.com/planting/

The Web pages are updated regularly. So if you find a URL in the book that no longer works—or if you prefer not to type out all those long Web addresses—use the online pages to make things easier. The Web pages also contain copies of some of the samples and examples provided in this book. For example, Chapter 6 includes HTML templates for a family group sheet and a basic Web page. Chapter 12 has text you can use in e-mail messages to make online announcements. The Web pages provide those files online so that you can easily copy and paste the text to your own documents or e-mail messages. These files and URLs will be a valuable resource as you work through the book and develop your Web site.

As your Web site expands and your enthusiasm for genealogy grows, you may find that you want to learn more about how to research your family history. For a basic introduction to all aspects of genealogical research, I recommend another book in the National Genealogical Society (NGS) series—*Genealogy 101: How to Trace Your Family's History and Heritage* by Barbara Renick. For a detailed guide on how to use the Internet for genealogical research, be sure to read the NGS book *Online Roots: How to Discover Your Family's History and Heritage with the Power of the Internet* by Pamela Boyer Porter, CGRS, CGL, and Amy Johnson Crow, CG.

Publishing your own personal family history Web site is now a vital part of genealogical research. The rewards of putting your research online and the almost immediate benefits make the effort well worth your while. When you stop to think about it, the ability to honor our ancestors by sharing their story with the rest of the world each day is astounding. During the last several centuries, many of our ancestors migrated across oceans and across nations—willingly and unwillingly—with family members becoming separated from one another. Now, as cousins meet online and share information, we come full circle and bring those family lines together again, meeting electronically and sharing our love of history and respect for our ancestors.

Now it is time for you to publish your own genealogy Web site and bring your family's history full circle.

CHAPTER 1

Why You Need a Genealogy Web Site

YOU NEED A GENEALOGY WEB SITE. TRUST ME, YOU NEED ONE.

You need a genealogy Web site to help you find those dozens of cousins who are waiting to meet you. The cousins who have boxes of family photos sitting in their attic. The cousins who know hundreds of stories that will enhance and help prove (or disprove) what you already know about your ancestors.

You need a genealogy Web site to help you find that one cousin you have been looking for over the past several years—the only cousin left in one of your family's lines. The cousin with the family Bible and the quilt made by your great-great-grandmother.

You need a genealogy Web site to help you begin the process of preserving your research, your family photos, and what you have gathered so far in the search for your ancestors. Starting the process of publishing your family history in small portions on a Web site sets you off on the road to publishing a larger, more complete work later.

You need a genealogy Web site to help you break down the brick walls that have stumped you throughout your research. Having a Web site is a great way for you to reach out to your family and your fellow researchers, anytime and anywhere in the world. Many veteran genealogists who have been researching their family tree for decades are now able to use personal Web sites to solve research puzzles that had mystified them for years—just by connecting with the right person online (a cousin, a fellow genealogist, or an expert on a particular topic). Their Web sites helped put the last piece into place to complete their hard-to-solve genealogical puzzle and prove a vital point in their research.

You need a genealogy Web site to help you and your fellow family historians learn better ways to research your families. A new site published with what you know about your family tree can be the outline from which you plan your next step to learn more about genealogical records and methods for research. It can be the tool that helps you evaluate where you are in your research and identify the areas that need more attention. In this way, your Web site can serve as an educational tool for you and for others who follow your research.

The Many Faces of Online Publishing

This book covers information about one significant method you can use to plant your family tree online—a personal genealogy Web site of your own. There are many other ways you can publish genealogical data on the Internet: e-mail messages, mailing lists, message boards, chat rooms, instant messaging, commercial databases, volunteer projects, and Web sites owned by others. Many of the same rules apply to publishing in those areas that apply to publishing your own Web site, especially principles involving privacy, copyright, sources, quality, and accessibility. However, the focus of this book will be to help you design a great family history Web site of which you can be proud.

Publishing in Pixels versus Publishing in Ink

Back in the "old days" (as far back as ten years ago), publishing your family history meant doing so in ink, on paper, generally in book form. Even now, if you want to publish your research in book form, you have a lot to consider. First is the concern about printing your *final* work. Many people prefer to finish their research before printing it in a book. They want to be sure they have all the facts straight before making such a big commitment to publish.

Once you put your words and data into ink, printed on paper, there is a feeling of finality. If you publish a book or an article in a newsletter or journal, that work is generally considered finished and then stands on its own. You can always publish updates or amendments to the book or the article, but these are separate publications that aren't always found with or near the original publication. You cannot control the distribution of the original material—or the amendments. You cannot guarantee that the amended details will always be attached to the original published data. Libraries may obtain copies of your book or copies of the amendment, individually or together. In the end, someone might have access to your book, but never learn about any updates you have published.

Lineage-Linked Databases

Rather than publish a genealogy Web site, some people opt for submitting their personal research databases to lineage-linked databases, sometimes known as pedigree-linked databases. These are common databases used by numerous people to pool their data with that of others. On the Internet you will find lineage-linked databases run by commercial enterprises, nonprofit groups, volunteer projects, and private individuals. In general, there are no criteria or standards for supplying proofs or sources for the data within these databases. Because of that, the information found in lineage-linked databases is made up of the good, the bad, and the ugly—the proven and the unproven. Additionally, once the data is submitted, it most often cannot be updated, edited, or deleted. Putting your data in a lineage-linked database is a one-time deposit to an archive, rather than a true opportunity to publish, manage, and control that data yourself the way you can do on a personal Web site.

Finances

Another consideration is the financial aspect of printing a book. You have to compile the book and put it into a format that can be printed. You may have to invest time and money in several software programs—a desktop publishing program, an indexing program, at least a word processor. If you plan to include pictures or documents in your book, you may have to invest in a scanner and scanning software in order to make copies of your family photos and precious documents. After preparing the book for printing, you must find a family history publisher. You must decide how many copies to have printed. Most likely, you want to have a copy for yourself, a few for various libraries and genealogical societies, plus several more for cousins. In deciding how many books to print, your budget often determines how generous you can be (do you plan to give away copies of the book?) or whether you should take orders for the book before printing. Many family historians opt for a short print run—a one-time printing with a small, limited number of copies. But for a short print run of thirty copies, you can easily spend a few hundred, or even a few thousand, dollars. The money alone often becomes the driving force behind a person's decision to wait and print *after* they feel they have completed their research.

When Will You Publish a Book?

Ask yourself these questions about printing your research in a book:

- When do I pause in my current research task and put the facts I have gathered to date onto paper?

- How do I determine when I am completely "finished" with my research on any one family line?

- At what point do I become comfortable enough with the data I have gathered to share it with others?

- What happens if I collect new information about my ancestors after I have published a book?

- Am I ready to spend the money to publish a book and have multiple copies printed?

The answers to these questions vary from person to person. Some people choose to research for a number of years and gather as much verifiable data as possible before publishing any of their findings. Others are comfortable publishing basic data about their family found early in their family history research. What most family historians discover as they work more and more on their research is that no one is ever truly "finished" with research. The answer to one question always leads to more questions. One found ancestor leads to the search for two other ancestors. It can truly be a lifelong task for those who want to carefully document and verify each fact before they publish what they know.

But generally, there comes a point in the research on one family line or another when you realize it may be time to publish what you know to date about that ancestor or family. You make your choice based on your budget, your comfort level with what you have done to date, and what your ultimate goal is—a long-term research project that culminates in a final published work for everyone or a short-term project to publish for current family members, a work that you or others can improve upon in the future.

Turn to the Web

If you take the long-term approach and prefer not to publish your research in book form for several years, turn your thoughts to publishing online instead. A Web site and the documents put online for others to read are not static like books. Web sites are living, dynamic creations that can change as often as you need them to. You can publish your Web site one day, locate a terrific new bit of genealogical data the next day, and update your Web site with the new data that same day. Because this is so easy to do, the question of whether or not you are "finished" is no longer an issue. You don't have to stop researching before publishing.

And publishing online doesn't have to be expensive. Because you aren't publishing anything in the physical realm, there's no cost for paper, ink, binding, or shipping. The only expenses you incur are the computer hardware or software you need to create the Web site. Most new Webmasters find that the necessary hardware and software are already available on their computer and through sources on the Internet. If you are connected to the Internet through an Internet Service Provider (ISP), most likely you already have Web space available to you as part of your monthly fee. The decision to publish online isn't driven by your financial budget.

Check your own Internet Service Provider's Web site to learn about the benefits your ISP provides to customers, including Web hosting services and helpful Web design tools. See Chapter 2 for more information about services provided by ISPs.

The only question that remains the same in regard to publishing in ink versus publishing in pixels is this: When do you feel comfortable enough with your research findings to share them with others? If you publish a book, only a few who visit a library can view your findings, only during the hours when the library is open to the public. On the Internet, your findings are available to the entire world, twenty-four hours a day, seven days a week. Search engines, link lists, bookmarks, favorites, and word of mouth all guarantee that more people will see your Web site than ever would have seen your book. This means you have an even greater responsibility to publish your work online with care and caution. As we proceed in this book, we will discuss all the important points you should consider in order to do just that.

Pixels are small units on your computer's monitor that use light and color to display an image on the screen.

Always a Work in Progress

Anyone who has been compiling a family history for more than a few months quickly becomes aware that genealogical research is never finished. It is always a work in progress. There is always one more fact to confirm and an endless number of questions to ask. And each answer you find leads you to a dozen more questions.

If you are researching each of your ancestors through your great-grandparents, you are working to prove the ancestral lines for fifteen individual people with eight different surnames—you, two parents, four grandparents, and eight great-grandparents. To do this right requires a great deal of time and energy. If you plan to finish researching one specific family line before you publish any of your findings, it will be many years before you publish your work about just that one family. If you plan to publish your research about each family line, you will spend many more years to accomplish your goal. This is one of the reasons that for many people, genealogy becomes a life-long hobby.

A responsible genealogist always identifies a work in progress as such, so as not to cause any confusion or mislead anyone into thinking that anything read on the Web site is a final conclusion or final outcome for research on any one individual or family.

Publishing on the Internet is a perfect complement to genealogical research. Just as your research evolves and changes with time, Web sites are always a work in progress. Therefore, publishing your family history online as you are doing the research is a perfect fit. What you publish on your Web site should reflect the progress you have made in your research on each family line. Think of your Web site as an ongoing research diary or virtual workbook that you publish online and update on a regular basis. In many ways, publishing your research on a genealogy Web site can be a prelude to publishing that final paper-and-ink version. The Web site may be the outline for the book you plan to publish later.

I mentioned earlier that researching your great-grandparents' generation means following the lines of eight surnames in your ancestry. That's the example used throughout this book. In fact, you can think of your own research as being sorted into at least eight different chapters or sections for your Web site. To begin with, each of the eight sections is brief. But as inspiration comes, you begin to flesh out one section or more at a time. As serendipity and fate intervene, you may find yourself spending more time on one section than another. While each section of your Web site grows—and as you become a better genealogical researcher yourself—it also changes, evolving into a more structured, accurate, and balanced representation of your family's history. As you grow, so does your Web site. As your research expands, so will your online publication.

Leave a Trail for Your Cousins to Follow

Traditionally, researching the family has been a solitary affair, with the family historian being the oddball who sits in the corner interviewing all the family members at every holiday and family get-together. It wasn't often that we found close family members who were interested in genealogy. Many cousins might have been interested in hearing about the family's history from you, especially those juicy bits filled with scandalous villains and ne'er-do-wells, but those same cousins didn't generally want to do the research themselves. Also, it wasn't often that we found long-lost, distant cousins with whom we share the same second or third great-grandparents. But the Internet has changed all that. The family genealogist is no longer alone. Cousins are now coming out of the virtual woodwork.

The Internet has made it easy for people to find lost family members, old friends,

The Sanderlin Genealogy Gene

My internal drive to locate my ancestors has to come from one of my paternal grandfather's lines. I know this now without a doubt—I have one specific gene in my DNA that can be traced directly back to my fourth great-grandfather, Thomas Jefferson Sanderlin. I know this is a dominant gene because at least forty other people share this gene with me. They are all cousins, they are all genealogists, and they all stalk me on the Internet.

It all began on 4 March 1996 when I published a story on my personal Web site about my third great-grandfather (Thomas's son), Isaac Spears Sanderlin. Within two months, the first Sanderlin cousin found me. Since that time more than forty Sanderlin cousins have contacted me after running across my story about Isaac online. In just a few years, I gained forty new, genealogically crazed cousins like me.

I haven't done any further research on my Sanderlin line. Yet I now know details about several lines of Isaac's family and his father's that I didn't know before. I have a copy of a Civil War photo of Thomas in his Union uniform. I have a copy of Isaac's Civil War diary, which I hadn't even known existed. And I have had the great pleasure of meeting several of my Sanderlin cousins in person. All because I took the time to publish just one story, about just one ancestor, on my Web site. The rest, as they say, is history—family history.

and misplaced acquaintances. People find one another in a variety of ways: mailing lists, message boards, chat rooms, and Web sites. Every day genealogists place queries on message boards or discuss their research roadblocks on genealogy mailing lists. But leaving your trail of breadcrumbs on these types of message forums relies on a hit-and-miss randomness for people to find your note. Message boards on Web sites aren't always included in search engine indexes, so leaving your message there means you must hope for a cousin to browse the same message on that message board at some point in the future in order to find you. Many mailing lists are archived and searchable, but these may not be further indexed by search engines. So again you cross your fingers and hope that a distant relation stumbles across your note. Instead, you should be sure to use every avenue available to you in order to post queries and messages online. Don't discount these valuable resources, but don't rely on mailing lists and message boards alone.

Publishing your own genealogy Web site puts you in the driver's seat. You do not have to depend on luck for fellow researchers to find you. Your genealogy site stands on its own, with distinct URLs for each Web page on your site. The manner in which you publish your Web site gives you the power to grab the attention of those cousins you hope find you. The name of your site, the way you arrange your site, and the features you include on it all help your cousins spot you quickly. You can work to have your Web site included in search engine indexes, and you can advertise the various URLs for your Web site on mailing lists and other message forums, as well as through links on other Web sites. Having specific URLs to reference means that you can leave a very visible trail for your cousins to follow and make contact with you. Your genealogy Web site is a billboard on the information highway—in plain sight for all your online cousins to easily notice.

A **URL** (Uniform Resource Locator) is the address for a Web site or file stored on a Web server. URLs are used in bookmarks, favorites, and hypertext links.

Help Fellow Genealogists and Set an Example for Others

Genealogists are helpful in nature, and sharing is a customary attribute. Ask twenty genealogists a question, and you can expect to receive twenty answers (sometimes even twenty *different* answers), along with numerous offers of help in the future. A Web site is the perfect vehicle for you to help other genealogists and for you to receive help in return. You can use your Web site to post requests for help—or offers of help. Your Web site can become your soapbox and the way you make your mark in the genealogical community. Reaching out to help others is one of the best ways to be sure that you get the help you need when the time comes.

Through our publications online, we can also help others to learn something new. The first exposure that most people now have to genealogical research is through the Web. These new family historians take what they learn online and apply it to their research. So publishing your site gives you the opportunity to teach by example. You might publish helpful tips and information, and share what you know with others.

You can post details and addresses for record repositories that you frequently use. You might share your success stories, as well as stories of your failures so that others learn from your mistakes. In fact, many researchers who have been at this for a while will learn from you when they visit your site. By clearly marking, labeling, and defining your research on your Web site, you can set an example for all genealogists, both new-bie and veteran, by publishing truthfully, honestly, and with integrity.

Now you know that you need a genealogy Web site for many reasons: Compared to publishing a book, a family history Web site saves you money and gets your research published more quickly in order to share with people worldwide. It serves as a working research tool to help you track down specific ancestors. A family history site puts you in contact with cousins and other genealogists, which serves to improve and enrich your entire research experience. As a work in progress, your genealogy Web site outlines and highlights your research and helps direct you on the cyberpath to your ancestors.

Your next step is to determine the type of site you want. Your genealogy Web site can be as small or as large as you want. It can be one page long with minimum information—a brief list of surnames, dates, and places. It can branch out to a handful of pages, with one page devoted to each surname you're researching. Or your site might be made up of hundreds of Web pages devoted to every person in your database. Your site may contain one photo or dozens of photos and digitized documents. The possibilities are endless.

Do you see yourself publishing only something small? Or do you have big dreams for your site? Perhaps you think you might start out small and work up to something larger as time passes. Do you want to bring one of your favorite ancestors to life online? Or would you like to honor several of them? No matter what answer you come up with, you need to know that you are committing yourself to a project that needs planning, attention to detail, and maintenance as time passes. In the chapters ahead, we will walk step by step through finding a place to publish your site, planning your site, creating your site, personalizing the site, testing the site, advertising the site, and maintaining the site over the long term.

CHAPTER 2

Find a Home for Your Web Site

IF YOU PLAN TO PUBLISH A BOOK OF YOUR FAMILY HISTORY, YOU normally consider how to write the book and you prepare the majority of it first, before starting to look for a publisher or printer to make the final product for you. But in preparing to publish a Web site, you do almost the complete opposite. Finding a home for your Web site first helps you make other decisions as you move on to the next step in planning and designing your site. Depending on which tools and features it makes available for your use, the host for your Web site influences how you design your site. Selecting your Web hosting service first is a bit like buying a plot of land before you begin to plant your trees. You need to know what the lay of the land is in order to properly till the soil, plant the seeds, and nurture the seedling.

Most people find a host and then plan their site. They want to explore available options before they commit time, energy, and money to publish on the Web. You may already have an idea where you want your genealogy Web site to be hosted, and you probably already have Web space allotted to you by your ISP. But you may prefer to plan the details of the Web site *before* looking for a Web site host. Then you have a clear idea of the size of the Web site and what special features you might use on the site. Having some specific figures for the size of the site ahead of time can be an advantage during your search for a Web host. If you prefer to plan your site first, skip ahead to Chapters 3 and 4, and then return to this chapter to learn how to find a host that suits your needs. Of course, no matter how much you plan ahead, your site will eventually change, evolving into something that you cannot see clearly now.

What to Look For

The first step is to locate a Web hosting service or a Web server on which you can place your Web pages. What is the difference between the two? A Web server is the physical piece of hardware—the computer—on which a Web site is stored and accessed by visitors. Some Web hosting services are specifically designed to host Web sites. They supply the Web server and storage space for your site. They generally offer you a variety of tools (hardware, software, guides) and the support that you need to publish your Web site. But you can also find Web server space for your Web pages elsewhere, including your current ISP, or through a friend or acquaintance. If you use Web server space in a place that isn't officially a Web hosting service, you may not have the same tools and support available to you.

A **Web server** is a computer that hosts files for Web sites—graphics, Web pages, and so on. Web servers can be large powerful computers or computers similar to yours at home. They run constantly each day and are identifiable on the Internet by a unique address. When Internet users visit a Web site, their browsers make a request of the Web server to view the pages and graphics located on that server, at that specific URL.

You must consider at least three important issues when seeking a home for your Web site. You need enough physical server space in which to publish your Web pages. You need a stable, reliable host server to serve up your pages. And you need a long-term home for your Web site that will supply you with an established URL for many years to come.

Space

As your research expands, your Web site grows. You need file space for the Web pages you create and for all the additional graphics (scanned photos, digitized documents, and such) that you place on the site. Each Web page is one file. Each photo is an additional file. You must consider the file size for each of these and have a general understanding of how large your entire site might be when you put it online. The file sizes of individual Web pages themselves are usually quite small because they are composed of plain text. They differ from other files you may use regularly, such as word-processing files, which contain a lot of extraneous file formatting that adds to the overall file size. But the majority of the space taken up on your Web site comes from scanned images (see Chapter 9).

MB is an abbreviation for megabyte, which is equal to one million bytes or one thousand kilobytes. **KB** is an abbreviation for kilobyte, which is equal to one thousand bytes. A **byte** is a unit of measure for the capacity of computer files that is roughly equal to one character.

To get a rough idea of the potential size of your Web site, add together the file sizes for all the graphics you plan to use. Then add approximately 1MB to 2MB for the plain-text Web pages. If you aren't yet sure how many photos you might put on your site, use these very rough estimates: Photographs on the Web vary in file size from 5KB to 100KB depending on each photo's resolution, file format, and image size as measured in pixels. Using the highest number, you could store up to ten photos and use about 1MB of your Web server space. Most people need about 5MB of space to begin with, and most sites easily grow to 10MB, 20MB, or more with the addition of photos and digitized documents over time.

Remember that you not only have to publish what you have now, but also have to accommodate growth in your site as you go along. Once you have a general idea of the size for your Web site, calculate the space you would need if the size of your Web site doubled or tripled over time. Will the server of the Web host you are considering have that much space available for you a year or two from now? Or does the host limit the space for each site? Find a host with as much space available to you as possible.

Stability

Relying on a stable Web hosting service saves you numerous headaches after your site has been published. Your site should be easily accessible to others on the Web and should not suffer from unnecessary downtime. Downtime is the time your Web site isn't available to others when they try to access it through their Web browser. Your Web hosting service may have scheduled downtimes, during which routine maintenance tasks are performed. Scheduled downtime is a necessity. Unscheduled downtime might happen when equipment malfunctions or other technological problems occur. Periodic downtime due to failing equipment is to be expected—after all, technology isn't perfect. But repetitive and frequent downtime is a sign of poor service and poor technical support by the Web hosting service. If the server is frequently down, it is also unavailable to you via FTP, so you won't be able to update your site. Be sure you have the access you need to easily update your site whenever you have to make changes.

FTP (File Transfer Protocol) is the method you use to transfer (upload or download) files back and forth between your computer and your Web server.

Many ISPs and Web hosting services have come and gone over the past several years. Nothing bothers Webmasters more than having to move their Web site to a new server because their Web hosting company went out of business or discontinued a service. So be sure to look for a well-known Web host with a long history online. There are several free, online mailing lists you can consult in order to ask others about Web site publishing for genealogy. These forums are the perfect place to ask fellow genealogists what they recommend for stable and reliable Web site hosting services:

- Freepages-Help (for anyone whose site is hosted on RootsWeb)
  lists.rootsweb.com/index/other/RootsWeb_Support/Freepages-Help.html
- GENCMP
  www.rootsweb.com/~jfuller/gen_mail_computing.html#GENCMP-L
- GEN-COMP-TIPS
  www.rootsweb.com/~jfuller/gen_mail_computing.html#GEN-COMP-TIPS
- GEN-WEB-DESIGN
  www.rootsweb.com/~jfuller/gen_mail_computing.html#GEN-WEB-DESIGN
- HTMLHELP
  www.rootsweb.com/~jfuller/gen_mail_computing.html#HTMLHELP

Once you receive recommendations for specific Web hosting services, locate and visit a genealogy site hosted by that same service. You can investigate further by browsing the Personal Home Pages links found on Cyndi's List *(www.CyndisList.com/ personal.htm)*. Send e-mail to the owner of the site and introduce yourself. Let the owner know that you're thinking about publishing your own Web site with the same provider and ask for feedback about the host:

- Are you happy with the service?

- What are its pros and cons?

- Is your site always accessible to others online?

- Is your site always easy to update via FTP?

- Have there been any problems with excessive amounts of downtime?

- Would you recommend this service as a long-term Web site host?

If you receive positive responses, and if that service offers the other features and support that are important to you, you can be confident that you are making an informed choice when it comes to the home for your genealogy Web site.

A **domain name** is the main portion of a URL that denotes the host or the owner of the Web site. Domain names are registered for a small yearly fee so that only one Web site can use it. In a URL, the domain name usually follows the protocol (*http://www*). For example, in the URL *http://www.ngsgenealogy.org*, the domain name is *ngsgenealogy.org*.

Longevity

Keep in mind you are seeking a permanent home for your Web site. Does the host you are considering have most everything you need in order to place your site there for years to come? People sometimes start out on a free Web server with the idea that they will eventually move their site to another home once the site is established and growing. *That is exactly the opposite of what you should do.* The idea is to make it easy for cousins and other researchers to find you and your Web site. Moving your site from Web host to Web host defeats that purpose because, unless you have your own domain name, your address changes each time. Your best bet is to find a home for your genealogy Web site and leave it there. That means you must pick the best home possible for your site, one that offers you flexibility and numerous options to explore in the years ahead. You may not yet know what options you will use. That's okay; we'll discuss how to plan your genealogy Web site in Chapters 3, 4, and 5 before diving into the creation of the Web pages themselves.

Forwarding Page

If you do find that you need to move your Web site to a new ISP or Web hosting service, consider setting up forwarding pages on the old host server. There may be a small fee to leave the pages on the server for a few months. The forwarding pages would supply links that point visitors to your new site on the new host. If you have a domain name of your own, transferring the domain to the new provider is all you need to do and forwarding pages aren't necessary.

Other Considerations

When searching for a place to publish your site, you also want to consider the availability of the following:

- Help files or FAQs (Frequently Asked Questions) about Web publishing with that hosting service. Having a set of helpful questions and answers readily available goes a long way to get you started on the right track with your new site.

- Additional tools available for Web publishing, such as software, graphics, or links to such resources. If your Web hosting service offers you these useful tools from their own servers, you will save time as you begin to create your new Web pages.

- Technical support for Web publishing. Once you launch your Web site live online, you may run into problems with some of the pages or features you have included on your site. Having technical support help available is invaluable to you, especially in the early days of your site.

Web page forwarding or redirecting services. You need these in case you decide to move your site from that provider to another at some point in the future. If you do move your site some day, you want to ensure that genealogists and cousins are still able to find your site.

Domain name hosting. Having your own domain name for your site is one way to keep a single, constant address for the Web site, no matter what provider is hosting it. This, in turn, ensures that your site is always easily found by others.

If you want to shop around for possible Web hosting services, there are many Internet directories that can point you to a variety of options (national, local, free, or fee-based):

- *www.yahoo.com*
- *www.webhostdir.com*
- *www.hostindex.com*

Where to Look

There are many places you can look for a Web hosting service. Start with your own Internet Service Provider. You probably already have Web space available to you with your current account. You might also have space available to you through the publisher of your genealogy software program. Many free and fee-based Web hosting services are also available. Visit family history sites on a variety of servers and get ideas from your fellow genealogists for places to host your site. To locate other family history sites and find out what Web hosting services are most often used by your fellow genealogists, scan the listings found in any of these directories:

Cyndi's List—Personal Home Pages
www.CyndisList.com/personal.htm

Cyndi's List—Surname Pages
www.CyndisList.com/surnames.htm

- RootsWeb Freepages
  freepages.rootsweb.com/directory/genealogy.html
- Genealogy Register
  genealogyregister.com/Personal_Pages/

Your Internet Service Provider

Most ISPs offer between 5MB and 10MB of server space to their customers for publishing a Web site. Some large, national ISPs even offer more than that (see Figure 2.1). When you originally set up your Internet account, your ISP, whether national, regional, or local, should have sent you a contract or an e-mail message that welcomed you as a new customer. In that message, the benefits of your account were detailed, including whether Web space is available to you. If you no longer have that original message, you should be able to find the same information, or perhaps more current information, on your ISP's Web site. Visit the home page for their Web site and look for sections such as these:

- FAQs—Frequently Asked Questions
- Customer Service
- Member Benefits
- Member Home Pages
- Your Account

Internet Service Provider	Web Space Available	ISP Help Online
America Online	14MB	*hometown.aol.com*
AT&T Worldnet	60MB	*help.att.net/care/ccforums/perspub/index.html*
Earthlink	10MB	*www.earthlink.net/home/tools/clicknbuild/*
MSN	30MB	*support.msn.com*

Figure 2.1 Web space and online help available from some major ISPs

Learning what your own ISP has to offer will help you weigh it against other options, such as free Web hosting services. Find out whether your account entitles you to any Web space for publishing your personal Web site. Your ISP may offer other services to enhance the Web space you already have on their servers. They may have more Web space available for an additional fee, as well as Web design tools and domain name hosting. If you are unable to find this type of information on the Web site for your ISP, send an e-mail message or call and talk to a real, live, customer service person. If your ISP does provide Web server space for customers, determine the following:

- How much Web space are you allowed to use? You want *at least* 10MB.

- Does your ISP provide additional Web space for a fee?

- Are you automatically charged a fee for going over a certain limit in file space? If so, what is the fee and what is the limit?

- Does your ISP provide customer service and technical support for Web site creation or maintenance? This is a very helpful benefit, if available.

- Does your ISP provide any additional tools that help you create your site (such as Web page generators, graphics, or HTML help)?

- Does your ISP offer domain name hosting?

- Are there any limitations or special rules regarding publishing Web pages? To answer that question, look for a link at the bottom of your ISP's Web page that points to any of these:

  - AUP or Acceptable Use/Usage Policy

  - Terms of Service

  - Terms and Conditions

Your Genealogy Software Manufacturer

The latest versions of many popular genealogy software programs offer the ability to create Web pages. In the past, a few had taken that one step further by providing space for Web pages on the software company's servers. Currently only one software company supplies Web space as a feature—Family Tree Maker (FTM). The Web space provided is limited and can be used only in conjunction with the genealogy software program.

FTM takes what you currently have in your database, generates Web pages, and uploads them to a predesignated URL on the software manufacturer's servers. This doesn't allow for much control on your part and leaves you at the mercy of the features built into the software. Some customization may be allowed, so read all the available Help files and FAQs regarding what you can and cannot do with the Web pages. No doubt, the genealogy software manufacturer has rules, guidelines, and limitations regarding the type of material you are allowed to post on your site if it is hosted on their server. Be sure you understand all the rules before you publish. Look for an Acceptable Usage Policy on the manufacturer's Web site, and familiarize yourself with the details.

Most other programs generate the Web pages from your genealogy database and allow you to upload the new pages yourself to the Web server of your choice (see Chapter 6). That way, you create a foundation for your Web site based on your genealogical data. Then you can easily edit and update individual Web pages any time you like. This is the best option for making your Web site work well for your research, allowing you the flexibility to customize the pages and host them on the server of your choice. In Chapters 7, 8, and 9, you learn the benefits of customizing your Web pages.

Free Web Space

There are numerous free Web site hosts online (see Figure 2.2). Two of those most frequently used by genealogists are RootsWeb *(freepages.rootsweb.com)* and GeoCities *(geocities.yahoo.com/home).* But remember what your parents taught you—nothing in life is truly free. The free Web pages offered by most Web servers allow you to publish

Free Web Server	Free Web Space Available	URL
Angelfire	20MB, with ads	*www.angelfire.lycos.com*
Bravenet	100MB, with ads	*www.bravenet.com*
Fortune City	25MB, with ads	*www.fortunecity.com*
RootsWeb	Unlimited, with banners	*freepages.rootsweb.com*
Tripod	20MB, with ads	*www.tripod.lycos.com/host/*
Yahoo! GeoCities	15MB, with ads	*geocities.yahoo.com/home*

Figure 2.2 Web space and online help available from some free Web hosting services

your Web site at no financial cost to you, but they do have other requirements for using their services.

Advertisements

The most obvious requirement is the banner advertisements that are placed on your Web site. Web hosts derive their income through paid advertisements. The hosting service chooses and approves the ads placed on your site, so you have no control over the types of ads that appear there. The banners are usually placed at or near the top of the Web page. In some cases, they are put on the site in the form of pop-ups—small windows that float over the top of a Web page. Visitors to a Web site are forced to view the ad and close the pop-up before they can view your Web page. Another variation on this idea is pop-unders. These launch windows under your current browser window, which you generally find after you close down your current browser session.

Banner ads are almost always found at the very top of a Web page, although they can be found anywhere on a site. Most banners are a common size of 468 x 60 pixels. Some banners are animated, and many banners alternate so that a variety of graphics appear on a Web site each time someone visits.

Advertisements on Web sites are a common occurrence, so most visitors are undeterred when they visit a site that has banner ads. Pop-up ads are a bit more of a nuisance because of the extra work required to close down a window. But there are software utilities that close pop-ups automatically. In the end, most people tend to become accustomed to ads of all types and view them as a necessary part of surfing the Web.

Limitations of Free Hosting Services

Free Web hosting services often have very basic or limited technical support for their users. Most likely, help is available only in the form of FAQs (prewritten questions and answers), tutorials, and instructions. Message boards might also be available, giving you a venue in which to ask others for help with your site.

Pop-up Prevention Utility Programs

Pop-ups have become an everyday occurrence on Web sites, so you may not be able to avoid having them appear as part of your site if your Web hosting service uses them. However, your Web site visitors can avoid this nuisance by using pop-up killer software utilities such as the following:

- Popup Killer
  www.popup-killer.info

- PopUpCop
  www.popupcop.com

- STOPzilla
  www.stopzilla.com

- Popup Smasher
  www.popupstop.com

Some free services limit the amount of bandwidth used by a Web site. Bandwidth refers to the amount of data that is transferred to visitors of the Web site. The amount is measured based on the file sizes of the Web pages and graphics that are viewed, along with the frequency that those pages and graphics are served up to the visitor. The limitation is generally a set number each month. If your Web site is popular, the amount of traffic to your site could exceed the bandwidth limit. Once the limit is reached, the site returns error messages telling the visitor that your site is unavailable. Once the new month begins, your site becomes available once again. Bandwidth limits and fees are common for commercial Web sites, but they generally aren't a normal occurrence on Web hosting services for personal Web sites. Each service is different, so read the terms of service to find out if there are any bandwidth limits at your Web hosting service of choice.

Also be aware that some free Web hosting services limit the amount of free Web space you can use. Some people work around the size limitations by splitting up their Web site among numerous free Web hosting services and the space already available to them at their own ISP. This can be a problem, though, because it means that numerous different URLs are associated with one Web site. This type of setup can work as long as the Web site is designed well and has good navigation tools so that a visitor can get to any part of the Web site from any other part of the site, without having to depend on identifying each URL for navigation. Read the Terms and Conditions for using the free Web hosting services. Some of them do not allow you to have more than one free Web account on their servers if you plan to use them all to create one continuous Web site.

Can You Change Your Mind Without Changing Your Address?

Some free services offer you a choice of free Web hosting or fee-based Web hosting. If you start out using a free service, you may later be able to switch to fee-based instead. Paying a fee may give you more Web space and remove the advertising banners and pop-up ads common to free Web hosts. You might prefer to begin with a free site but have the flexibility to change your mind later; if so, look for one of the services that offers both options.

Questions to Ask If You Are Considering a Free Web Hosting Service

If you are thinking of using a free Web hosting service, consider these issues:

- Do you mind having advertisements on your site? Advertisements may not bother you if you don't think they'll interfere with the way your site appears or behaves.

- Will visitors to your site be bothered by the advertisements there? While most people aren't fond of online advertisements, they tend to accept them, just as they do the ads in a newspaper or magazine.

- Will you be content knowing you have no control over the type of advertisements placed on your site? If you are the type of person who wants to control every aspect of your publication, this may be something that you won't be able to deal with.

- Can you live with having the advertisements on your site for the entire life of your Web site? You hope your site remains on its current Web host for many years to come. If you think that you might not mind the ads now, but may eventually tire of them, the free Web space may not be the place for your site.

- Will your genealogy Web site outgrow the space limitations on the free Web server? If your plans for your site are focused on long-term research and continual updates with new text and photos, I guarantee you will eventually outgrow any space limitations that you run across.

🍃 Does the same service offer additional Web space for a fee, in case your site outgrows the free Web space? When you run out of the free space allotted to your site, having the ability to expand your site on the same server for a small fee is a wonderful way to avoid moving your site and changing your address.

🍃 Are there any limitations, rules, or guidelines on the free Web hosting service that will hinder the plans you have for your genealogy site? For example, perhaps you hope to eventually add video files or searchable databases to your site. If so, the free Web hosts may not give you the ability to use these types of advanced features.

🍃 Will the Web space always remain free? You have no way of knowing whether the space will always remain available to you or be free. So don't pin all your hopes just on the fact that the space is free. Weigh your options and make the best choice overall.

Fee-Based Web Hosting Services

If you have already determined that your own ISP or the free Web hosting services don't give you flexibility and stability, or allow enough Web space for your plans for the site, your next option is to look at fee-based hosting services. A fee-based host for your site doesn't have to be expensive. You may even find that paying a small fee for the service gives you the stability and space that you can't find anywhere else.

There are many benefits to hosting your Web site on a server for a fee (see Figure

Fee-Based Web Server	**URL**
Network Solutions	*www.networksolutions.com*
Tripod	*www.tripod.lycos.com/host/*
Yahoo! GeoCities	*geocities.yahoo.com/home*
Yahoo! Web Hosting	*webhosting.yahoo.com/ps/wh/prod/*
The List of Web Hosts (directory of hosting services)	*webhosts.thelist.com*

Figure 2.3 Fee-based Web hosting services

2.3). The size of your site is limited only by your budget. No advertisements and pop-ups appear, so your site's appearance and content remain entirely under your control. Because you are paying a fee to host your site on the server, customer service and technical support help are available to you. Fee-based hosting services generally have several tools available to help you create and maintain your Web site.

Ask yourself the same types of questions about fee-based services that you asked about your own ISP:

- How much Web space are you allowed to use for the fee paid?

- Can you easily add more space to your site for an additional fee?

- Are customer service and technical support for Web site creation and maintenance provided as part of the fee?

- Does the Web hosting service provide any additional tools to help you create your site (such as Web page generators, graphics, or HTML help)?

- Does it offer domain name hosting?

- Are there limitations or special rules regarding Web pages? Look for an Acceptable Use/Usage Policy or Terms of Service.

Domain Name Registration and Hosting

Let's talk a bit about what domain names are and how you get one yourself. In a common URL, the domain name is the part that generally ends in .com, although many other extensions are available for use with domains today, such as .net or .info. To use a specific domain name, you must register that domain and pay a small yearly fee to have the exclusive use of that domain. One of the biggest benefits of having your own domain name is that your URL—your address—stays the same as long as the domain registration remains in your name. You can move your site from provider to provider without changing the URL. So no matter where you move your site, visitors can always find you. If you don't have your own domain name for your Web site, your URL is based on the address of your Web hosting service. So if you move your site to a new Web hosting service, your URL changes to reflect the address of the new hosting service.

Domain Registration Web Sites

When you decide to register your own domain name for your Web site, you can make use of one of the many domain registration services on the Internet. These services allow you to obtain your own unique domain name to help give an identity to your site. Some also offer Web hosting services, professional Web design help, and a variety of tools you can use to enhance your site. The following are a few of the domain registration services:

- Network Solutions
  www.networksolutions.com

- Register.com
  www.register.com

- Yahoo! Domains
  domains.yahoo.com

- Yahoo! Directory—Domain Name Registration Resources
  dir.yahoo.com/Computers_and_Internet/Internet/Domain_Name_Registration/

If you are planning a long-term commitment to your genealogy Web site, you probably have already given thought to having your own domain name. Visit domain registration Web sites to find an available domain name and register it for your own use. You can look up domain names and those that are already registered to others in a "whois" search on any domain name registration service. A search of the whois database will tell you who has registered a domain name and it will provide you with contact information for that person or company. Examples of whois databases can be found at *www.networksolutions.com/en_US/whois/index.jhtml* and *www.uwhois.com*. Be sure your Web site hosting service can host a domain name for you. There may be additional fees involved to do so.

Renew Your Domain Regularly

Don't forget to renew your domain name registration each year. If you don't renew it, someone else may be able to take over the registration and use it for themselves. You can register your domain name for multiple years. This is the best option you have to make sure the domain is yours for the long term.

Extra Tools and Features

Once you find a hosting service for your Web site, explore its Web site to learn what extra tools and features are available to you as a user of that service. Earlier we discussed the minimum in features that you should look for in a hosting service. Having selected a specific Web host, you may find that you have a whole bunch of extra goodies to work with. You may find features such as these:

- A library of Web graphics to use on your site
- Web page templates
- Online Web page generators
- CGI scripts for items like e-mail forms and counters
- Copy-and-paste JavaScript utilities
- E-mail addresses
- Web page forwarding services
- Web site reports and statistics about traffic to your site

What Is the Best Choice for You?

Use the checklist in Figure 2.4 as a guide to help you weigh the pros and cons, and determine which type of Web hosting service is best for you.

	Option 1	Option 2	Option 3	Option 4
Web host name				
Free				
Fee				
Type of ads				
Amount of space				
Bandwidth limit				
Tech support?				
Domain hosting?				
Extra tools?				

Figure 2.4 Checklist for pros and cons when choosing a Web hosting service

Many options are available to you as you search for a place to plant your family tree online. Investigate the options available to you through your own ISP, a free hosting service, or a fee-based hosting service, and compare the details and features most important to you. Weighing the answers you find for each of the questions you ask yourself helps you determine which Web host is right for you. Always keep in mind the purpose of your site and the long-term goals you have set—and your site will surely succeed.

CHAPTER 3

Plan Ahead for a Successful Genealogy Web Site

THE NEXT FEW CHAPTERS DISCUSS HOW TO DESIGN THE STRUCTURE OF your genealogy Web site. Thoughtful planning has to be your first priority to ensure success as you create your site. After you find a Web hosting service and determine what help, tools, and goodies it provides, you can begin working on your site's appearance and layout. But first, decide what your ultimate goal for the site—or for individual parts of the site—should be. Your goal for the site is determined by who you think will visit your site and how you want to share what you know about your ancestors. After that, you can decide what to include on your site, how it will be formatted, and how you will present the information. Spending the time to plan ahead and organize yourself now will save you a lot of time and effort as you begin creating Web pages later.

Who Will Visit Your Site?

Who do you hope visits your site? Cousins? But what sorts of cousins? Fellow genealogists and family historians? Or cousins who have only a slight interest in the family tree? We genealogists get so focused on our research that we tend to think every cousin online will be thrilled to find us and bestow on us every bit of family lore, every name and date, and every ancient family heirloom in their possession. You may be overestimating the draw of your new Web site if you design it with only the genealogist in mind, rather than the cousin with a lighter interest in your family's history.

Web: The portion of the Internet that contains pages written in HTML, hypertext-linked from one page to another, creating an interconnecting "web" of information.

Web page: One plain ASCII text file, written with HTML tags, that tells a Web browser how to display formatted text and graphics.

Web site: One Web page or numerous Web pages, along with supporting graphics, databases, and other features, published together for one purpose or by one person.

Home page: The front (or first) page to a Web site. Most often it is also the main index page.

Webmaster: The person who creates or manages the Web site. A Webmaster may or may not also be the author of the content published there.

Web browser: A software program (such as Netscape Navigator or Microsoft Internet Explorer) that allows you to view a Web page.

As you design your site, the first rule is this: Know your audience. Who is truly likely to visit your site? Perhaps a few cousins are genealogists themselves. They'll have a working knowledge of family group sheets and the importance of accuracy in names, dates, and places. But your visitors are more likely to be a variety of cousins who are just a bit curious about their family tree. They may have a few things to share with you, but for the most part, they want *you* to share with them.

Few real surveys or statistics tell us how many people are interested in genealogy. Genealogy is rumored to be the second most popular topic online and to surpass coin and stamp collecting combined. Surely everyone has an interest in knowing who they are and where they come from. And every family has at least one dedicated family member who becomes the historian and keeper of the family artifacts and stories.

Don't Forget the Nongenealogical Cousin

One of the reasons you are a genealogist is almost certainly because you want to honor your ancestors and share what you learn about them with the rest of your family. What happens when you meet in person and talk with your nongenealogical family about genealogy? As you rattle off names, dates, and places, do they look at you with a blank stare? Does it take you a while to notice their glazed eyes because you are so busy telling them the oh-so-fascinating story of those four weeks you spent in the library trying to prove Great-Aunt Mathilda's death date? Your Web site must grab your family's attention so they really absorb what they find there and read it thoroughly. You want to give them something so interesting that they return to the site over and over again. Most important, you want everyone in your family who visits your Web site to share with you, helping add more to your research and your site.

The Internet is a true medium for the genealogist—it almost seems designed just for us. A genealogy Web site can breathe life into your family's history and stories. A Web site allows you to enhance family stories with photos of ancestors and to prove your assertions by including scanned copies of a family Bible or World War I draft registration. Do you have the voice of your grandmother captured on audiotape? Convert the tape to an audio file, and allow your cousins halfway around the world to hear her also, via the Web. Bring the true multimedia strength of a Web site into how you share your genealogy with your cousins—and you'll keep them interested in what you are doing.

How Should Your Site Look and Behave?

The most important step in this planning phase is to remember that your site will be available to everyone, everywhere on the Internet. Genealogists, nongenealogists, and people with all types of computer hardware and software will use your genealogy site, so aim for the most common denominator. A genealogy Web site should be

- Easy to read
- Easy to navigate
- Simple and straightforward
- Appealing to the eye and interesting—but not hyperactive

A Baseline

Not everyone who visits your genealogy site has the same type of computer. While you might have the latest and greatest Cadillac of computers, others are still happily using their Model T. To be successful, your Web site should be accessible to everyone, everywhere, no matter the type of hardware or software. To reach the largest possible number of cousins online, you should gear your site to the following "baseline" setup. The list doesn't reflect the status of your own computer, but the computers of the potential visitors to your Web site.

- A computer that is *at least* three years old
- Software programs, such as Web browsers, that are *at least* two versions out of date
- A 14.4 or 28.8 kbps dial-up modem
- A monitor with a 640 x 480 screen resolution at 256 colors
- An environment with only one phone line that cannot be tied up for long periods

If you design your site with those minimum parameters in mind, you can be reasonably sure that you won't exclude anyone from visiting your site. Targeting your site for a common population of computers is a courtesy to the online community. I often see brand-new Web sites launched with every bell and whistle imaginable—usually by an overly enthusiastic Webmaster who went a wee bit overboard. A general rule of thumb when it comes to the fancy stuff is this: Just because you *can* use it doesn't mean you *should* use it (see Chapter 10). If some features won't work within the limitations described above, don't use them. Statistics tell us that if people have trouble accessing a Web site, they leave almost immediately *and don't return.* So do your best not to chase away any of your long-lost cousins because the super-duper, high-tech extravaganza on your Web site crashes their computer. Chances are it will happen to the cousin who has the family Bible—and I know you don't want to miss that opportunity!

Easy to Read

Another reason your visitor will leave almost immediately is if your site is difficult to read. Use a standard font common to every computer. The default for most computers and Web browsers is Times New Roman or Times. If you do not specify a font type or size when you design the site, Web browsers automatically display the defaults. And those defaults are the safest choice—especially if you're not sure how the font will appear on your visitor's computer. If you want to use a specific font, choose a sans-serif font—a font with straight lines and no curly doo-dads on it. In paper publications, serif fonts are preferred because they make text easier to read. The opposite is true of fonts on a monitor. Web designers all agree that sans-serif fonts such as Arial are easier to read on the screen. With a serif font, the pixels of light that display the serifs tend to make the letters blotchy and hard to read. The font you choose should be straightforward, simple, and available to most computer users. And it should always be a dark color, displayed on a light background (see Figure 3.1).

Once you select a font and color that are easy to read, decide how you want to display the text. How much text should appear on a page? Should you use single-line or double-line spacing? The answers to those questions depend on the structure and organization you choose for your Web site. For example, if you include biographies of your ancestors, use single-spaced paragraphs of text. If you publish outlines or family group sheets, some double-line spacing helps create a more attractive and useful display.

You don't need to put everything on one Web page. Instead, create several pages for your site, with a separate page devoted to each item or topic of interest.

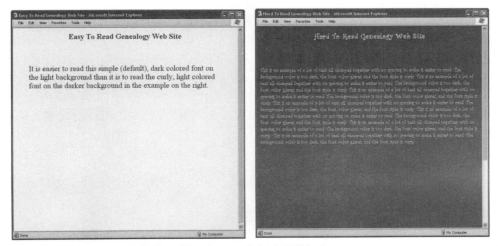

Figure 3.1 Easy to read *(left)* and hard to read *(right)* Web sites

One common mistake in early genealogy Web page development is to create just one Web page for the entire site. Such sites list multiple topics on a page that scrolls on and on and on. If you have more than one topic, create a separate page for each topic. Your home page should function as a title page and index only—not as a page setting the record for the longest vertical scroll bar.

Your only limitation is the server space available to you. Each Web page on your site can vary in length depending on what you want or what you have to publish on those pages.

Many of the rules that apply to publishing a newsletter also apply to Web site design. To make the pages easy to read, plan the layout and organize the text logically. Leave plenty of "white space" around and between text and graphics. White space refers to the empty space and margins around blocks of text. White space pulls the reader's eye through the page and makes the text easier to scan or read. Most important, don't let the page look crowded. Leave margins along the top, bottom, and sides just as you would on any letter or printed page. Break up sentences or paragraphs that are too long. Unbroken chunks of text are much harder to read online than on the printed page. If you have lists of names, facts, or items, use bullets or icons. Balance the text on your page with pictures and graphics. But don't get carried away with graphics. Too many pictures make the page look busy and messy, and draw attention away from the text. We will return to fonts and formatting in Chapter 7.

Draw Yourself a Picture

In this early planning stage, draw a rough draft on paper of how you might like your Web pages to appear. Sketch in where you want to put the title, buttons, text, photos, and other graphics. Refer to your sketch as you test your Web pages.

Easy to Navigate

Another key element to good Web site design is navigation. Navigation is the way a visitor reaches the other pages of your Web site from any one page. In many ways, a Web site is like a book and the individual Web pages serve as chapters and pages within that book. This analogy will be used more as we discuss the structure for the site in Chapter 4. Genealogists have been known to walk through the library, pull a book off a shelf, and open that book to a page in the middle. Better yet, we head straight to the index at the back of the book to search for surnames or place names that we recognize. Very rarely do we take down a book and start with the cover, the table of contents, and then the first page, working consecutively through the book. That's the way people surf the Internet, too. They find your Web site, open it up, and head straight for the index—the part of the site that gets them to the good stuff. Many times, they actually begin in the "middle of the book" of your Web site, led there directly by search engine hits or favorites and bookmarks shared by others. So don't assume that visitors will always begin at your home page and navigate your site from there.

Good navigation on a site means visitors can easily reach the rest of the site from any individual Web page on the site—not just from the home page. You should at least allow visitors to hop back to main sections within your site. A navigational aid such as a standard set of text links or a graphical toolbar can be replicated on every page on your site. Such navigational aids (also known as nav bars) usually appear across the top or bottom of a Web page, or down the left side (see Figure 3.2). The easiest nav bar to find and use generally appears at the top of a page. But a nav bar at the bottom of the page means that those visitors who have read the page don't have to scroll back to the top to find the nav bar.

Easy navigation also means using clearly identifiable names and labels for pages and sections within your Web site. As you set up links from one page on your site to another, be sure the name of the link matches the name on the page. When your visitors click a link labeled "Smith Family in Arkansas," but arrive on a page titled "Descendants of John Smith," their first impulse is to think they landed on the wrong page. I have reached just that point and invariably gone back to the previous page and clicked the link again just to be sure. *The name of the link to a Web page should match the name on that Web page.* Again, the structure resembles a printed book. If a chapter in the table of contents is called "Ted's Genealogy," you expect to

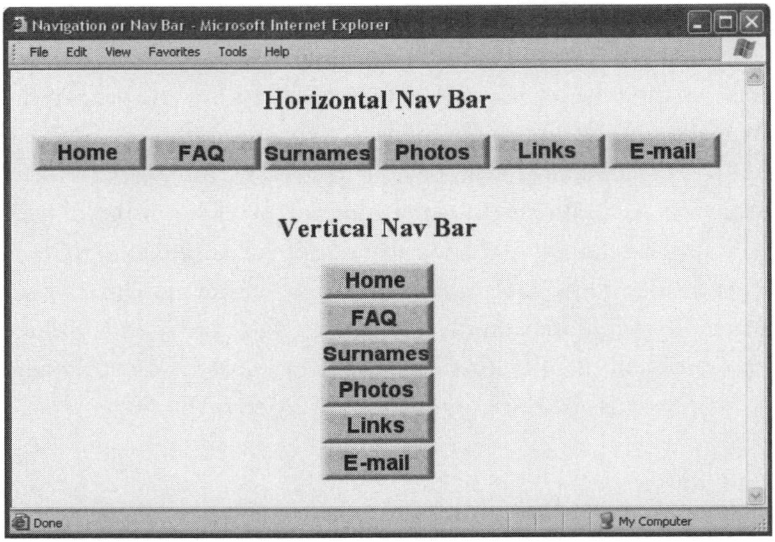

Figure 3.2 Examples of a horizontal and a vertical navigation bar using buttons

turn to that page and find "Ted's Genealogy" at the top of the page. Web page and section headings should match what is shown in the index or within any navigational links throughout the Web site. We will explore navigational tools in more detail in Chapter 8.

Simple

A Web site easily becomes more complex as it grows and evolves. Sometimes we get carried away, working too hard to accomplish something specific or to achieve a particular goal. Other times we look at the site we have created and think, "This is boring, just names, dates, and places. It really needs some pizzazz." Not necessarily. Your site need not wow your visitors—it need not showcase the latest in JavaScript 3-D Virtual Reality Cemetery Time Travel Tours. It is most likely just fine as it is—a representation of your genealogical research to date. Again, just because you *can* include a pop-up that allows visitors to consult with genealogical psychics doesn't mean you *should* add such a complex feature to your site. Simple is best. Simple makes it easy for you to maintain the site and easier for your family to find and absorb the information you provide there.

Straightforward

Be straightforward on your site—be honest about what visitors can expect. Providing a mission statement near the top of the home page or on the first page in each section of your site helps you explain what your site is about clearly and concisely. Don't overstate the contents or mislead the visitor—or you lose your credibility. I have been to sites that claim to be "The ultimate Web site for SMITH genealogy" or "The only genealogy site you'll ever need." As Webmaster of Cyndi's List, I see thousands of sites that all make similar claims. But the casual online genealogists who visit your site may believe exactly what they read there. Be straight with your visitors. Tell them exactly what your site contains. We will further explore the vital issue of correctly representing what is on your site in Chapter 5.

Say It Like It Is

You put a lot of work into both your genealogy research and your Web site design. You deserve to have your research taken seriously. To ensure that there will be no misunderstandings and no assumptions made about any of the material published on your site, be sure to be completely honest about that material. Be straightforward as in the following examples:

- Clearly mark, label, and define the limits of your research.

- Indicate if your site is a work in progress or if you are focusing on one specific family more than the others on your site.

- Let others know if you are new to genealogy or new to publishing your research. Conversely, let them know if you are a seasoned researcher.

- If parts of your site contain data derived from verifiable sources, cite those sources clearly.

- If some data on your site is only your best guess, be sure to identify that clearly so that others know to look at that information with a more discerning eye.

- Label transcriptions, extractions, and abstracts appropriately.

- Set an example for all genealogists, both newbie and veteran, by publishing truthfully, honestly, and with integrity.

The secret to keeping your site simple and straightforward is to stay focused on your purpose and goal. Always keep in mind why you created your Web site and what you hope to achieve with it. Then you'll stay on the right track.

Appealing to the Eye and Interesting, but Not Hyperactive

Keeping your site simple doesn't mean it has to be ugly or boring. As we'll see in Chapter 7, you can use pretty graphics and a variety of the fonts commonly found on most computers. And a color scheme goes a long way toward making your site pleasing to the eye. But whose eyes should you please? Your own or your visitors'? Your goal should be *both*. Color choice is an issue when it comes not only to viewing and reading, but also to printing. Have you ever tried to print a Web page that uses a light-colored font—on a black and white printer? The printer attempts to emulate the light shade, resulting in a faint gray printout that is sometimes nearly impossible to read.

Choose a color scheme that is easy to read and comfortable to look at, and that results in a crisp printed page. Dark text on a light background is always best. Remember that visitors will view your Web site in a variety of settings: large and small monitors, high and low resolutions, dark rooms and rooms filled with light.

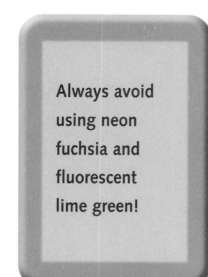

Always avoid using neon fuchsia and fluorescent lime green!

Some visi-tors will have glasses or limited vision. A small computer monitor with low screen reso-lution can make some colors appear blotchy and incorrect. Some colors you choose for your site might appear differently under these conditions than they would on a monitor set to a higher screen resolution. The higher the resolution, the crisper the picture, and the better the chance that the colors will be more true to your intent for the display. Select a color scheme that will be soothing for all your visitors and that also satisfies your artistic side.

The same rules for colors apply to the graphics you use on your site. The buttons, bars, banners, and icons should follow that same soothing, easy-on-the-eye scheme. If you decide to include scanned photographs on your site, you have a lot more latitude when it comes to the colors. You can't control the fact that Aunt Mabel wore her flamingo-pink stretch pants in the last family reunion photo. So don't worry whether the photo matches the rest of the color scheme on your site.

The background for each page should be solid or have a faint, low-key pattern. Be sure the background you choose doesn't interfere with the most important part of the page—the text. The background should support the text so that the text stands out crisp and clear for the reader.

A million animated graphics and cursors are available to use on your site. But do you truly need them? If they don't serve a purpose, don't use them. Otherwise, they just interfere with what your visitors come for—information about your family. In fact, most visitors quickly leave a Web site when faced with animated graphics. Instead, you want them to settle in for a long visit so they can read and absorb what they find. See Chapter 10 for more about animation on genealogy Web sites.

In my experience, most people spend so much time fussing with the appearance of the site that they fail to give the proper attention to the site's purpose: its content. Again, focus on your goal for the site—to publish your genealogical research and family history. Rely on the purpose and content of your site to interest the visitor, rather than on outrageous colors and wild graphics.

Learn from My Mistake

I learned my poor color choice lessons the hard way. The first year that Cyndi's List was online, I thought I would "decorate" the site for the holidays. I found a graphic showing Santa Claus at a computer. I used it to make a border that ran the length of the page, with the remainder of the background in a nice holiday red. I changed all the font colors to white, gold, and evergreen. It was beautiful—for about two hours. Almost immediately after putting my artistic creation online, I received two e-mail messages from gentlemen kindly asking me to change the colors I used. Why? They were colorblind—neither visitor could read a thing on my site. For the first time, I understood that if I truly wanted my site to be useful to others, I could not afford to spend time entertaining myself. I switched the colors on my site that day and have kept a user-friendly color scheme ever since.

What Is the Purpose of Your Site?

Why have you decided to publish a family history site? Perhaps to share your findings with fellow family historians. Or to create a research center for your cousins to work together on the same project. Or you may want your site to be a focal point for everyone who researches a specific surname or in a specific locality. The way you lay out your site should be influenced by your research plan and methodology, rather than by a desire to entertain others.

As we go through the next several steps in the planning process, ask yourself the following questions. Your answers will help you decide what your site needs to do.

- What is the purpose of my site?
- Who do I want to visit my site?
- Who do I think might be interested in visiting my site?
- Who else might visit whom I haven't anticipated?
- Do I hope to reach out to a few cousins, or do I want to track down every descendant of a specific ancestor?
- Do I want to attract other genealogists?
- Do I want my site to be an online diary that reflects my ongoing research, or do I see the site as a one-time publication for posterity?
- Do I want it to be an archive of family records and documents to share with the world?

Types of Genealogy Web Sites

Having answered the questions in the previous section, you should have a better idea how to choose the type of genealogy Web site you want. Let's explore some of the more common examples of sites that family historians publish online.

A Personal Genealogy Database Site

A large number of personal genealogy Web sites are based on Web pages generated from a personal database in a genealogy software program. That ready-made structure is one of the simplest options; it provides the foundation you need to easily build and customize your Web site. You can sort your database by surname or family group, and create several individual sets of Web pages based on the content and purpose of your site. You can include photographs and other personal touches. The examples discussed in this book are based on this type of site.

A Surname or Descendant Site

Some genealogists create Web sites devoted to one specific surname. Their site might represent a one-name study or a family association. Or the site may be created for research on the descendants of one person or couple. Many of these sites are developed from one-name studies or family associations that already exist offline. The Web site becomes an electronic newsletter for the group, a virtual meeting place, and a research center for members of the surname group to coordinate their research findings.

A Family Newsletter or Meeting Place

A genealogy Web site is a terrific way to create a newsletter or meeting place so that your family can stay in touch online. Along with the usual genealogical information about ancestors, your site can be full of photographs, news, events, and announcements about contemporary family members. This hive of activity is a great way to draw your cousins back to your site time and time again just to see what's new.

A Person Site

Everyone who has been bitten by the genealogy bug has a favorite ancestor. Usually it is that one ancestor who inspired the search in the first place—or who continues to inspire the genealogist to follow each new trail. A Web site dedicated to that ancestor can be a terrific way to honor his or her memory. A biographical story, photographs, and historical documentation of the events in an ancestor's life can truly help bring him or her back to life.

A Topic Site

During the research process, you may find a topic you love or even one in which you become an expert. You become so familiar with the topic that the next logical step is to share your knowledge with fellow family historians. You can find genealogy Web sites dedicated to all sorts of topics—historical events, the military (wars, specific regiments), genealogical records (census, immigration, wills), and how-to information for just about anything having to do with genealogical research.

A Locality Site

After spending several years researching an ancestor or an entire family in a specific locality, the family historian knows quite a bit about that locality and how to make the most of research there. A Web site created about that locality is a terrific way to reach out and help others. It might also be a good way to transcribe records for that area and preserve them electronically. A locality genealogy site contains lists of records repositories, along with information about those repositories and how to use them. Your site could educate genealogists about the types of records available for research in a certain locality. In fact, your site might even be an overall genealogy portal for everyone with ancestors in that area.

A Research Project

Historically, a genealogist tackling a research project did so mostly alone. And the project was often long and involved. Not so anymore! A genealogy Web site can be a public forum for a coordinated genealogy research project. Cousins can work together to research a common ancestor, using the Web site to keep track of what others are doing. The site becomes an electronic research log and a place for cousins to post—and discuss—what they have accomplished.

A Community Service Site

The genealogical community is made up of a large group of volunteers. Genealogists volunteer to participate in genealogical and historical societies; libraries; Family History Centers; and many online forums, such as mailing lists, message boards, and chat rooms. Volunteer genealogists can maintain a Web site that highlights such community services.

A Combination Site

A combination site is made up of all or some of the components found in the preceding examples. In fact, a Web site often starts off as one type of site and then later develops into a combination site as the Webmaster enhances and expands the site to reflect her own expanding genealogical research.

Knowing both whom you want to visit your Web site and what type of site you want it to be are the first major hurdles in planning your genealogy site. Those decisions drive every other decision you make for the site. We have examined many types of genealogy sites. From this point on, the example I use is the personal genealogy database Web site. But all the ideas concerning the structure and creation of Web pages apply to any of the types of genealogy sites discussed here.

CHAPTER **4**

Structure Your Genealogy Web Site

THE NEXT STEP IN YOUR PLANNING IS TO DESIGN A LAYOUT—A structure and organization—for your genealogy Web site. The key to layout is to mimic what you have already done in your research. Your family tree has structure and organization. It has a specific layout, as illustrated in a basic ancestor chart. You start with yourself, branch out to your parents, then your grandparents, great-grandparents, and so on. If you plan to include on your Web site a bit about all the branches in your research, look at your ancestor chart and envision each person or each individual surname line as a separate chapter or section on your Web site. Similarly, if you choose to create a Web site for all the descendants of a specific person, each new generation could be given its own section on your Web site.

Folders and Directories

Each page on your Web site is a unique file created by you and stored on the Web server. Each file on your site has its own unique URL (Uniform Resource Locator)— that file's address on the Internet. A URL is more than an address, though; it illustrates the *path* to where a file is located on a Web server. If you read the URL from right to left, you can detect a filing system that shows a specific file stored in a folder/directory that is in turn stored on a specific Web server. Figure 4.1 shows the components of the URL for a basic Web page.

Throughout this book, I refer to *directories* or *subdirectories* and to *folders*. In

49

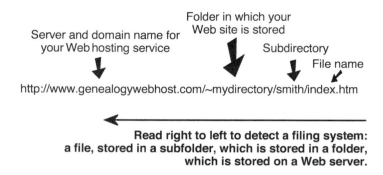

Figure 4.1 Diagram of the URL for a basic Web page

computer jargon, these terms can be interchangeable depending on the user, computer platform, and context in which they are used. Most often, we refer to *directories* on a Web server and *folders* on your personal computer. Their function, however, is the same: file storage organization.

Let's relate file storage organization on a Web server or home computer to how you might organize your printed reports and research files. Would you file everything in one hanging file in one cabinet drawer? Or would you sort your research by surname and then by family group into individual hanging files? Would you put all your research into one large three-ring binder? Or would you sort that binder into tabbed sections by surname, or even into individual smaller binders by surname? Whatever filing system you choose, your Web site can easily mimic it. Your Web site's folders or directories can be organized to duplicate the filing system of hanging folders or tabbed sections in a binder.

It's easy to forget about organizing when you're looking at the big picture. We genealogists often get tunnel vision as we work on our family history. We view our records and database as a single large project—"my ancestors." Similarly, we tend to think in terms of one large Web site rather than the individual pages or sections that compose the site. Let's return to our analogy of a printed book. If you were publishing a book, would you publish your family history all in one large book without any sections, or would you divide it into chapters? Your Web site can be like one large book with chapters for each family or surname.

Logical organization is important to printed books, but it's essential to Web sites. The larger your project becomes, the more sense it makes to start sorting material by surname. Unlike books, Web sites are dynamic—they evolve, changing and growing over time. The example we began with in Chapter 1 is a book that traces your history through your great-grandparents. That book could logically be organized into eight chapters, one chapter devoted to each surname. Similarly, if your site is devoted to another subject (as opposed to the surname theme), you should find a logical break-down for the information that you plan to publish and assign a separate chapter to each topic. Whether you organize your site by surname or some other topic, be sure each "chapter" is self-contained. Not only should the chapter stand on its own, but you should be able to easily expand, update, and maintain the content over time.

Once you break down your content into distinct chapters, assign each chapter to a sepa-rate directory within your site. Then each chapter will have a unique URL that people can reference in correspondence, bookmarks, and source citations for their research.

A Model for Web Site Structure

Let's look at a basic model for a Web site. You can create your entire family history site based on this model, or you can use whatever bits and pieces of it you like. The model has four basic structural elements:

1. A main index page (your home page) for your site

2. A directory for each chapter (section), with an index page for each chapter in your site

3. Supplementary pages in each chapter for information such as stories, pictures, and multimedia—whatever you want to include in that chapter

4. Data pages that you create manually or generate from your genealogy database

You can easily expand this model (see Figures 4.2 and 4.3) to better fit the contents of your site. The model also helps you update your site easily—it limits the number of pages that you have to create manually or maintain when you use genealogy soft-ware to generate the data pages for your site. You create the index pages and any optional supplementary pages using an HTML editor or by writing the HTML code with a text editor. (See Chapter 6 for more about HTML editors.) The data pages can be simple pages—perhaps just one page with names, dates, and places for the ances-tors in that chapter. Or the data pages can be sets of pages created directly from your genealogy software or GEDCOM file. See Chapter 6.

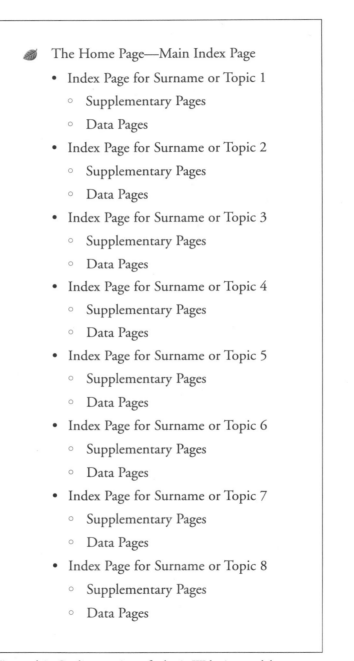

Figure 4.2 Outline version of a basic Web site model

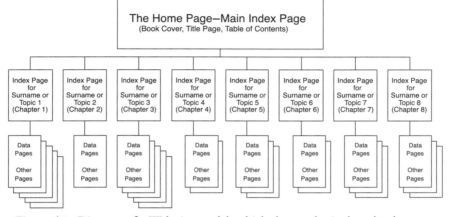

Figure 4.3 Diagram of a Web site model, which shows a basic three-level structure and illustrates that each chapter may have just one page or many pages within

Every Tiny Bit Counts

Like many genealogists, you may find that you have little information on one surname branch in your family tree, but a ton of data for another. That's common, particularly for female family lines. So don't worry if your Web site has some chapters that are very small or nearly empty of information beyond the surname itself. Go ahead and create the chapter for the surname so that it is ready when you begin your research. That particular chapter can simply be one brief Web page with a message—something like "I don't know anything more about this family than the surname, as found on the birth certificate of my grandmother. I hope to add more to this page as my research progresses."

Let Your Ancestor Chart Be Your Guide

Using the model for Web site structure just described, let's see how to logically organize the supporting sections for your site by surname. You can use the following ideas or expand upon them to come up with something that works best for you. Using your ancestor chart or a descendant outline report as a map, determine how many chapters or sections you want to create for your site. For example, the ancestor chart in Figure 4.4 has eight surnames. The eight-chapter model we've been using is based on that chart.

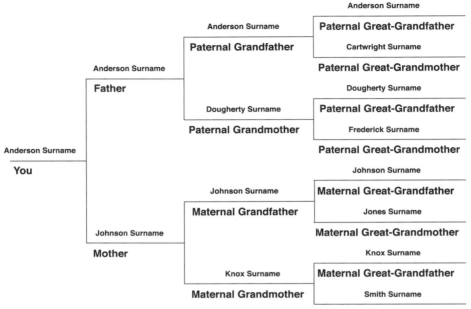

Figure 4.4 An ancestor chart that displays four generations, fifteen individuals, and eight surnames

The Home Page—Your Main Index Page

The front page of the Web site is known as the "home page." It is like the cover on a book, displaying the title, a subtitle, and the name of the author. Generally, the home page also serves as the table of contents and introduction to the site. It

Home Page File Name

The home page for most personal Web sites is given a default file name such as index.htm, index.html, or default.asp. The file name depends on the operating system used by your ISP, by the defaults set on the ISP's servers, and by the HTML editor you use, if any. In general, you are bound to use whatever convention has been set for that first page. Other Web pages and directories are then yours to name, as you like, based on the operating system and software being used.

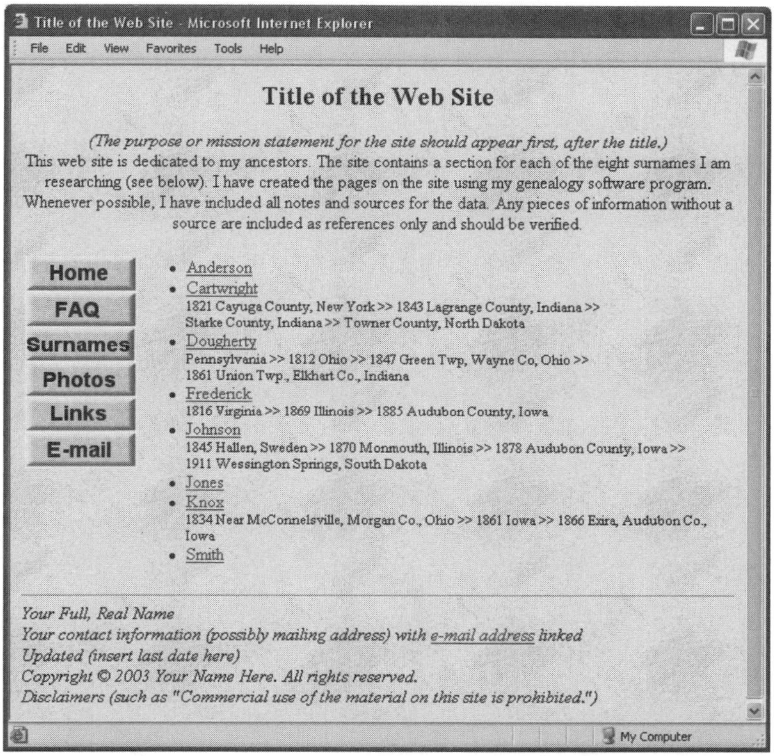

Figure 4.5 A sample home page based on the model. The home page shown here is set up as a guidepost to everything on the site.

provides links to each of the index pages for the chapters or sections contained within the Web site. Starting with your home page, a visitor should be able to quickly learn what your site is about, and then easily navigate through all the chapters within your site.

You can use a predesigned template (see Chapter 6) to create your home page, or you can model the layout of your home page on others you have seen online. (See the model home page in Figure 4.5.) You can design it completely by yourself, if you prefer. Just be sure your home page reflects you, your personality, and your research. After all, you want to make a good impression on your visitors because you want to encourage them to use your site, revisit your site, and refer others to your site.

Your home page should follow all the rules of good Web site design (see Chapter 10). But it has several additional functions to accomplish. Your home page should

- Convey the purpose of your site
- Clearly identify who you are and how to contact you
- Serve as a guidepost for the remainder of the Web site
- Tell people what they will find on your site, and then clearly outline how to find it
- Be updated regularly, with new information or messages indicating the current status of your research or your project
- Communicate everything that is important for you to share about your Web site (such as disclaimers, dedications, caveats, or personal remarks)

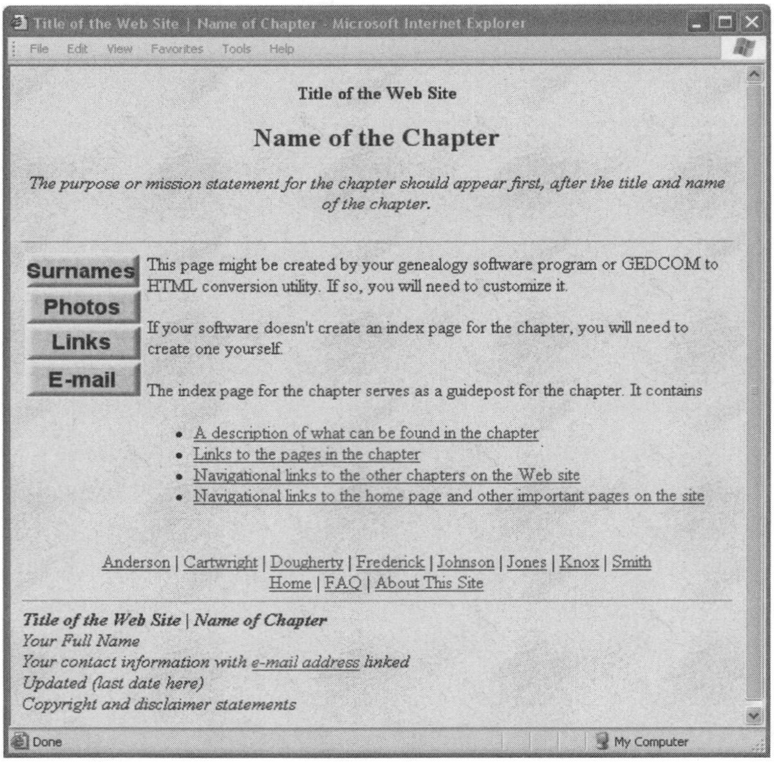

Figure 4.6 A sample index page based on the model. As in the home page in Figure 4.5, the chapter index page shown here is set up as a guidepost to everything within the chapter.

Index Pages for Each Chapter

The introductory page in each chapter acts as the index for the pages within that chapter. That first page in each chapter is like a mini home page. It serves as the entry point to the chapter and includes links to all the other pages within that chapter (see Figure 4.6). Each chapter has its own name. The title of the Web site and the chapter name appear on each page within that chapter. As with every page on your Web site, the index page includes a common footer and navigational aids (see Chapter 8 for details). You can create the index page for each chapter yourself, or you can use index pages that are created by your genealogy software.

Directories = Folders = Chapters

One way a Web site is more versatile than a book is its use of directories and sub-directories. A directory on a Web server is part of the storage space and is designated by a specific name. Having directories within other directories on a Web site is similar to the chapters that make up a broad section of a book (for example, Part 1 of a book might comprise Chapters 1–4). In a URL for your Web site, the Web host server's domain name is followed by a forward slash (/) and your directory name on that server *(http://www.genealogywebhost.com/~mydirectory)*. Following that, you insert a directory name (*http://www.genealogywebhost.com/~mydirectory/Anderson*). If you want to insert subdirectories within directories, use another forward slash, followed by the subdirectory name, and so on. For example, using the eight surnames in the ancestor chart in Fugure 4.4, the URL for each chapter would be as follows:

http://www.genealogywebhost.com/~mydirectory/Anderson

http://www.genealogywebhost.com/~mydirectory/Cartwright

http://www.genealogywebhost.com/~mydirectory/Dougherty

http://www.genealogywebhost.com/~mydirectory/Frederick

http://www.genealogywebhost.com/~mydirectory/Knox

http://www.genealogywebhost.com/~mydirectory/Johnson

http://www.genealogywebhost.com/~mydirectory/Jones

http://www.genealogywebhost.com/~mydirectory/Smith

Case-Sensitive URLs

URLs (Web site addresses) are case-sensitive. This means that visitors must type the address into their browser exactly as it is shown, with lowercase and uppercase letters as appropriate. Domain names (*cyndislist.com* in the example below) aren't case-sensitive by themselves, but everything that follows the domain name is (the directories and file names). For example, if you try to visit the following two URLs, you will be taken to two different Web pages. This URL is all lowercase:

http://www.cyndislist.com/planting/case.htm

This URL is mixed-case, with an uppercase *P* in the directory name, and an uppercase C in the file name:

http://www.cyndislist.com/Planting/Case.htm

Subdirectories = Subfolders = Sections within Chapters

After starting with a directory for each surname, if you plan to publish extensive information for one of your family lines, or for specific ancestors within that family line, you might decide to insert a subdirectory for each couple or each male ancestor with that surname. For example:

http://www.genealogywebhost.com/~mydirectory/Knox/Thomas

http://www.genealogywebhost.com/~mydirectory/Knox/Tilman

http://www.genealogywebhost.com/~mydirectory/Knox/Xerxes

http://www.genealogywebhost.com/~mydirectory/Frederick/Albert

http://www.genealogywebhost.com/~mydirectory/Frederick/Jacob

You will create directories on your Web site and transfer files using an FTP (File Transfer Protocol) software program. Your ISP will supply you with instructions on how to "FTP" to your Web site.

Web Pages = Files = Pages within the Chapters

File names for each Web page usually end in an extension such as .htm or .html, depending on the software program you use to create your Web pages. You can create an individual Web page for each person or couple—or create multiple pages for each person, with a different topic on each page. Each page is then stored within the proper directory or subdirectory, which ultimately assigns each page a distinct URL. In the third example above *(http://www.genealogywebhost.com/~mydirectory/ Knox/Xerxes)*, I might create several Web pages devoted to my research on my third-great-grandfather, Xerxes Knox—a main page for information about Xerxes (similar to a table of contents), a page with a biography, a page about his Civil War service, and a page about his first wife. So I would use at least four Web pages to share Xerxes' story with the world, each with a unique URL depicting the file and directory structure (see Figure 4.7).

Server and User's Directory http://www.genealogywebhost.com/~mydirectory	Directory	Subdirectory	File Name
The main index page, serving as a Table of Contents for the Xerxes directory, within my Knox surname folder	/Knox	/Xerxes	/Xerxes.htm or use the default name for index pages on the host server (such as index.htm)
Supporting page with a biography of Xerxes	/Knox	/Xerxes	/Xerxes_bio.htm
Supporting page with details of his Civil War service	/Knox	/Xerxes	/Xerxes_cw.htm
Supporting page with information about his first wife	/Knox	/Xerxes	/Xerxes_Phoebe_Huntley.htm
Data pages generated from my Genealogy database—three generations of descendants of Xerxes Knox	/Knox	/Xerxes	Page names and additional subdirectory names are generated by the genealogy software.

Figure 4.7 File structure for four Web pages within a chapter for a specific surname

Never create Web page file names or directory names that have spaces in them. They create problems when you try to share a URL with other people via e-mail, they are awkward to copy and paste, and they word-wrap in strange places within text. Use an underscore (_) instead of a space.

Duplicate the Organization on Your Computer's Hard Drive

When you begin the process of generating pages for your Web site, you should create and store the Web pages on your computer's hard drive in a specific folder created just for storing that set of pages. You should make a separate folder for each set of pages that you generate by family or surname, as shown in Figure 4.8. If you create the folders on your computer's hard drive in the same fashion that you plan to create the directories on your Web site, you can easily transfer pages from your computer to your site with few errors. Otherwise, it's easy to transfer a copy of a file to the wrong directory.

If you plan to further structure your Web site with sections or chapters for specific people within those families and surname groups, you can create additional subfolders within folders (see Figure 4.9). The organization is up to you, but again you should be sure that the way you store your Web pages on your hard drive duplicates the way you

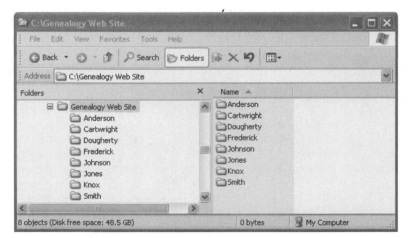

Figure 4.8 The structure of folders for a Web site as stored on your computer's hard drive

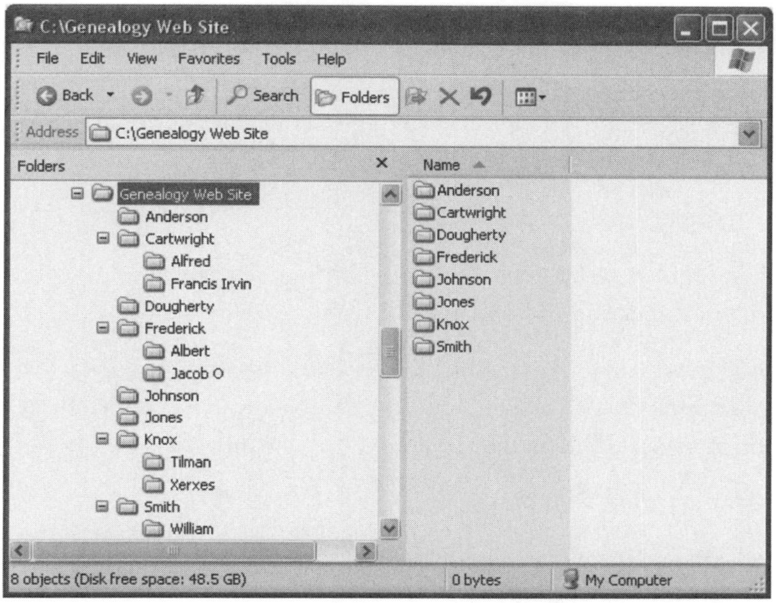

Figure 4.9 The structure of Web site folders, and subfolders used to store Web pages on your computer's hard drive

organize them on the Web server and vice versa. Doing so ensures a much smoother transfer when you move files back and forth between your computer and your Web site.

Plan Ahead—Avoid Broken Links and Lost Cousins

Your initial plans for your Web site may be a few simple pages, perhaps only one Web page for each of the eight surnames. Or you may envision numerous data pages for each person in your family tree. Either way, planning your file and directory structure ahead of time ensures that you have plenty of room to grow. One of the problems I see most often with new genealogy Web sites is that after the Webmaster creates the site, it begins to expand over the next few months. The Webmaster then reorganizes and shuffles files around, which changes the directory structure and the URLs within the site. Changing URLs after the fact means that previous links, favorites, bookmarks, and search engine hits all become broken and previous visitors are unable to return to your site. A stable site relies on static URLs that can be used over and over again. Broken URLs mean losing a repeat visitor or a cousin who has no other way of finding you. The following partial summary outlines the structure of our eight-chapter model:

🍃 Home Page (the cover and table of contents for our book)

- Chapter 1 (representing one surname, family group, or topic)
  Index page for the chapter, outlining the information to be found in that chapter, with links to the remaining pages within the chapter

  - Supporting Web pages for Chapter 1

  - Possible subchapters or sections within this chapter, each with its own directories and index pages

- Chapter 2 (representing one surname, family group, or topic)
  Index page for the chapter, outlining the information to be found in that chapter, with links to the remaining pages within the chapter

  - Supporting Web pages for Chapter 2

  - Possible subchapters or sections within this chapter, each with its own directories and index pages

- Chapter 3 (representing one surname, family group, or topic)
  Index page for the chapter, outlining the information to be found in that chapter, with links to the remaining pages within the chapter

  - Supporting Web pages for Chapter 3

  - Possible subchapters or sections within this chapter, each with its own directories and index pages . . .

You can continue this general layout for each additional chapter and each section within those chapters.

🍃

Use your ancestor chart to outline the structure for your own site. You should mimic the model and the naming conventions detailed in this chapter to set up folders and directories on your computer. Keep in mind that you will expand the site over time, so be as flexible as possible in your naming patterns and conventions. One major benefit to partitioning your genealogy Web site by surname comes when it's time to update the Web pages. If you generate Web pages from genealogy software or a

GEDCOM utility (see Chapter 6), it is much easier to generate a new, updated set of Web pages for one surname in one directory on your Web site. It is much harder to generate your entire database and a completely new set of pages. Once you decide how to structure and organize your site, you can take the next step—planning the content for the Web pages themselves.

CHAPTER 5

Select the Contents for Your Genealogy Web Site

BY NOW YOU HAVE A GOOD IDEA WHAT THE PURPOSE OF YOUR SITE IS and how to organize the content. Let's look at what kind of content you want to publish on your site. Of course, you want to publish information and stories about your ancestors. But what else should you include—and what should you be sure *not* to include on your site?

The Title

You've selected the type of site you want, you've mapped out its structure, and you have a clear sense of its purpose. Now choose a title for your Web site that clearly reflects that purpose. Keep the title short and useful—and easy to understand at a glance. Most important of all, choose a title you will be happy with for quite some time. Changing the title of your site confuses those visitors who try to return to your site. You can choose one main title for your entire site, and then use specific and more descriptive titles for each section on your site. This is similar to having a title for your book, with different names for each chapter in the book. For example, your Web site might be called "Daisy's Family Tree" and the chapters might be called "Dougherty Family in Indiana" and "Cartwright Family in North Dakota" and so on. For a complete discussion of the dos and don'ts of Web site titles, see Chapter 10.

What You Should Include

The purpose of your site dictates the content. Your site can be short and sweet, detailing the bare essentials about one or more of your ancestors. Or it can be all-inclusive, with copies of everything you've worked on to date. The ideas are endless:

- Full names, dates, and places
- A brief sentence about each of the ancestors you are researching—or your entire research project copied directly from your own genealogy database and research notes
- Stories and biographical text about your ancestors
- Charts and reports generated from your genealogy software (see Chapter 6)
- Individual photographs or a comprehensive photo album (see Chapter 9)
- Digitized copies of records and documents (with proper permissions for reproduction when necessary; see Chapter 9)
- Audio or video files of family members (see Chapter 9)
- Sources for your data—or a statement that source citations are available on request
- A consistent title across the site (see Chapter 10)
- A consistent footer on every page across the site (see Chapter 8)
- Full contact information to make it easy for people to find you online and offline (see Chapter 10)
- Navigational aids that make using the site easy (see Chapter 8)
- A Web page that focuses on the information and help that you hope to get from visitors in order to break through the brick walls in your research or find answers to some of your research questions

What You Should Not Include

In the zeal to create genealogy Web sites, many people inadvertently step into areas that get them into a bit of trouble. They have the best of intentions but are simply unaware that they have stepped over a line. These basic rules of online publishing should help you avoid making those same mistakes:

- Don't include information about living individuals. Respect the privacy and rights of others.

- Don't include copyrighted material unless you obtain permission from the copyright holder.

- Don't include redundant information that can easily be found elsewhere, like census indexes or family data that has already been published by others online or offline.

- Don't include misleading statements. Unproven information or assumptions about your research should be clearly labeled as such.

About Privacy

Privacy is a hot topic in this electronic world, and genealogy databases contain a lot of personal information about living people. Names, birth dates, mother's maiden name, and other sensitive bits of information that end up in the wrong hands can easily be misused. And some information may cause family members embarrassment or discomfort if you make it available to the outside world. Our cousins share information with us because we are the designated family historians. That means it is our job to use their information responsibly. Is it appropriate for you to share personal information about your cousins with the rest of the world via your Web site? Is it polite to share stories that include sensitive family secrets with total strangers online?

Determine a personal policy regarding privacy, and make it well known to people who contribute data to your research. If you plan to include information about your cousins, be sure you first have their permission to publish that information online. But even if you have their permission, stop to think about whether you truly need to publish that information online. For the most part, genealogists work backward in time. We connect online with cousins who share a common great-grandparent or an ancestor further back in the family tree. It usually isn't necessary to publish information about living family members. I publish *nothing* about living people—and that's the policy I recommend to every genealogist publishing online.

So set some guidelines to follow as you publish your family history information online—on your Web site and in e-mail correspondence. Do not publish information about anyone in your database who is currently labeled as "Living." This includes private information about you, such as your birth date. Use a time guideline for privacy such as the seventy-two-year rule observed by the government for the U.S. Federal

Standards for Sharing Information with Others
Recommended by the National Genealogical Society

Conscious of the fact that sharing information or data with others, whether through speech, documents or electronic media, is essential to family history research and that it needs continuing support and encouragement, responsible family historians consistently

- Respect the restrictions on sharing information that arise from the rights of another as an author, originator or compiler; as a living private person; or as a party to a mutual agreement

- Observe meticulously the legal rights of copyright owners, copying or distributing any part of their works only with their permission, or to the limited extent specifically allowed under the law's "fair use" exceptions

- Identify the sources for all ideas, information, and data from others, and the form in which they were received, recognizing that the unattributed use of another's intellectual work is plagiarism

- Respect the authorship rights of senders of letters, electronic mail, and data files, forwarding or disseminating them further only with the sender's permission

- Inform people who provide information about their families as to the ways it may be used, observing any conditions they impose and respecting any reservations they may express regarding the use of particular items

- Require some evidence of consent before assuming that living people are agreeable to further sharing of information about themselves

- Convey personal identifying information about living people—like age, home address, occupation, or activities—only in ways that those concerned have expressly agreed to

- Recognize that legal rights of privacy may limit the extent to which information from publicly available sources may be further used, disseminated, or published

- Communicate no information to others that is known to be false, or without making reasonable efforts to determine its truth, particularly information that may be derogatory

- Are sensitive to the hurt that revelations of criminal, immoral, bizarre, or irresponsible behavior may bring to family members

Census. Better yet, due to extended life expectancy, observe your own privacy rule—publish nothing about anyone born within the past hundred years. Use a utility or software option to "clean" your database file and remove information about living individuals before you publish anything on a Web site or send it in e-mail correspondence. The following software programs (also known as GEDCOM cleaners) are designed to protect privacy in GEDCOM files:

 GeDStrip Program
freepages.genealogy.rootsweb.com/~hotrum/gedstrip.htm

 GED2GO (GEDCOMS TO GO)
www.geocities.com/yosemite/trails/4849/evb/

 GEDClean32—GEDCom File "Cleaner"
www.raynorshyn.com/gedclean/

 GEDLiving
www.rootsweb.com/~gumby/ged.html

 Res Privata
members.ozemail.com.au/~naibor/rpriv.html

> If your grandmother is living, you might choose not to publish her mother's maiden name—it may well be her security password at her bank.

If you do publish information about living people, do so only with their *written* permission. An e-mail message may or may not suffice, depending on the circumstances, because it can be hard to prove that it came from a specific person. When you ask your cousins for permission to include their information on your Web site, be sure you clearly indicate what your intent is for that publication. For example, explain in detail that you plan to publish a Web site with the family history and that their personal data will appear on your site, on the Internet, available to anyone worldwide.

Once you publish information online (on the Web or via e-mail), it is forever out of your control. It can easily be copied, distributed, and used by others. You might publish it on your site or share it with a cousin and believe that you "know" where the data is. But if you share the data with Person X, she can easily share it with Person Y, who then shares it with Person Z. Or a visitor to your site may copy the data without your ever knowing. In either scenario, the data may eventually find its way into the publications (books, Web sites, online databases, CD-ROMs) of others, which may never have been your original intent. If you have any reservations about publishing anything on your site, follow your instincts—don't publish it.

About Copyright

When it comes to copyrights, misinformation and misinterpretation abound. Briefly, copyright gives the author of a work the right to

- Reproduce the work
- Permit copies to be made by others
- Prepare derivative works
- Display the copyrighted work publicly

Your work is automatically covered by a copyright upon creation in a fixed medium—paper, computer media, disk, Web site, and so on. You don't have to display a copyright symbol or statement in order to maintain a copyright on your work. But you *should* display a copyright symbol because doing so makes it easier for you to defend your copyright and protect your work. Similarly, you don't have to register your copyright in order to protect your ownership of your work. But if you ever find yourself in a legal suit, your copyright must be registered if you want to enforce the full benefits of copyright protection.

Before you include anything on your site that originally belonged to someone else, find out whether it is under copyright. Most of the material you might want to use is protected by the copyright of the owner. If you aren't sure, always ask permission—never make assumptions. If the owner of the material permits you to publish the information on your site, be sure to give the owner credit. Tell your readers that some of the material on your site is used with permission of its author, and supply them with a name and e-mail address. If that material is contained in a paragraph or on a specific Web page, you can acknowledge the author there. If the borrowed material

Something to Think About

One of the sad side effects of copyright infringement is the proliferation of inaccurate genealogical data. People who are tempted to copy things from others run the risk of copying incorrect information. If that faulty data is published online, it is easily repeated by others who may believe it to be factual. The accessibility of the inaccurate material becomes magnified because everyone online will be able to view it in more than one place. Additionally, if you copy something from someone else, do you even know whether the information was that person's property to begin with? You may be contributing to a problem that goes deeper than you thought. To avoid making matters worse, use the work of others only when you have obtained proper permission.

is merged with your own data throughout the site, consider creating a separate Web page for acknowledgments. An acknowledgments page is a good place not only to indicate that you have used others' material with their permission—and list them by name—but also to thank those who have helped you.

Web pages are protected by a copyright. Information contained on those Web pages and all original information that is not in the public domain are protected by copyright. Graphics and other multimedia that appear on a site are protected by a copyright, unless they are clearly marked as public domain. A collection of works, including a set of compiled links, *is* protected by copyright. URLs to Web sites are not under copyright protection by themselves because they are *facts*, just as telephone numbers are facts. But a *link* is not the same as a URL:

$$URL + HTML\ code + descriptive\ text = A\ link$$

Source code for a Web page is also protected by copyright. Just because you *can* copy it doesn't mean you *should* copy it. Doing so constitutes a copyright violation. Besides, the Web makes it easy for you to link to another person's work online. So there's no reason to copy it.

Your Web site is protected by copyright as soon as you create it. You are not required to display a copyright notice. *But you should.* To receive the full benefit of copyright protection, include a copyright statement at the bottom of every page of your Web site, preferably in the common footer (see Chapter 8). A standard copyright statement should appear this way on your site:

Copyright © 2003 Your Name Here. All rights reserved.

The following are some common copyright myths, misinformation, and misunderstandings I have seen online:

Myth: It's on the Internet. Everything on the Internet is free.

Fact: It may be free for you to view (aside from pay-for-use sites), but not free for you to take. You are free to go to a library and look at books. But you can't take a book, put your name on it, and call it your own work. The same goes for the Internet. You are free to visit Web sites and look at the information found there. But you can't copy that information, put your name on it, and call it your own. You must ask permission of the author before you copy from a site.

Myth: It is all right to copy information from a cousin's Web site because it is my family too.

Fact: The information may be about your ancestors, but it isn't your work or your research. You must ask permission first.

Myth: It is all right to copy information because I'm not going to make any money from it.

Fact: The copyright is in place to protect the intellectual property—the creative work—that went into authoring the information. Whether someone derives income from the work isn't the issue. What matters is that the work belongs to the author.

Myth: It is all right to copy information because I'm doing this as a volunteer service, for the good of genealogy and online researchers.

Fact: Again, your reasons and intentions for taking the copied work are not the issue. You aren't the author. It isn't yours to copy.

Myth: Genealogy is just a bunch of facts. Facts can't be copyrighted.

Fact: True, facts such as names, dates, and places that are publicly available information are not protected by copyright. But the way facts are compiled and presented is unique—compilations are protected by copyright. Genealogical research and your family history information are much more than just facts, though. How you choose to organize and present facts, the facts you choose to present, your analysis of the data and your conclusions, all reflect your unique perspective and creativity!

For more information about copyright, see these Web sites:

- 10 Big Myths About Copyright Explained
  www.templetons.com/brad/copymyths.html

- COPYRIGHT Mailing List
  www.rootsweb.com/~jfuller/gen_mail_general.html#COPYRIGHT

- Cyndi's List—Copyright Issues
  www.CyndisList.com/copyrite.htm

- U.S. Copyright and Genealogy
  stellar-one.com/copyrightgenealogy/

- U.S. Copyright Office
  lcweb.loc.gov/copyright/

About Redundancy

It's this simple: Don't waste time (yours and your visitors') publishing information that appears elsewhere online—unless there are differences and discrepancies that fellow researchers need to know about. Links on Web pages allow us to point to other online references that relate to our own publication and research. So if you already know about the existence of the Web site "The Definitive Life Story of Frederick Jones in Simpleville, USA," do you really need to publish "A Simpleton in Simpleville: The Life Story of Frederick Jones"? I see examples of online redundancy on a regular basis, particularly when it comes to transcriptions, extractions, and indexes of records. You are certainly welcome to publish everything you have accomplished in your own research. But why waste your energy, time, and Web space duplicating already available information when you have so many tasks to accomplish to get your family history online and to share records with others?

If you do choose to publish something that exists elsewhere in another version or format, try to find a unique way to present your material—another spin on the old story, a new perspective on the research. Add something new or correct an error that appears on the existing site.

About Misleading Statements

The Internet and the electronic environment lend a feeling of legitimacy to materials published online. We think of the Web as one huge reference library, but *anyone* can publish *anything* online. The statement, "I found it on the Internet!" is often said with faith and enthusiasm. Consider information that you find online as only a helpful hint or clue. Unless it is a digitized copy of an original record or source, what you find on the Internet is far from the final word.

Because of visitors' tendencies to believe what they read online, a Webmaster must publish information responsibly and with care, as we noted in Chapter 3. Visitors to your site believe what they see on your site. If you make overblown statements like the following, you do a disservice to yourself and your site's visitors:

- "The only Web site you will ever need for Smiths in New York."
  (Hint: How do you know it is the only site they will ever need?)

- "Everything you need to know about my family is here!"
  (Hint: *You* don't yet know everything about your family.)

- "I have been working on my family history for a year now, and I'm done with two of my families."
  (Hint: You are never done with any family.)

- "The Snicklefritz family never lived in Pennsylvania."
  (Hint: Never say never.)

How can you be a responsible Webmaster? Full disclosure. Tell your visitors when you are unsure about something. Let your visitors know when one of your statements is based on assumptions or an educated guess. You can even tell them how you arrived at that conclusion. In fact, presenting the reasons for your conclusion may help you: Cousins and fellow researchers may see something in your brick wall that you didn't see and may tell you how to find a definitive answer or the proof you need.

Food for Thought: NGS Standards and Guidelines

Now that you have planned your site, you are probably anxious to dig in and start building your Web pages. But first, take a few minutes to review the "Guidelines for Publishing Web Pages on the Internet" recommended by the National Genealogical

Guidelines for Publishing Web Pages on the Internet
Recommended by the National Genealogical Society

Appreciating that publishing information through Internet Web sites and Web pages shares many similarities with print publishing, considerate family historians

- Apply a title identifying both the entire Web site and the particular group of related pages, similar to a book-and-chapter designation, placing it both at the top of each Web browser window using the <TITLE> HTML tag, and in the body of the document, on the opening home or title page, and on any index pages

- Explain the purposes and objectives of their Web sites, placing the explanation near the top of the title page or including a link from that page to a special page about the reason for the site

- Display a footer at the bottom of each Web page that contains the Web site title, page title, author's name, author's contact information, date of last revision, and a copyright statement

- Provide complete contact information, including at a minimum a name and e-mail address, and preferably some means for long-term contact, like a postal address

- Assist visitors by providing on each page navigational links that lead visitors to other important pages on the Web site, or return them to the home page

- Adhere to the NGS "Standards for Sharing Information with Others" (see page 68) regarding copyright, attribution, privacy, and the sharing of sensitive information

- Include unambiguous source citations for the research data provided on the site, and if not complete descriptions, offering full citations upon request

- Label photographic and scanned images within the graphic itself, with fuller explanation if required in text adjacent to the graphic

- Identify transcribed, extracted, or abstracted data as such, and provide appropriate source citations

- Include identifying dates and locations when providing information about specific surnames or individuals

- Respect the rights of others who do not wish information about themselves to be published, referenced, or linked on a Web site

- Provide Web site access to all potential visitors by avoiding enhanced technical capabilities that may not be available to all users, remembering that not all computers are created equal

- Avoid using features that distract from the productive use of the Web site, like ones that reduce legibility, strain the eyes, dazzle the vision, or otherwise detract from the visitor's ability to easily read, study, comprehend, or print the online publication

- Maintain their online publications at frequent intervals, changing the content to keep the information current, the links valid, and the Web site in good working order

- Preserve and archive for future researchers their online publications and communications that have lasting value, using both electronic and paper duplication

Society *(www.ngsgenealogy.org/comstandards.htm)*. You can find the other NGS Standards and Guidelines on page 68 and in the Appendix. Throughout the next five chapters, you will see references and recommendations that are heavily influenced by these standards and guidelines.

Now that you have a clear idea what to include and what *not* to include on your site, gather your database files, reports, photos, tapes—and your creative flair. All the planning you've done to this point will make the next few steps much easier. It's time to create and customize the pages for your family history Web site!

Chapter 6

Create the Basic Web Pages

NOW THAT YOU HAVE A PLAN FOR WHAT TO INCLUDE ON YOUR WEB site and how your site should appear, it's time to create the Web pages.

Let's look first at some of the software programs available to help you generate genealogy Web pages. This chapter, indeed this book, will not teach you how to use the various software programs from a technical standpoint. Because software has so many variables and updates come so frequently, you should refer to your user manuals for specific information about your software. Here, we'll explore the features common to genealogy software in general, rather than address the details of specific programs.

As you create your Web pages in this chapter, you may need to make some design choices for your site, such as color, font style, or graphics. Refer to the guidelines in Chapters 7, 8, and 9 for detailed information on making the best design choices for your site. Once you have created your basic pages, those chapters show you how to enhance and personalize them.

Using Genealogy Software

Since you are creating a genealogy Web site, it is safe to assume that you have a computer. If you have a computer, it is likely that you already have a genealogy database software program. Genealogy software (such as Family Tree Maker, PAF, or Legacy) helps you maintain a database of your ancestors and their descendants in your family tree. These programs also allow you to create reports and charts in order to share your research with fellow genealogists and family members. Most of the popular genealogy database software programs, particularly the most recent versions, also give you the ability to build Web pages directly within the program's features. If you haven't upgraded your genealogy software in the past two or three years, consider doing so in order to take full advantage of the latest features, such as Web page building. Figure 6.1 lists some of the most common genealogy software programs that also help you generate Web pages. If you plan to have a comprehensive site that includes most of the individuals and families found within your database, using your genealogy software program to create the Web pages is the best way to go. It provides you a structure to work with—and saves you time.

Software Program	Web Site	Creates Web Pages
Ancestral Quest	*www.ancquest.com*	Yes
Ancestry Family Tree	*aft.ancestry.com*	Yes
Brother's Keeper	*www.bkwin.org*	Yes
Family Origins	*www.formalsoft.com*	Yes
Family Tree Maker	*familytreemaker.genealogy.com*	Yes (Limited Web space is available)
Generations	*www.genealogy.com*	Yes
Legacy Family Tree	*www.legacyfamilytree.com*	Yes
The Master Genealogist	*www.whollygenes.com*	Yes, with supplemental software *(www.johncardinal.com/ss/)*
PAF—Personal Ancestral File	*www.familysearch.org/eng/paf/*	Yes
Reunion	*www.leisterpro.com*	Yes
RootsMagic	*www.rootsmagic.com*	Yes

Figure 6.1 Some genealogy software programs that generate Web pages

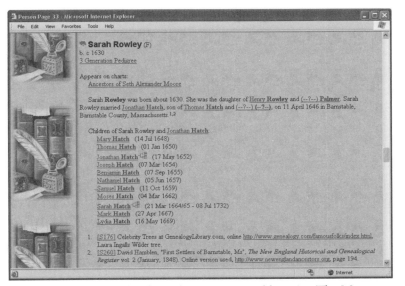

Figure 6.2 An example of a Web page generated by using The Master Genealogist and Second Site can be found on Thomas Clough's genealogy site *(freepages.genealogy.rootsweb.com/~tclough/SS/p33.htm#i815).*

Each genealogy program has its own format and layout for the Web pages it creates. For the most part, the programs all generate a similar set of Web pages that are usually designed to mimic traditional printed genealogy reports and charts—family group sheets, ancestor charts (also known as pedigree charts), descendant reports, ahnentafel reports, and so on (see Figure 6.2).

Read the user manual and help files that accompany your genealogy software program to determine what options are available. You may be able to choose any of the following before the pages are created from your database:

- Type of report or format for your Web pages
- A title to apply to the site or to pages within the site
- Colors for your site (background, text, links)
- Privacy options to remove living individuals from the reports

In Chapters 7–10 we will discuss a variety of ways you can modify your Web pages so they will become the best possible genealogical resources for others to use.

Your Entire Database or Portions?

Your genealogy software program offers at least two options: You can create one large Web site using everyone in your database (after removing the references to living individuals to respect their privacy), or you can sort your Web site by family line and surname. I recommend the second option; it's more logical, easier to organize, and more appealing to cousins as they attempt to navigate through your site.

The one element common to all the people in your database is that they are all related to you. But keep in mind they are not necessarily all related to one another. The cousins who visit your site are related to you through one or more family lines, but not through each and every one of the lines that you might include on your site (see Figure 6.3). They will be interested in learning about one or two of the family groups, but not about every single line.

Sorting your Web site by family and surname helps your cousins make sense of your site and easily see the connections to their own family and genealogical research. You might choose to sort by surname using the ancestors of one specific person or the descendants of one specific person in your database. Either way, your genealogy software

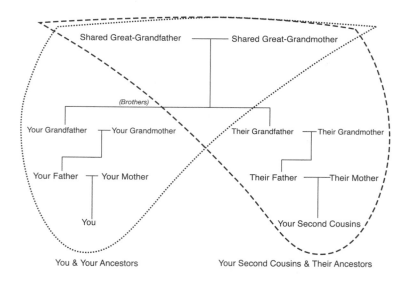

Figure 6.3 Diagram showing that cousins share some ancestors with you, but not all ancestors. For example, these second cousins would not be interested in your mother's family line.

program allows you to partition and sort your database to create several sets of Web pages for specific surnames or family groups.

During the planning phase discussed in Chapters 3 and 4, you determined the organizational structure for your Web site. You may be using the model to which we refer throughout the book and be partitioning your site into eight surnames (which takes you back to your great-grandparents' generation). Or you might sort instead by the earliest known generation on each family line in your database, which will vary for each surname depending on where you are in your research for that family. Your site might be devoted to one surname and all the families in that one-name study. Or you may have decided to publish information for just one person or couple in your family tree. For the sake of this discussion, we'll refer to the eight-surname model, but the concepts below can be adapted to fit your site's purpose and structure.

Don't settle for the default output for the Web pages generated by your genealogy software program. Often the defaults don't include many components necessary to make your site easy to navigate. It is vital that you include contact information, consistent page titles, and other custom bits of information that convey your intentions to all visitors. So be sure to customize your pages using the tips outlined in Chapters 7, 8, and 9.

Sorting Your Database by Surname

In most genealogy software programs, you first open the record of the person in your database on whom you want to focus—generally, the earliest known individual with that surname. From there, you choose the button or menu option to create the Web pages. In some software programs, this option is under Reports. Next, you may be presented a set of choices about what you want to include in the Web pages you are about to produce. These are typical:

- Whether to display the ancestors or the descendants of that person

- The number of generations to incorporate, including that person

- Which database fields (birth, death, marriage, occupation, etc.) to feature for each individual

- Whether or not to include sources for the data

- The title of the page or additional text to be included on the pages

- The name of the file (or files) that will be created

- The name of the folder on your computer's hard drive where you will store the copies of the Web pages you create

For example, if I were to create a Web site for my third great-grandfather, Xerxes Knox, I would first locate his record in my genealogy database. In the Web page options, I would choose Descendants and limit it to three generations (see Figure 6.4). This means I would generate Web pages that display information about Xerxes as the first generation. The resulting Web pages would take us through his descendants for two more generations, stopping at his grandchildren—the generation of my great-grandmother. For privacy reasons, I wouldn't publish anything about the

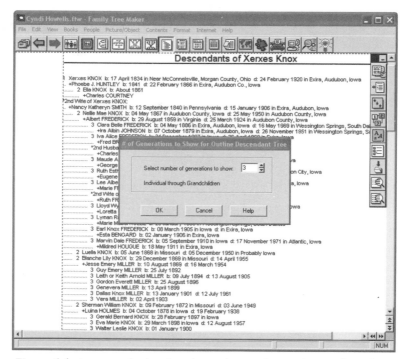

Figure 6.4 An example showing the option to choose the number of generations included in a report, and thus in the Web pages that will be generated using Family Tree Maker v.9

next generation, which includes my grandparents. For more information about privacy and Web page publishing, see Chapter 5.

For each surname you plan to include on your Web site, you repeat the process: Find the common ancestor for that surname, create the Web pages for a fixed number of generations, and include the options that you prefer. Each new set of Web pages you create for each surname then represents a "chapter" in your Web site. You can then customize each chapter and place it on your site within the appropriate directory or folder (as outlined in Chapter 4).

GEDCOM Web Page Conversion Software

If you keep your research in a genealogy software program database, you may want to generate Web pages directly from your database as outlined above. But what if you aren't happy with the resulting pages? You have another option: Several available software programs convert your GEDCOM file into Web pages. Creating Web pages this way becomes a two-part process: First use your genealogy software to create the GEDCOM, then use the conversion software to create the Web pages.

For more detailed, highly technical information on GEDCOM files, such as technical specifications, the data model, and so on, see the GEDCOM Standard Release 5.5, *homepages.rootsweb.com/~pmcbride/gedcom/55gctoc.htm.*

What Is GEDCOM?

GEDCOM stands for GEnealogical Data COMmunications. GEDCOM is a generic, database format designed to allow users to share family history database files between differing genealogy software programs. For example, if you want to share your Family Tree Maker file with your cousin who uses Legacy genealogy software, you first convert your database file into GEDCOM format. GEDCOM files can be shared easily with others via e-mail attachment or disk. They can be uploaded to user-contributed lineage-linked databases online. GEDCOM files can also be converted for use in companion software programs and utilities that create such items as specialty charts, books, scrapbooks, and Web sites.

To create a GEDCOM file (in most genealogy software programs), go to File, Export to GEDCOM, and create a new file with a .ged file extension after the name. Read the user manual and help files for detailed instructions on how to do this in your particular program.

Creating the GEDCOM File(s)

For the most part, the process of creating Web pages using your GEDCOM file is the same as described in the previous section for using your genealogy software. You create one large GEDCOM file from your entire genealogy database file that includes everyone, or you create several smaller GEDCOM files, one each to represent individual surnames or chapters in the Web site you are building.

In most genealogy software programs, you can create a GEDCOM by starting with one ancestor and choosing options to include the descendants of that person for a specific number of generations. More recent versions of genealogy software give you a variety of options to choose from in order to incorporate certain fields or features in the resulting GEDCOM file. For example, you may be able to choose a basic set of data fields (birth, marriage, death) or to include all the data fields in your database (baptism, divorce, occupation, notes, sources, etc.). As you create the GEDCOM files, choose the fields that you want to appear on the Web pages that you produce in the next step.

Building the Web Pages from Your GEDCOM File(s)

Once you generate the GEDCOM files from your database, you can begin to convert them into Web pages. Numerous software utilities can help you create the Web pages from a GEDCOM file. (See Figure 6.5 for an example of a page created using a typical GEDCOM-to-HTML conversion program.) Some programs are freeware, some are shareware, and some are online conversion utilities. Just as with genealogy software programs, each of these GEDCOM-to-HTML conversion programs produces a resulting set of Web pages. Some programs create a separate Web page for each person or family group, while other programs group several related families on one Web page. Most programs generate a surname index that lists all surnames alphabetically. Some also produce an index of individual names in the GEDCOM. Evaluate several programs to find one that is right for you and that produces the type of Web pages you want. Visit the Web sites for each of the utilities in the list below to view examples of what the program produces.

- GED2HTML: A GEDCOM to HTML Translator
  www.gendex.com/ged2html/

- Ged2Web
  www.wtoram.co.uk/ged2web/ged2web.htm

- GED2WWW
  www.lesandchris.com/ged2www/

- GED4WEB GEDCOM to HTML Genealogy Webpage Software
  www.ged4web.com/

- GEDCOM to HTML service on RootsWeb.com
  www.rootsweb.com/~nozell/gedcom-service.html

- GedHTree
  www.gedhtree.com/gedhtree.htm

- Gedpage
  www.frontiernet.net/~rjacob/gedpage.htm

- Genealogy Site Builder
  www.bargeron.com/software/gsb/index.htm

- GeneWeb (in French, Dutch, Swedish and English versions for Unix and Windows)
  pauillac.inria.fr/~ddr/GeneWeb/

- Indexed GEDCOM Method for GenWeb Authoring
  www.rootsweb.com/~gumby/igm.html

- Kinship Archivist
  www.kinshiparchivist.com

- Oxy-Gen: The Ultimate GedCom Converter
  www.ifrance.com/oxy-gen/index_en.html

- PerlGed (a shareware Perl script that generates Web pages on the fly from a GEDCOM file)
  www.etgdesign.com/perlged/

- phpGedView
  phpgedview.sourceforge.net/

- Publish Your Own PDF Genealogy Book Electronically on the Web
  www.ldpierce.com/publishpdf.html

- "Relatives" Genealogical Software
  mypage.direct.ca/v/vdouglas/RelIntro.html

- RootsView
  www.natural-software.com/rootsview.htm

- Sparrowhawk (a GEDCOM-to-HTML conversion program for the Macintosh)
  www.bradandkathy.com/genealogy/sparrowhawk.html

- uFTi homepage (Windows software for creating HTML Web pages)
  www.ufti.com/

- UncleGED
  gatheringleaves.org/uged/index.htm

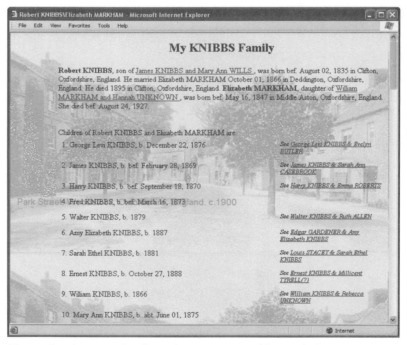

Figure 6.5 An example of a Web page generated by UncleGED to convert a GEDCOM file to HTML can be found on Don Knibb's genealogy site *(knibbs.family.users.btopenworld.com/fam010.html).*

Freeware is software that is free to use, without a fee to purchase it. **Shareware** is software that generally requires a small registration fee after a period of evaluation. Some functions that freeware and shareware programs provide are also available in online utilities on Web sites.

You might even download demos of the programs and try them yourself by using your GEDCOM file and displaying the resulting Web pages on your home computer.

Like genealogy software programs, GEDCOM-to-HTML conversion programs present options that allow you to customize your Web pages. See "Using Genealogy Software" on pages 77–83.

Customizing the Software's Output

Using the Web pages generated by your genealogy software or a GEDCOM conversion program is usually the easiest option, particularly if your database contains thousands of individuals. The software program has a predefined hierarchy of pages and directories in which the branches of your family tree will be organized. The genealogy program or GEDCOM software also generates an index of the surnames that can be found on your Web site, with each of the surnames hypertext-linked to specific pages within that hierarchy. If you have a large personal database, generating a site from a genealogy software program certainly has its advantages; it gives you a solid foundation on which to build your Web site, taking much of the organizational headaches out of the building process. It's one of the simplest ways to produce pages quickly and easily. Consequently, people often use the resulting set of pages "as is," without taking the time to customize the pages. But those pages are merely the foundation for your Web site.

Make the best use of your genealogy software program or GEDCOM utility: Customize the output as much as your software allows. Unfortunately, every software program works differently. Some programs offer several sought-after options, while others are very limited and give you few or even no options. Some have odd page-naming conventions, and others ignore common Web design elements that are necessary for good Web page layout and functionality. So be sure you take a good look at what your software allows. If the genealogy software or GEDCOM utility doesn't offer the options you want, you must edit your Web pages manually and add those features yourself. You edit your Web pages with an HTML editor or text editor (see pages 94–97).

One of the reasons to edit the pages in order to customize them is for consistency and clarity across your entire Web site. If your software doesn't already incorporate the following elements, you should do so yourself:

- Consistent titles and chapter headings. If several different names or titles appear in various places on your site, from one page to another, visitors will be confused as they attempt to find their way around your site.

- A common footer across the entire site that contains:
  - Contact information
  - Navigational aids for the main index page(s) on your site
  - Copyright and disclaimers (if applicable to your site)

  Having the same information at the bottom of every page makes it easy for the visitor to find your home page and to get in touch with you.

- Common navigational aids and information on every page. These help visitors find their way around your site. If you use the same types of graphics or links to point visitors to chapter index pages or your home page, you make it simple for them to surf from page to page and find what they are looking for.

- The last "update date" for that page or for the site as a whole. The update date indicates the last time you made a change to that Web page. Visitors can use this date each time they visit your site to help them determine whether you have new information to share.

Similarly, you can customize your Web pages to suit your creative impulses. You might tailor your Web pages to include such items as these:

- Personal choices for graphics and design elements
- A specific background color or graphic

Photographs and documents to accompany the data

Personal messages or text to enhance the data published in the pages

Additional text such as copyright statements and disclaimers

See Chapters 7, 8, and 9 for more about customizing your Web pages.

Supplemental Software Utilities

You can use a variety of methods to customize your Web pages:

- Edit the pages with an HTML editor software program (such as FrontPage, HotDog, Arachnophilia, Dreamweaver, BBEdit, Coffee Cup, or NoteTab).

- Manually edit the pages with a text editor (such as Notepad or NoteTab), which requires some basic knowledge of the HTML programming language.

- Use a text-replacement software program that can help you add, edit, or delete bits of text and code on your Web pages. Use its find-and-replace function to make numerous changes across several Web pages all at one time. This works great for repetitive updates such as dates, names, copyright, new links, and updated URLs. Three such programs are

  - NoteTab Pro
    www.notetab.com

  - TextPipe Pro
    www.crystalsoftware.com.au/textpipe.html

  - XReplace-32
    xreplace.vestris.com

Displaying the Data without Genealogy Software

If you are not yet using a genealogy software program to maintain your database, I strongly urge you to find a program that suits you. Several free programs, as well as shareware programs, are available online. To learn more about genealogy software, go to *www.CyndisList.com/software.htm*.

However, you don't have to own a genealogy software program in order to display your family history on a Web site. You can create the Web pages yourself using an HTML editor or text editor (see the next two sections) and manually enter genealogical information about your ancestors. All of the guidelines outlined in this book apply to creating your Web pages, whether you use genealogy software or not. If you create your pages manually, though, you may want to keep them small and simple. The structure of your site should be the same as described in Chapter 4—you should include one home page and one index page for each surname. You can include one Web page for each person or couple, unless you want to leave the majority of that information on the main index page for each surname.

Display a Few Simple Facts

Your information for each family might simply consist of one line—surname, dates, and places, as shown in Figure 6.6. Or you could display that same information in a

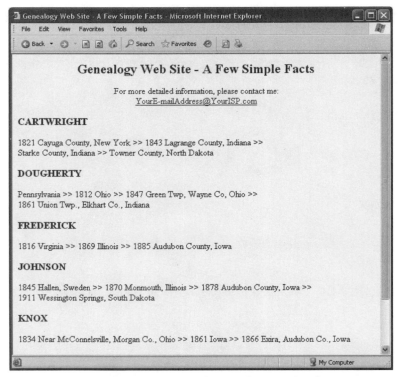

Figure 6.6 A simple, one-page genealogy Web site with a few names and facts displayed in one line

short, line-by-line list as in Figure 6.7. At the top or bottom of each Web page, you should provide a simple contact statement such as those shown in the following examples:

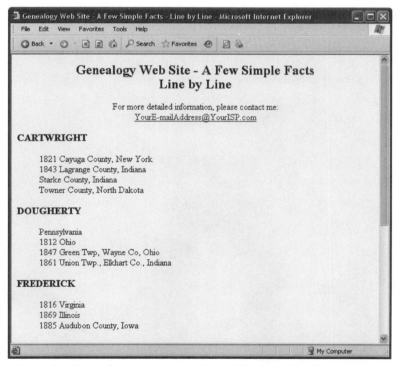

- For more detailed information, please contact me: YourE-mailAddress@YourISP.com

- Sources are available upon request by e-mail: YourE-mailAddress@YourISP.com

- I am happy to share my database via e-mail attachment. Contact me for more information: YourE-mailAddress@YourISP.com

- Please contact me with new information and corrections: YourE-mailAddress@YourISP.com

Figure 6.7 A simple, one-page genealogy Web site with a few names and facts displayed line by line

Use a Family Group Sheet

If you want to publish more details, you might use a typical family group sheet as a guide for laying out the information on your Web page. Include full names, dates, and place names for each event. You have several options: You can create your own format for the family group sheet, you can use a free template found online *(www.ida.net/users/elaine/pedigre2.HTM)*, or you can create a page like the one shown in Figure 6.8 by using the basic template in Figure 6.9 and filling in your own family's data. If you use the template, then for each additional child, repeat the part of the code shown for the first child. Replace each of the items that appear in bold italics, and customize the title and footer to your own specifications. We will discuss using HTML code in more detail later in this chapter.

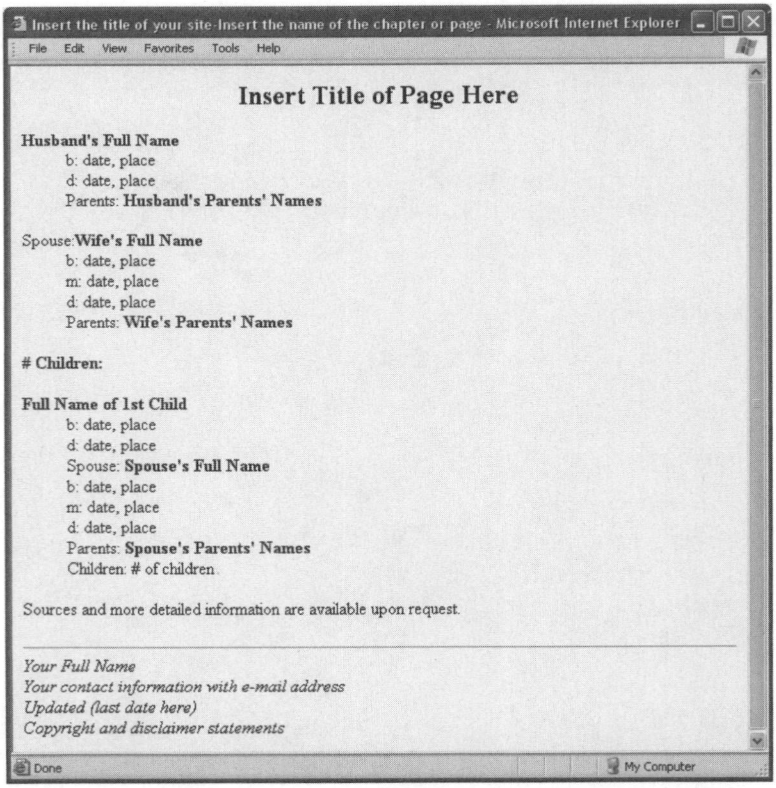

Figure 6.8 A family group sheet Web page created from the HTML code in Figure 6.9

```
<HTML>
 <HEAD>
  <META NAME="Author" CONTENT="Your Name">
  <META NAME="Keywords" CONTENT="Insert your list of surnames here">
  <META NAME="Description" CONTENT="Insert a one line description of your site.">
  <TITLE>Insert the title of your site—Insert the name of the chapter or page</TITLE>
 </HEAD>
 <BODY>
 <H2 ALIGN=CENTER>Insert Title of Page Here</H2>
  <DL>
  <DT><B> Husband's Full Name </B>
  <DD>b: date, place
  <DD>d: date, place
  <DD>Parents:  <B>Husband's Parents' Names</B>
  </DL><P>

  <DL>
  <DT>Spouse:<B>Wife's Full Name</B>
  <DD>b: date, place
  <DD>m: date, place
  <DD>d: date, place
  <DD>Parents:  <B>Wife's Parents' Names</B>
  </DL><P>

  <B># Children:</B><P>

  <DL>
  <DT><B>Full Name of 1st Child</B>
  <DD>b: date, place
  <DD>d: date, place
  <DD>Spouse:  <B>Spouse's Full Name</B>
  <DD>b: date, place
  <DD>m: date, place
  <DD>d: date, place
  <DD>Parents:  <B>Spouses' Parent's Names</B>
  <DD>Children:  # of children
  </DL><P>

  <I>Sources and more detailed information are available upon request.</I><P>

  <HR SIZE=1>
  <ADDRESS>
     Your Full Name <BR>
     Your contact information with e-mail address <BR>
     Updated (last date here) <BR>
     Copyright and disclaimer statements <BR>
  </ADDRESS>
 </BODY>
</HTML>
```

Figure 6.9 A template with HTML code for a basic family group sheet

Using HTML Editors

An HTML editor is a software program designed to write hypertext markup language so that you can create Web pages. With an HTML editor, you can create Web pages from scratch or edit preexisting pages such as those you created with your genealogy software program or GEDCOM conversion utility. Many HTML editors are available to choose from, including several shareware options:

- Arachnophilia
  arachnoid.com/arachnophilia/index.html

- BBEdit
  www.barebones.com/products/bbedit/index.shtml

- Coffee Cup
  www.coffeecup.com

- Dreamweaver
  www.macromedia.com/software/dreamweaver/

- FrontPage
  www.microsoft.com/frontpage/

- HotDog
  www.sausage.com

- Macromedia HomeSite
  www.macromedia.com/software/homesite/

- NoteTab
  www.notetab.com

Many are WYSIWYG editors, while some allow you to edit the HTML code yourself.

WYSIWYG (pronounced *whiz-ee-wig*) is an acronym for "What You See Is What You Get." In Web page creation, a WYSIWYG HTML editor is one that lets you design your Web page visually. Instead of writing the HTML code and then viewing the results in your Web browser, a WYSIWYG editor allows you to create the Web page within a browser and see your design as it is being fashioned. For new Webmasters, WYSIWYG editors are easy to use and a great way to get started if you have little technical background. Most people start off using WYSIWYG editors and later learn more about the HTML code behind the Web page, as well. That's what I recommend.

One of the disadvantages to using a WYSIWYG editor is that you have less control over the final output and display than if you were to write the HTML code yourself. Some WYSIWYG editors tend to add extraneous code that is unnecessary. Excess HTML code makes the file larger. A large file takes longer to load in the Web browser than a smaller file. Therefore, the more you know about HTML, the easier it is for you to manually edit problems out of your Web pages.

Using a Text Editor to Write HTML Code Yourself

Text editors are programs such as Notepad, WordPad, or a word processor. They allow you to create and edit plain text files (ASCII) such as those written in HTML for the Web. Before HTML editors were developed, HTML was always written with plain text editors. Over time, some text editors have been enhanced to make writing HTML easier. I use NoteTab Pro *(www.notetab.com)*, which is both a text and HTML editor. It is easy to use and has several automated features for making repetitive updates. It also has a find-and-replace feature that allows me to make a change across several Web pages all at one time.

Basic HTML
If you want to write your own HTML code for your Web pages, you need to know a few basics (see Figure 6.10). HTML is a formatting language that uses tags to assign certain behaviors to text on your Web page. Each function has an opening tag and a closing tag. For example, to apply bold formatting to text, insert the text between this opening tag <B> and this closing tag </B>. Within some tags you can also apply certain "attributes" to control the behavior of the tag. For example, in the <FONT> tag, you can specify a font name, color, or size attribute:

<FONT Name="Arial" Color="#000000" Size="+1">

This particular tag produces black text in the Arial font, one font size larger than the default that would be displayed in the Web browser.

Creating a New Web Page from Scratch
Using your text editor, open a new document. Give the file a name appropriate for the content on that Web page. For example, if you are creating your home page, the

A Few Basic HTML Tags	
Link	<A HREF="URL">Title of Link</A>
E-mail link	<A HREF=mailto:"YourE-mail@YourISP.com">Your Name</A>
Image/graphic	<IMG SRC="graphic_file.jpg">
Font	<FONT COLOR=... SIZE=... FACE=...> text </FONT>
Bold	<B> text to be shown in bold </B>
Italics	<I> text to be italicized </I>
Center	<CENTER> text or image to be centered </CENTER>
Paragraph	<P> text in a paragraph </P>
Left align text	<P ALIGN=LEFT> text </P>
Center align text	<P ALIGN=CENTER> text </P>
Right align text	<P ALIGN=RIGHT> text </P>
Heading, levels 1–6	<H1> text </H1>, <H2> text </H2>, <H3> text </H3>, <H4> text </H4>, <H5> text </H5>, <H6> text </H6>
Line break	 (similar to a single carriage return)
Horizontal rule	<HR> (horizontal line across the page to divide sections)
Page background	<BODY BACKGROUND="URL for the background graphic">
Line item bullet	<LI> (no closing tag necessary)

Figure 6.10 Some of the more common HTML tags you might use in your Web pages

name of the file will be index.html (or index.htm, index.asp, default.asp, etc.) and it will be stored in the top level of your directory structure. To save and name the file, follow these four steps:

1. From the menu choose File, Save As.
2. Save the file in the appropriate folder on your hard drive.
3. Type in the name of the file: index.html (or whatever file name and type is designated by your Web hosting service).
4. Save file type as HTML, Text Only, or ASCII.

HTML Tutorials Online

Learning how to write HTML is easy. Better yet, it's free. There are numerous HTML tutorials and guides online. The following are some of my favorites. They are easy to understand and quick to work through for people with all levels of computer experience.

- Barebones Guide to HTML
  werbach.com/barebones/

- HTML Help by the Web Design Group
  www.htmlhelp.com/

- Writing HTML—A Tutorial for Creating WWW Pages
  www.mcli.dist.maricopa.edu/tut/index.html

Use the template in Figure 6.11 for a very basic Web page. Use your own content to customize each of the items that appear italicized in bold print.

The Home Page and Index Pages

Your Web site needs a home page, which functions as the main index page. The home page for your site is the one page that should connect to every other significant section of your Web site. It deserves special care and attention. If you don't get all the noteworthy tidbits of information on any other page on your site, you should at least be sure that your home page includes everything of importance.

Each directory (or chapter) on your Web site also needs its own index page, which serves the same important function as a sort of mini home page for that chapter. These pages are all pivotal pages for your site. They also need special care and attention. The index page in each Web directory is the main entry page for that directory. These index pages should be updated any time you have a change in your research that you want to share online.

Most of the genealogy software programs or GEDCOM utilities generate rudimentary index pages with the bare bones of information that you need to share

```
<HTML>
 <HEAD>
  <META NAME="Author" CONTENT="Your Name">
  <META NAME="Keywords" CONTENT="Insert your list of surnames here">
  <META NAME="Description" CONTENT="Insert a one-line description of your site.">
  <TITLE>Insert the title of your site – Insert the name of the chapter or page</TITLE>
 </HEAD>
 <BODY>
  Title of the Site
  Insert graphics, text, data, etc.
  <ADDRESS>
   Your Full Name <BR>
   Your contact information <BR>
   Updated (last date here) <BR>
   Copyright and disclaimer statements <BR>
  </ADDRESS>
 </BODY>
</HTML>
```

Figure 6.11 A template with HTML code for a very basic Web page

Home Page—Main Index Page	Directory Index Page
Title of the Web site	Title of the Web site—name of chapter
Purpose or mission statement for site	Purpose or description for the chapter
Links to each chapter on your site	Links to each page in this chapter
Personal messages and other information you want your visitors to know about you and your family history research	Personal messages about the research in that chapter
Common Footer That Repeats Across the Entire Site	
Navigational links to important pages on the site	Navigational links to return visitors to the home page and other important pages on the site
Your full name and contact information	Your full name and contact information
Update date for that page	Update date for that page
Copyright statement and disclaimers (if any)	Copyright statement and disclaimers (if any)

Figure 6.12 The most necessary items to include on your main index page and on the index pages for each directory or chapter on your site

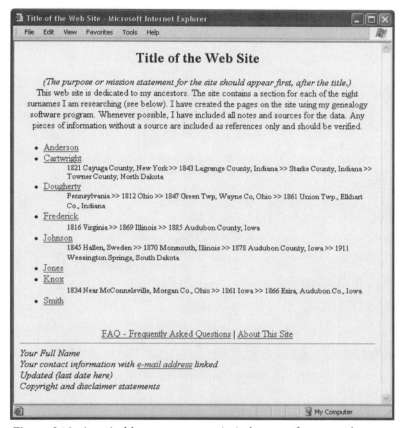

Figure 6.13 A typical home page or main index page for a genealogy Web site

about each surname. But these are not necessarily the same index pages I am referring to for each directory. The index page in each Web directory is the main entry page for that directory. Those are not always created by genealogy software. So you should create a main index for your home page and the directory index pages yourself using an HTML editor or text editor, incorporating the details in Figure 6.12. If your genealogy software or GEDCOM-to-HTML conversion program created index pages for each of the directories or subdirectories in the set of Web pages generated, you should edit them to incorporate each of the features outlined in Figure 6.12. See examples for the main index page and directory index pages in Figures 6.13 and 6.14.

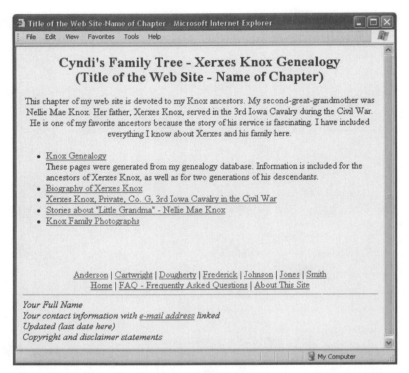

Figure 6.14 Example of an index page for a directory or chapter within a Web site

Checking Your Work

If you used your genealogy software program or a GEDCOM conversion utility to create your Web pages, you can now edit any of those pages using your HTML editor or text editor. After editing those pages, or after you have created any new Web pages from scratch, be sure to view the results in your Web browser. Checking the final output in your Web browser is important so that you can be sure the pages appear the way you want them to appear. Many times this part of the process highlights items you forgot or an odd placement of text or graphics. Viewing your pages in the browser enables you to see your publication from a different perspective. Use this opportunity to proofread the pages and look for errors.

To check the Web pages, open your Web browser. Choose File, Open from the menu at the top of the browser. Open the Web page file that you are currently working with. How does it look? If you find things that you want to change (such as the placement of text, or the size or color of text), go back to your HTML editor or text editor, make the changes, and save the file again. On your open Web browser, hit the Refresh or Reload button on your toolbar to get the new version of your Web page to load in the browser. Congratulations! You just created and edited your own Web page!

Getting Help from Friends and Professionals

If you find working with HTML, text editors, or Web page software programs a bit intimidating, you might look for help from others. When all else fails, ask a computer-savvy friend or family member to give you a hand tweaking your Web pages. If you don't know anyone who might be able to help you with your Web pages, you may be able to find the help you need from fellow genealogists who participate in the following free mailing lists online:

 Freepages-Help (for anyone whose site is hosted on RootsWeb)
   lists.rootsweb.com/index/other/RootsWeb_Support/Freepages-Help.html

 GENCMP
   www.rootsweb.com/~jfuller/gen_mail_computing.html#GENCMP-L

 GEN-COMP-TIPS
   www.rootsweb.com/~jfuller/gen_mail_computing.html#GEN-COMP-TIPS

 GEN-WEB-DESIGN
   www.rootsweb.com/~jfuller/gen_mail_computing.html#GEN-WEB-DESIGN

 HTMLHELP
   www.rootsweb.com/~jfuller/gen_mail_computing.html#HTMLHELP

You might also consider hiring a professional. If you find that you need a professional Web site designer, take some time to shop around. Before hiring someone to create your Web site, you should

 Ask for references from people who have used the Web site designer's services. Contact some of those people and ask whether they had a positive experience.

 Ask for addresses to some live, online examples of Web sites they have created. Visit the sites yourself to see how you like their work.

🍃 Make sure you agree to pay a flat fee for work on your site, rather than pay an hourly rate. Paying by the hour can result in having work on the site go on for more hours than you allowed in your budget. Don't pay the entire amount up front.

🍃 Get all estimates, promises, rates, and fees in writing.

🍃 Obtain the professional's full, real name; e-mail address; phone number, and physical address. It is easy for people to remain anonymous on the Internet. If you plan to do business with someone, that person should not be anonymous to you.

🍃 Prepare a set of instructions and a list of your goals and needs for your Web site.

🍃

You now have a set of new Web pages waiting on your computer's hard drive. What are they waiting for? Your personal touch. It's time to personalize, customize, and enhance the pages to make them your own. Let's turn those drab, generic Web pages into something that appeals to you and works well for your visitors.

CHAPTER 7

Personalize Your Web Site with Color and Style

NOW THAT YOU HAVE CHOSEN A FORMAT FOR YOUR WEB SITE AND created a basic set of Web pages, you are ready to move on to the next step—enhancing your site to give it your own personal flair. However, enhancing your site isn't merely the process of decorating and beautifying. It means customizing the site to make it easy to use and to give it additional features that help support the family history information you are publishing.

Remember Your Mission and Audience

As we talk about enhancing and personalizing your Web site, one of the key things you must keep in mind is your purpose and mission for the site. Are you creating your site for your own personal entertainment, or as a way to reach out to fellow researchers and long-lost cousins? Your genealogy Web site will be available worldwide, twenty-four hours a day, seven days a week. It will be seen by people at all levels of genealogical and computer experience—beginners and veterans alike. People both young and old, those with twenty/twenty vision or with bifocals, will all see your family history site. So you must work out a balance between what appeals to you and what is acceptable to the majority of your potential visitors. It is never possible to please everyone all the time. But you can do your best to make things work for the greatest possible number of your online viewers. Let the following principles, which we first explored in Chapter 3, guide you through this next phase of your creative process:

- My Web site will be easy to use.
- My Web site will be easy to access.
- My Web site will be easy to read and print.
- My Web site will accurately depict my family history research efforts.

Refer to Chapter 10 for a discussion of dos and don'ts—those elements you should be sure to include in your site and those you should avoid.

Colors in Backgrounds, Text, and Links

As we saw in Chapter 3, the color choices you make for your Web site are vital. Most people mistakenly choose their color schemes based on personal favorites, without much thought to how the colors might affect visitors to the site. Think about our book publishing analogy; most of us would not choose to publish a family history book on black paper with fluorescent pink ink. The vast majority of us would choose a traditional black font on white or cream paper. What works as a standard for us in traditional print publication also works for us in online publications. The rules do not change merely because we are now publishing in pixels of light on a monitor instead of ink on paper. Presenting your text in dark colors sitting on a light background is the only way to be sure that everyone can view and print your pages with clarity.

You must choose colors for four basic items: background, text, hypertext links, and visited hypertext links (those already viewed).

Don't design your site so that everything hinges on specific colors. Users can change the default settings in their Web browser and choose their own font colors. So no matter how you may want your Web site to appear, you don't ultimately have the final word. Your safest bet is a light background because the majority of visitors will be using a dark font.

Background Colors

First, think of a color scheme that appeals to you or that complements a set of graphics you have in mind for your site. From there, choose a light color for your background. You can choose a plain, solid color for the background when you create the Web page, or you can incorporate a Web graphic with a specific color and pattern. Picking a light background doesn't mean that you are stuck with just white, cream, or light beige. You can use very pale or faded versions of darker colors, as long as they offer just a tint of shade—but not enough to overpower the text that will appear on top (see Figure 7.1).

Font Colors

You need to choose three distinct font colors for your site—for the text, the hypertext links, and the visited links. The text on your Web pages makes up the majority of what your visitor sees, reads, and prints. So, using your preferred color scheme, pick a color for the text font that is easy to read on the computer monitor and dark enough to stand out on the lighter background. Be sure it's also dark enough to be readable when printed on any type of computer or printer. For example, if you have a faded periwinkle blue background and you use a font color in the blue or purple range, you must choose a *very* dark blue or purple to stand out on top of the periwinkle. Black is a much more reliable choice. Test your color selections by printing one version in color and another in black and white.

Colors on a computer screen can give very different results when printed in ink on paper. Always evaluate your page onscreen and on paper to make the best possible color choice for both.

Link Colors

A hypertext link is the part of the text your visitor can click on to go immediately to a specific page in your Web site or a different section on the same page. It is made up of the following elements in HTML:

```
<A HREF="insert full URL here">Name of Link Here</A>
```

Background Colors	Hex Number	RGB Number
Alice blue	F0F8FF	240, 248, 255
Antique white	FFEFDB	255, 239, 219
Azure	E0EEEE	224, 238, 238
Blue (pale)	CCFFFF	204, 255, 255
Gray (pale)	CCCCCC	204, 204, 204
Green (pale)	CCFFCC	204, 255, 204
Honeydew	F0FFF0	240, 255, 240
Ivory	FFFFF0	255, 255, 240
Lavender	E6E6FA	230, 230, 250
Lavender blush	FFF0F5	255, 240, 245
Lavender (pale)	CCCCFF	204, 204, 255
Light blue	BFEFFF	191, 239, 255
Light cyan	E0FFFF	224, 255, 255
Light yellow	FFFFE0	255, 255, 224
Linen	FAF0E6	250, 240, 230
Mint cream	F5FFFA	245, 255, 250
Misty rose	FFE4E1	255, 228, 225
Pink (pale)	FFCCFF	255, 204, 255
Rose (pale)	FFCCCC	255, 204, 204
Slate gray	C6E2FF	198, 226, 255
White	FFFFFF	255, 255, 255
Yellow (pale)	FFFFCC	255, 255, 204

Figure 7.1 A selection of browser-safe, pale colors suitable for background

When viewed in the Web browser, only the name of the link is displayed (the URL and the HTML code are hidden). The link is usually underlined and appears in a contrasting color that pops out from the rest of the text. If you are using an HMTL editor, it already has a standard set of link colors chosen as the default—usually dark blue or a similar dark color. As Webmaster, you can change those defaults and choose the colors that appear in each of your links. Good Web designers use different colors for the hypertext links, the visited links, and the rest of the text. For example, if you choose black text, you might make your hypertext links a bright, royal blue. Whatever color you choose, be sure it's easy to read and print.

Visited or Viewed Links

When your visitors click on a hypertext link to jump to another page on your Web site, they can then click the Back button on their browser to return to the previous page. If the Web site has been designed properly, the link they clicked should then be a different color from both the text and the other hypertext links. That color change comes from a design element called a visited link (or a viewed link). Like a trail of breadcrumbs, the visited link tells the visitor "you have already been there."

The color of the visited link should be quite distinct from those links that haven't

Web Browser History

Your Web browser software has an important history feature that performs at least two handy functions. The browser keeps track of all Web pages you visit and logs them by URL and by the date and time you last visited. It also tracks your visited links. After a certain number of days (twenty is the default for Microsoft Internet Explorer, nine for Netscape Navigator), the color of the visited link returns to the original link color. As a research tool, this color change helps alert the researching Web surfer that a certain number of days have passed since they last visited that URL. You can adjust the settings in your browser's options menu to increase or decrease the number of days that are used for the history.

Tip: Change your browser settings to thirty days for a fresh, monthly reminder of which links you need to revisit. To do this in Microsoft Internet Explorer, go to Tools, Internet Options. In Netscape Navigator, go to Edit, Preferences, Navigator.

yet been viewed—a lighter color that appears faded works best. For research purposes, a visited link has much value. Genealogical surfers use the color-changing aspects of visited links on a Web site to help them methodically visit each page on that site or to systematically visit one link after another in a long list of links on a page. If you have ever visited a Web page with a long, ongoing index of family names in someone's GEDCOM file, you know why having a different color for the visited links is an important timesaving tool for researchers.

Where Do You Specify the Colors?

As you create your Web pages, you may have several opportunities to specify your choice of colors for the background, fonts, and links. If you use a software program to generate your Web pages, you may be able to make a series of color choices before the new Web pages are created. The software program then applies your color choices to the HTML code it creates for your Web pages.

If you use an HTML editor or if you write the HTML yourself, you specify your default color choices at the beginning of each Web page within the <BODY> tag. The <BODY> tag is found following the <HEAD> tag at the top, or near the top, of every Web page. Within that tag, you identify the color attributes that you want the body of that Web page to display (see Figure 7.2), as in the following example taken from Cyndi's List:

```
<BODY BACKGROUND="http://www.CyndisList.com/graphics/cyndibak.gif"
BGCOLOR="#FFFFFF" TEXT="#521800" LINK="#660099" VLINK="#004000">
```

Type of Attribute	HTML Code
Background graphic	BACKGROUND=
Background color	BGCOLOR=
Text color	TEXT=
Link color	LINK=
Visited link color	VLINK=

Figure 7.2 HTML attributes to include within the <BODY> tag to designate the colors you have chosen for that Web page

Cascading Style Sheets

Another option for specifying your colors (and other design and layout elements) is to use Cascading Style Sheets (CSS). With your text editor or Web design software program, you can create one set of color and style instructions for your Web site and store that information in a Cascading Style Sheet. Each Web page on your site then has code that refers to that one style sheet. Anything you specify on the style sheet applies to your entire site. Using style sheets can be an easy way for you to make changes across your entire Web site, especially when you have hundreds of individual Web pages. The details of creating and implementing a system with Cascading Style Sheets are beyond the scope of this book, but there are numerous sites online, such as those listed below, that can help you develop your own CSS for your Web site:

 Cascading Style Sheets
www.w3.org/Style/CSS/

 Web Design Group, Guide to Cascading Style Sheets
www.htmlhelp.com/reference/css/

 WebDeveloper.com's Guide to Cascading Style Sheets
www.webdeveloper.com/html/html_css_1.html

 WDVL: Cascading Style Sheets
wdvl.internet.com/Authoring/Style/Sheets/

216 Colors—by Name or by Number?

As you learn more about Web site design, you may see references to the "Web-safe" or "browser-safe" color palette of 216 colors. These non-dithering colors are solid and appear exactly as you intend, regardless of the visitor's browser or monitor. Colors that dither are outside the 216-color palette. Dithering colors attempt to create new colors by superimposing dots of one color on top of another color. These can look blotchy on your Web pages and can ultimately alter the way you want your site to appear. Choose your color scheme from the 216-color Web-safe palette found on the following Web sites:

 Color Cube with Hex Number and RGB
www.html46.com/Color_Cube_Vr3.html

 Non-Dithering Colors by Hue
www.lynda.com/hexh.html

🍃 Non-Dithering Colors by Value
www.lynda.com/hexv.html

🍃 Non-Dithering Colors
htmlgoodies.earthweb.com/tutors/non_dithering_colors.html

🍃 Web-Safe Color Picker
templates.cgi101.com/colors/

Web browsers read colors by name or by hexadecimal values. The original standard is for the HTML in a Web page to use the hex number specific to each color. Newer browsers can read the more common color names like "black," "white," "red," or "blue." But older versions of Web browsers cannot recognize color names at all. To be safe, always use the hex values instead of color names. Use the tables found on the Web-safe color palette sites listed above to determine the hex values of the colors you choose.

As you begin to work with your scanner and graphic-editing software programs—such as Paint Shop Pro *(www.jasc.com)*, Adobe Photoshop, or Adobe Photoshop Elements *(www.adobe.com)*, you will also see the term RGB in regard to colors in graphics and photos. RGB is an acronym for "Red-Green-Blue"—the base colors that are combined to create all colors on computers. Several online utilities can convert a color's RGB value to a hexadecimal value so that you can match colors in your HTML fonts to the graphics and scanned images that appear on your site. For example, you might

Playing with Colors

Here are some fun, interactive sites online that allow you to pick and choose from several color schemes and preview how they look together:

- Colormaker
  www.bagism.com/colormaker/

- NetLingo: Web Coloring Book!
  www.netlingo.com/more/color/index.cfm

- Two4U's Color Compose Engine
  www.two4u.com/cgi-bin/color/compose/

like the blue of your grandmother's skirt in a photo that you are scanning to include on your site. If you want to match the font color for your text to that blue in Grandma's skirt, use your graphic-editing software to determine the RGB color value for that blue. Then convert the RGB value to the hex value and use it to customize the font color so that they match. RGB conversion tools can be found at the following sites:

- Decimal RGB to Hex RGB Value Conversion Utility
  www.yvg.com/twrs/RGBConverter.html

- RGB to Color Name Mapping
  Web2.ucs.ubc.ca/newcounter/rgb.txt.html

Fonts and Formatting

Picking the right font style is just as important as picking the right color scheme. If you choose the wrong font, your site may end up being difficult to read and hard for a visitor to quickly scan. The first thing visitors to your Web site do is scan the home page; they scroll up and down, looking for a list of the surnames in your family tree or for the links that will lead them to your research. So make the site easy to scan and read quickly.

Browser-Safe Fonts

As we noted in Chapter 3, Web browsers display text using a common default font: Times New Roman (or Times). When it comes to fonts, the first rule is to design your Web site knowing that most people will see it using that default font. You can specify certain fonts for text on your site. But visitors can specify the fonts they wish to view in their browser. So no matter how much you attempt to control how fonts appear on your site, you may be thwarted by the flexibility of the visitor's browser.

Browser-safe fonts can be seen whether your visitor is using a PC or a Macintosh. Each of these fonts has a compatible equivalent across platforms. So your best course is to draw from a common set of browser-safe fonts, such as those listed in Figure 7.3.

You can use other fonts on your Web pages. But keep in mind that in order for your visitors to see the font you specify, that font must already be installed on their computers. If they don't have that font, the browser will attempt to substitute another font—generally the default browser font, Times New Roman. Microsoft

PC	Macintosh
Times New Roman	Times
Arial	Arial, Helvetica
Verdana	Verdana
Courier New	Courier

Figure 7.3 Typical browser-safe fonts

Internet Explorer (IE) is more forgiving about displaying a variety of font types than Netscape Navigator is—especially on computers using Windows. In general, any font installed with a Microsoft software program is viewable in IE. Most are viewable in more recent versions of Netscape. But Macintosh users or visitors using an older version of a Web browser most likely won't be able to view a font that is a bit offbeat. So if you were thinking of using the "Chihuahua Dog Prints" font or the "Clown Makeup Tattoo" font, please reconsider. To learn more about browser-safe fonts, go to these Web sites:

- Browser News: Resources—Fonts
  www.upsdell.com/BrowserNews/res_fonts.htm
- Design Tip: Finding Safe Fonts
  www.netmechanic.com/news/vol2/design_no3.htm
- Principles of Good Web Design: Browser Safe Fonts
  www.stevegarwood.com/classes/design/bsfont.htm
- Specify Browser-Safe Fonts
  builder.cnet.com/webbuilding/pages/Graphics/Type/ss01c.html
- What's Wrong with the FONT Element?
  www.mcsr.olemiss.edu/~mudws/font.html

Specifying Fonts in HTML

The first place you specify a font attribute is in the <BODY> tag at the beginning of the page, where you specify the color for your text and links. If you use Cascading Style Sheets, you can also specify font colors and types for your Web site. For all other font choices, use the <FONT> tag in HTML. If you use a software program to generate your Web pages, you may be able to choose fonts or to customize the <FONT> tags as you create the pages. When writing HTML, indicate the name of the font you want to use as follows:

```
<FONT FACE="Arial">
```

You can insert additional, alternate font names for the browser to use in case the first font is unavailable on the visitor's computer. In the next example, if Arial is unavailable, the browser will look for Helvetica instead. If neither can be found, the browser will attempt to use the next available sans-serif font.

```
<FONT FACE="Arial, Helvetica, Sans-Serif">
```

Font colors and sizes can be designated in the same bit of code. To display green text using Arial, the code looks like this:

```
<FONT FACE="Arial, Helvetica, Sans-Serif" COLOR="#009900">
```

For the same display, but one font size larger than the default, the code looks like this:

```
<FONT FACE="Arial, Helvetica, Sans-Serif" COLOR="#009900" SIZE="+1">
```

Formatting Text

HTML allows for other formatting options that you may be accustomed to using in a regular word-processing software program. Three basic HTML formatting tools are shown in Figure 7.4.

You can also insert bullets for lists, highlight text, insert lines to separate sections, organize information into tables, and much, much more. As you organize the information on your Web pages, find the appropriate bits of HTML to

Bold	<B>your text goes here</B>
Italics	<I>your text goes here</I>
Underline	<U>your text goes here</U>

Figure 7.4 Basic text formatting in HTML

accomplish the look and feel you want for your site. Refer to other Web sites you have visited and note what you like about the format. You can find many good Web design ideas by paying attention to what others have done right—or wrong. Look at other sites to learn, but avoid copying the work of others. You want your site to have your own, personal touch.

Another source for great formatting design ideas is print, as we saw in Chapter 3. Look at your favorite newsletters and magazines. They use a standard font size and color for the main text, while they use larger fonts in bright colors for the headings. Between and around paragraphs of text, they include plenty of white space. This makes it easy for the reader to differentiate between sets of data. The formatting rules that apply to print publications also apply to Web sites. Don't reinvent the wheel. Instead, use the resources readily at hand to organize the layout of your Web pages and to help you make the right choices.

Graphics: Backgrounds, Bullets, and More

Besides colors and fonts, graphics are one of the popular ways that Webmasters can dress up a Web site. Web site graphics include backgrounds, banners, buttons, bars, and bullets. You can find matched sets of such graphics online, some even specifically designed for genealogy Web sites. In choosing the graphics for your site, keep in mind the guidelines we have discussed so far. Don't overload your site with too many graphics. Each graphic is a separate file incorporated into your Web page. A Web page is a basic ASCII text document, which can be small in file size. But each graphic you include on that page is referenced in the HTML and is basically tacked onto the page. Each graphic on your Web page enlarges the file size of the overall site. Multiple graphics on one page means more time for that page to download and display in your visitor's Web browser. The consequences are simple: the more graphics on a site, the more cumbersome and time consuming the site becomes for a visitor. However, you can streamline your choice of graphics without taking away from the decorative appeal of your pages.

Pick a small set of graphics with items that can be used over and over again throughout your site. Free Web graphics are abundant online. Many sites offer themed sets of graphics. A minimal set of graphics includes a background, a title banner (if available), a horizontal bar to divide sections, and one or two small bullets or buttons. Not all these items are necessary, but they are typical of graphics sets online.

The following are just a few of the sites that offer genealogy Web graphics you can use on your site. Most of these graphics are linkware—they are free to use as long as you set up a link that points back to the owner's site:

- Free Graphics from the Timberlake Family Home Page
  www.geocities.com/Heartland/Plains/7906/freestuff.html

- Glee Graphics
  www.geocities.com/Heartland/Woods/5503/

- Graphics by Shawna—Genealogy Sets
  www.geocities.com/SoHo/Coffeehouse/5922/gen.html

- Genealogy graphics by Rhio's Sampler
  www.rhiossampler.com

- Cyndi's Genealogy Home Page Construction Kit (links to genealogy graphics)
  www.CyndisList.com/construc.htm

When you find an available set of graphics that you like, download the graphics to your own computer. From there, you will upload all the Web graphics to your host server, along with each of the Web page files for your site. Each graphic then has its own URL on your host server.

A Graphics Directory

To better organize your filing system, upload your graphics to a special/graphics directory on your Web site. This housekeeping trick stores graphics files separately from the text files. In general, you won't need to change or update your graphics as often as you will the text on your Web pages, so storing them elsewhere helps reduce clutter and makes uploading and downloading each page a simpler process.

When referencing the graphics on your pages, be sure to specify the full path in the URL so that the extra directory isn't forgotten. For example, the title graphic on Cyndi's List can be found at *http://www.CyndisList.com/graphics/cyndititle.gif*.

There is no need to use one of the overly abundant "Under Construction" Web graphics on your site. By the very nature of genealogy and the Web, your site will always be changing, growing, and evolving. The graphic is redundant.

GIF and JPG

Web graphics generally come in two common formats: GIF and JPG. GIF files (.gif) are an image format used most often for line art in buttons, bars, and banners. JPG files (.jpg) are compressed so they are suitable for large images such as photographs and digitized documents.

If possible, look for Web graphics that have been "Web optimized" or streamlined. This means the files have been compressed as much as possible so that the file size is small and quick to load in a Web browser, without losing any quality in the resolution of the graphic. Some image-editing software programs, such as Adobe Photoshop Elements *(www.adobe.com)* or JASC Paint Shop Pro *(www.jasc.com),* have a built-in Web graphic feature. If you have a scanner, you probably also have image-editing software. You may be able to streamline your Web graphics with that program.

HTML Code for Your Graphics

This simple line of HTML code adds a graphic to your Web site:

```
<IMG SRC="full URL for the graphic" BORDER="0">
```

As the graphic loads in the Web browser, the browser must first determine the dimensions of the graphic in order to make space for it in the display. If you tell the browser what the graphic size is ahead of time, you help speed up the load time. First, determine the height and width of the graphic in pixels. You can do this with your image-editing program. You can also determine the size by viewing the graphic in your Web browser. Place your cursor on the graphic and click the right mouse button. Choose Properties from the pop-up menu to view the dimensions and the URL for the graphic. The HTML code for the graphic, with dimensions included, is

```
<IMG SRC="full URL for the graphic" BORDER="0" WIDTH="xx" HEIGHT="yy">
```

In this example, *xx* is the number of pixels in the width of the graphic, and *yy* is the number of pixels for the height.

Text-Only Alternatives

If your Web pages are heavy with graphics and photos, consider creating a separate *text-only* version of the site—or at least text-only copies of the index pages. Offering your visitors text-only pages gives them a quick way to tour your site. You can set up links from the text-only pages to the pages with the graphics and photos, giving visitors the option to choose whether or not to look at them.

Another bit of code you must be sure to add to your <IMG> tag is the ALT attribute. If you pass your cursor over graphics on a Web site, you may see a pop-up text window appear showing the name of the graphic or the link attached to the graphic. The text entered into the ALT attribute is what appears in that pop-up window. Additionally, text-only browsers can read the ALT text and display that in place of a graphic. This is especially helpful for browsers used by people with vision disabilities. Those browsers read the text, including the ALT text, to the visitor. Insert a short line of text, usually something that describes the graphic or the link, into the code as follows:

```
<IMG SRC="full URL for the graphic" BORDER="0" WIDTH="xx" HEIGHT="yy"
ALT="Description of Graphic Here">
```

Turning a Graphic into a Link

Graphics can also be used in links on your site. You may find a set of graphics specifically designed to aid in the navigation on your site. Buttons labeled "Home" or

Accessibility

For more ideas on making your Web site accessible to people with disabilities, see "Bobby" at *bobby.watchfire.com/bobby/html/en/index.jsp.* To learn more, listen to a lecture on audiotape by Birdie Monk Holsclaw, FUGA: "Accessibility Issues When Designing Your Web Page" at *www.audiotapes.com/product.asp?ProductCode='BCBS37'.*

"E-mail" are some of the more common choices. You might also use buttons or banners that link to some of your favorite genealogy Web sites. Foreign language sites often put an English version online and link to that page from a U.S. or UK flag graphic.

To make a graphic a clickable link, you must surround the HTML code for the graphic with the code for a link. For example, to create a link to RootsWeb with a graphic, use this code:

```
<A HREF="http://www.rootsweb.com/"><IMG
SRC="http://img.rootsweb.com/links/RootsWeb.gif" WIDTH="66" HEIGHT="75"
BORDER="0" ALT="Visit RootsWeb"></A>
```

Always specify graphic dimensions in width and height for faster loading in the Web browser.

Now you know the importance of making the right choices regarding color, fonts, and graphics for your site. Your site can be attractive and still be easy to access and use for all your visitors. The next step is to begin customizing the pages to make them highly useful research tools. Adding links, good navigational aids, contact information, and other administrative touches to your site is sure to make your site helpful to you—and your cousins online.

CHAPTER 8

Customize Your Web Site

FOR THE AVERAGE GENEALOGY WEB SURFER, NOTHING IS WORSE THAN visiting a new Web site and being unable to make sense of it. The key to making your site a useful research tool for you and for those who use your site lies in how you customize the Web pages, particularly after you have created a default set of pages from a genealogy software program.

Navigation Tools

One element that will make or break the successful use of your Web site is navigation. How easy is it to travel throughout your site? For you it may be simple, because you designed it. However, as we saw in Chapter 3, you need to keep in mind that your visitors may be new to your site, new to the Internet, or new to genealogy. The site layout must make logical sense to them. Nothing chases visitors away more quickly than being lost in a maze with no way to get out except to hit the Back button on their browser a few dozen times. These basic rules for navigation help to ensure that your visitors do not become hopelessly lost on your site:

- The home page is the hub from which visitors can reach all other pivotal pages on your site (such as index pages or a site map).
- The home page should have a link to each chapter's index page.

119

- The home page should have links to other important pages on your site that you want your visitors to know about (such as a FAQ page or a "What's New" page).

- Every page on your site should have a link that takes visitors back to your home page. This allows them to start all over again with the rest of your site whenever they find themselves wandering lost in one of your chapters.

- Every page in a chapter should have a link back to the index page for that chapter. This way visitors can go back to the start of a chapter whenever they find themselves buried several layers deep within that chapter.

Navigational Links

If you use a genealogy software program or a GEDCOM utility to create your Web pages, some navigational links are already present on those pages. Generally, those links point to a surname index page created by the software and to each page that contains the data about your ancestors. But the pages created by your software won't have links back to your main home page or chapter index pages that you manually created. You must insert those essential navigation tools yourself.

> Don't label any navigational links or graphics with the word "Back." The link you label with the word "Back" may not point to the same place that the Back button in the Web browser does. As the Webmaster, you may intend "Back" to point the visitor back to the index page for that section or chapter of the site, or back to your home page. But the visitor to your site might assume that "Back" takes them to the previous page they visited.

Navigational links can be created with a simple bit of HTML code inserted at the bottom of each Web page above or within the common footer. If you create the navigational code once, you can copy and paste it repeatedly on each of the other pages on your site. Or you can use a find-and-replace feature in your text editor to insert the code across numerous pages. Figure 8.1 shows what the navigational links might look like for your home page, using the eight-surname model from Chapter 3.

Copy and Paste

Follow these steps to copy text from one place and paste it in another:

- Hold down the mouse button and drag the cursor across the text you want to highlight.
- Choose Edit, Copy from the menu, or press Ctrl+C (Apple+C for Mac users) on your keyboard.
- Place your cursor on the spot where you want to paste the copied text.
- Choose Edit, Paste from the menu, or press Ctrl+V (Apple+V for Mac users) on your keyboard.

Using the Knox surname as an example, Figure 8.2 shows what the navigational links might look like for each surname chapter index page. Figure 8.3 shows what the navigational links might look like for each page within a chapter for a specific surname. The example in Figure 8.4 uses button graphics to display navigational links on a main index page.

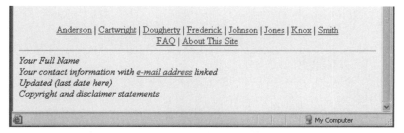

Figure 8.1 Navigational links on a home page that point to all the major chapters on the Web site

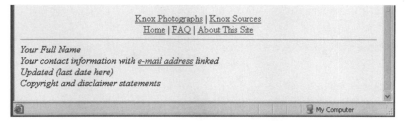

Figure 8.2 Navigational links found on a typical index page for a surname chapter on a Web site

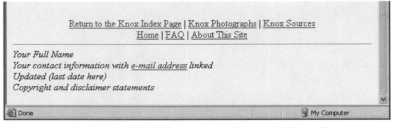

Figure 8.3 Navigational links found on each page within a chapter on a Web site, pointing to all the major pages elsewhere in that chapter

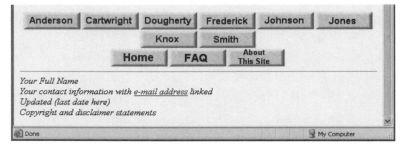

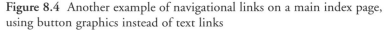

Figure 8.4 Another example of navigational links on a main index page, using button graphics instead of text links

Making Links Obvious

When the Web first became a mainstream place for the publication of personal home pages, HTML and Web browsers displayed hypertext links in a very obvious manner by presenting them with an underline. An underlined link tells the visitor to the site "you can click here" by making it stand out from the rest of the text. Newer versions of Web browsers and HTML standards allow Web designers to remove the underline. Some designers are now removing the underline *and* choosing to use the same color for both the link and the text. Those hypertext links aren't easy to spot because the

Make all your links stand out from the rest of the text so they are obvious to the visitor. Use a color different from the rest of the text—and don't remove the underline.

links blend in with the rest of the text. But if your visitors can't see the link, they won't click on the link. Hidden links defeat the purpose of using links at all! You *want* your visitors to be able to follow your links to other pages and features on your site. So make the links easy to spot and easy to use.

Rollovers

Another new trend is the use of rollovers. Rollovers, sometimes known as mouseovers, are created with a bit of JavaScript or inserted into a Cascading Style Sheet. When you roll over a link, the link performs a specific trick as designated by the rollover code. Popular rollovers make a text or graphical link pop out, change color, change formatting, or become highlighted in some other fashion. Done well, rollovers can enhance a site and make it attractive. The problem is that your visitors have to know to pass their cursor over that bit of text in order to make the rollover trick happen. If it's not obvious, they won't roll over it. If they don't roll over it, they don't get to use the feature and won't be able to navigate the site successfully. Rollovers, and the text used in the rollover link, aren't often obvious to the casual Web surfer.

There is no need to use the words "Click Here" in a link. The underlining tells visitors that they can click there. Instead, use the text in the link to describe the Web page so that the link matches the title of the page it points to.

Using rollovers and removing the underline (and contrasting color) from links can contribute to very poor Web design because they hinder the visitors' ability to easily navigate your site. They prevent your visitors from being able to see your site's navigation at a glance. If you highlight rollovers with color choices and icons that draw the visitor's attention, they may serve their purpose. Be sure your rollovers and hypertext links are obvious to someone who sees your Web site for the first time. If not, leave the underline option in place for your links and don't use rollovers. Your first goal is to make movement around your site straightforward and effortless for fellow family historians.

The Common Footer

A common footer contains a specific, consistent set of text, and sometimes links, that is displayed repeatedly at the bottom of every Web page across your site to create a sense of continuity from page to page. If visitors enter your site through a page deep inside, which isn't an index page or a main navigational page, the footer can help them identify you, the name of your site, and your home page. The common footer should include these elements:

- Your full name and contact information (see Chapter 10 for a full discussion about contact information)
- Date of most recent update to that page or section
- Copyright statement and disclaimers (see the next section)

See Figure 8.5 for an example of a common footer. You can create the code and text for the common footer once and then copy and paste it on each page. Or you can use the find-and-replace feature in your text editor to have the footer placed on each page

Find and Replace

Text editors and word processors have a find-and-replace feature that makes it easy to change words, phrases, sentences, and entire sections of text within a document. In most software programs, these features are listed on the Edit menu. For example, you could change every instance of the word "red" with the word "blue." If you last updated your Web pages on January 14 and you are now updating them on March 3, you can use the find-and-replace function to look for every instance of "Updated January 14" and insert "Updated March 3" instead. If your software has the ability, you might even be able to make this type of change all at once on every Web page on your site. But be cautious. For example, you don't want to attempt to change every instance of the date "28 January" across your entire Web site because you might accidentally alter a birth date or death date for one of your ancestors listed in your database. When using a find-and-replace function, be sure you search for unique phrases or entire sentences to avoid such errors.

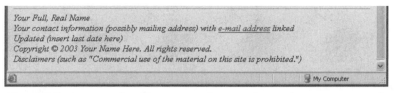

Figure 8.5 An example of a common footer to be used on every page of a Web site

```
<HR SIZE=1>
<ADDRESS>
Your Full, Real Name<BR>
Your contact information with <A HREF="MAILTO:YourE-mailAddress@YourISP.com">YourE-
mailAddress@YourISP.com</A> linked <BR>
Updated (insert last date here)<BR>
Copyright © 2003 Your Name Here. All rights reserved.<BR>
Commercial use of the material on this site is prohibited.
</ADDRESS>
```

Figure 8.6 The HTML code to use for the common footer found in Figure 8.5

for you. I created the footer shown in Figure 8.5 using the HTML code in Figure 8.6. The text for your footer should be inserted into the <ADDRESS> HTML tags. The <ADDRESS> tag was created specifically for this purpose. It italicizes the text automatically and helps browsers and search engine robots (automated indexing software) recognize the text for what it is—the author's address information.

You can also insert into your footer the navigational links we discussed in the preceding section. But because some navigational links are customized specifically for each section on your site, they shouldn't be included in the portion of the common footer that appears on every page of your site. The common footer applies across the entire site, but the navigational links might be specific to one area or chapter on your site. Make those links a separate entity displayed just above the common footer. Most sites display the navigational links above the footer, sometimes separated with a thin horizontal line using the <HR> tag in HTML. The example in Figure 8.7 shows all the information, including a general set of navigational links, that can be used as a common footer across an entire site. You can use

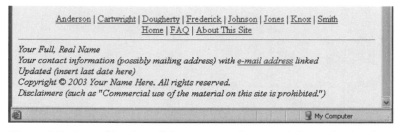

Figure 8.7 A combination of the common footer and the navigational links on a main index page

this layout as a template for the footer, and then customize the navigational links as appropriate for each area on your site.

Disclaimers

There may be many elements of your research that only you know about, which may not be clear to the casual observer. For example, you might not publish your sources on your Web site because you don't have any sources or because you don't want to share them with the general public. You may know that your research for the Anderson family is in its beginning stages, while you are much further along in your research on the Smith family. You might have made some assumptions or educated guesses based on circumstantial evidence regarding certain pieces of data on one or more of your Web pages. You may have inherited all your genealogical materials from a deceased relative, so you may not have verified the proof for any of the information in your database. You may have obtained everything you know about your Snodgrass family during a rare, uninhibited discussion with Great-Aunt Gertrude, most of which you have yet to verify and confirm by researching the records of the events.

On the flip side, your visitors may make certain assumptions about what they see on your site. Many, after seeing how beautifully designed and formatted your site is, may assume that you are a veteran genealogist and that everything on your site is 100 percent accurate. Other visitors may assume that you don't have any sources at all if you don't publish any sources for the data on your site. Some visitors may even believe that everything on your site is theirs for the taking. They may think they can blithely copy and paste into their own database without any thought to the time and energy you put into your research and creating your Web site.

Whenever you make assumptions or provide information based on your best guess, label your research findings to reflect that. Identify any incomplete research as a *work in progress.*

Publishing a disclaimer, or a set of disclaimers, should help alleviate any misunderstandings about your Web site, how it should be used, and the material it contains. The seriousness of the disclaimers—how they are phrased and how numerous they are—is up to you. For example, the site shown in Figure 8.8 displays a disclaimer reminding researchers to verify information for their own records. If you have several

Samples of Disclaimers

Use the following examples of typical disclaimers to create your own:

- Sources are available upon request.

- Sources are included wherever available.

- Some information on this Web site [or "in this section" or "on this page"] has not yet been proven and requires verification.

- Some information on this Web site derives from previous research done by cousins and fellow researchers. Attribution is included wherever available.

- Research for the Snodgrass family is in the beginning stages. Information published here about the Snodgrass family is based on an interview with Mathilda Dippy Snodgrass in 1972. Portions are still not proven.

- Information for the Anderson family is based on twenty years of research, which is still ongoing. Sources are published here. Information without sources has yet to be confirmed.

- Commercial use of the material on this site is prohibited.

- Information on this site may be used for personal research only.

- This site may be freely linked to but not duplicated in any fashion without my consent.

- Photographs and other graphics may be downloaded for personal use, but may not be reproduced or published elsewhere without my consent.

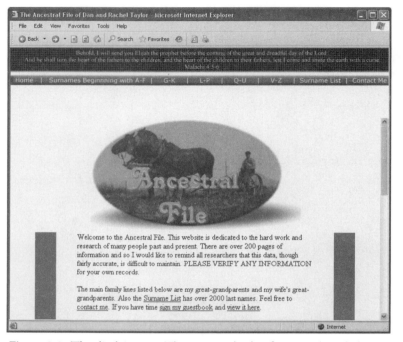

Figure 8.8 The disclaimer in The Ancestral File of Dan and Rachel Taylor *(www.geocities.com/Heartland/Bluffs/2473/ancestral_file.html)*

disclaimers, you might create one Web page that lists them all. You can then insert a link to your disclaimers page within the common footer or in the navigational links found across your site to ensure that visitors have a chance to read them. If you have just one disclaimer that applies to your entire Web site, you might insert the text for that disclaimer in the common footer. If a disclaimer is specific to one surname, include that disclaimer on the surname index page in the appropriate section on your site. If you have one disclaimer for a specific individual, include it on the Web page that contains the data for that person.

Getting Search Engines to Notice Your Site

One question most people ask is how to get their Web site noticed by search engines. If you follow each of the points made in this book, particularly in Chapters 7 through 10, you will be well on your way to having your site picked up and listed accurately in search engine databases. The secret to getting search engines to notice your site lies in the text that you, the Webmaster, choose to include on the pages of your site. Here are some guidelines:

- Choose a relevant, succinct title for your site without using any unnecessary verbiage such as "Welcome to my home page for. . . ."

- Use the <TITLE> tag appropriately, as described in Chapter 10.

- If you use a title banner graphic on your site, don't rely on that alone. Publish the title in text in the body of the Web page, as well. Search engines cannot read text on a graphic image.

- Use ALT attributes in the HTML code for the title banner graphic that defines your site. (See the discussion about graphics in Chapter 7.)

- Use the description and keyword attributes for Meta tags. (See the discussion on Meta tags in the next section.)

- Clearly identify the purpose of your Web site with a brief description in the body of your home page. You can duplicate that description as a purpose or mission statement (see Chapter 10). Place the statement at or near the top of the page, just under the text copy of your title.

- Submit your site to all the major search engines and link lists (see Chapter 12).

- Ask others to set up links to your site.

The way in which you personalize your site, insert new text, and edit to improve the generic format created by most HTML editors and genealogy software programs determines your success. And search engines aren't the only indexes that rely on your text, titles, Meta tags, and descriptions for your site. Bookmarks, favorites, link lists, and human indexers and authors use these tools, as well.

Meta Tags

Meta tags are special HTML tags used to provide information about a Web page. Meta tags are located at the top of a Web page within the <HEAD> tag. They do not display in the Web browser. The following is a standard set of common Meta tags:

- <META NAME="Author" CONTENT="*Your Name Here*">
- <META NAME="Description" CONTENT="*Insert a one-sentence description of your site.*">
- <META NAME="Keywords" CONTENT="*Insert a series of keywords that describe your site. Separate each with a comma and a space.*">

Some search engines read the information stored in Meta tags and use that information when building their databases. Most of the major search engines use at least the description Meta tag to one degree or another. So be sure you use the description tag effectively by inserting a clear, concise description for your site. One or two short sentences work best. You can duplicate the same description that you use in the body of the home page as a purpose or mission statement (see Chapter 10).

A few search engines use the Meta keywords. This field works best for specific words that accurately describe the content on your site—most likely, the surnames found in your research. Following the surnames, you might insert some place names, as well as the word *genealogy* for good measure. Place the most important keywords toward the beginning and the least important at the end. Using our eight-surname model, the keyword Meta tag might appear this way:

```
<META NAME="Keywords" CONTENT="Anderson, Cartwright, Dougherty, Frederick,
Johnson, Jones, Knox, Smith, Audubon County, Iowa, Morgan County, Ohio, genealogy,
family history">
```

Comments

Comments are a special syntax that you can insert into your HTML. Anything you include in a comment shows in the HTML source code, but is invisible in the Web browser. Comments allow you to insert notes, messages, dates, and other text that you may not want a visitor to see, but that you need in the HTML to help you maintain your site. A basic comment tag looks like this:

```
<!-- Insert your description here. -->
```

According to some Webmasters, a few search engines are able to read and index the text found in comments. Place the comment between the </HEAD> and <BODY>

tags. Use the same description that you used in the Meta tags and in the body of the document.

The most important thing to remember as you create your genealogy Web site is that you shouldn't settle for the default output from any software program. Your genealogy site is your own personal publication, created by you to represent your family history research in your own unique way. By the time you have committed yourself to the creation of your Web site and worked through the steps to plan and create it, you have invested a lot of yourself in the site. Taking the time to customize the pages in your site to make them easy to navigate and use is an important step toward making your site a success. Adding details to make it easy for people to find your site, and to find you and contact you, ensures that all your efforts are well worth the time spent.

CHAPTER 9

Enhance Your Web Site with Extras

You have created a basic set of Web pages with your family history information in a format of your choosing. And you have personalized the pages with custom text, colors, fonts, graphics, and navigational tools. Now it is time to enhance your site with even more personal touches. Helpful research tools, family photographs, digitized documents, and file sharing are some of the ways your site can be even more special.

Links and Bibliographies

One thing you are sure to find on almost every site on the Web is a set of links to other Web sites. If you want to recommend favorite genealogy Web sites to others, you can include a set of links to those sites. A list of genealogy links is a bibliography of Web sites for genealogy references online. But why stop with online sources? Your research takes you to all types of records and references beyond the Web. Why not create a bibliography of all references important to your research—records, books, periodicals, microfilm, CD-ROMs, audiotapes, videotapes, *and* Web sites?

Publishing a more comprehensive bibliography both educates others and enhances your own credibility as a genealogist. Visitors who are new to genealogy learn that they must use a combination of live records *and* electronic references in their own research. And you demonstrate that your research involves more than dabbling in a few online databases. Your bibliography tells visitors that you have research experience—and

133

proves that you have sources for the data in your family history research. And of course, it accomplishes the primary purpose of any bibliography: It provides a way for your visitors to follow up on any information they find on your site.

You might place your bibliography on the main index page of your Web site and label it "Bibliography," "References," or "Favorite Resources." If you have several

Citing Your Sources

The phrase "source citation" gets mixed reactions from genealogists. Many who are new to genealogy have been known to dismiss source citations as something that only professionals do. Not true. Anyone—and everyone—who wants their research to be taken seriously should use source citations. A source citation is a notation in your research that indicates what your source is for a piece of data. A source might be a birth certificate, a census return, or a conversation with Uncle Charlie. If your data or your research conclusion came from a birth certificate, you indicate that by including a source citation with that data, for example, "Oscar Howells, birth certificate no. 12-3456-78 (2002), Tacoma-Pierce County Health Department, Tacoma, Washington."

Every genealogist should have a copy of *Evidence!: Citation & Analysis for the Family Historian* by Elizabeth Shown Mills (Baltimore: Genealogical Publishing Company, 1997). *Evidence!* is the definitive guide for writing genealogical source citations and bibliographies. For more on sources, see Cyndi's List—Citing Sources at *www.CyndisList.com/citing.htm*.

Recent versions of most genealogy software programs have source citation fields built right in so you can enter the sources as you enter the data. When you generate reports and pages for Web sites, the sources can be included in the output you choose to include. This means that you can easily share the sources you have found with other researchers online. If you generate your Web pages manually, rather than with genealogy software, you will need to manually enter your sources along with the data. See terrific examples of sources generated by genealogy software on the Doyle Genealogical Database at *www.gentree.com/databases/Doyle/*.

At the very least, your Web site should indicate that you have sources for your data. If you don't plan to publish them online, tell your visitors whether or not they can write to you to get more information about your sources. Some people prefer not to publish the sources online because they first want to know whom they are sharing the information with. They would rather share their sources after starting an e-mail relationship with others. Choosing to share—or not to share—your sources is entirely up to you.

references that are specific to a certain surname in your research, you might create separate bibliographies for each chapter in your site and place them on each index page. If your bibliography is extensive, you can sort it into several smaller lists by locality; if it's fairly short, just list the items alphabetically by title. Your bibliography doesn't have to include everything you've ever looked at in your research. It can be a list of highlights, emphasizing resources that you believe are necessary or particularly well done.

> When creating links to a Web site, use the full URL, including any trailing slashes after a domain or directory name if shown in the browser. For example, the URL for the USGenWeb archives is this: *http://www.rootsweb.com/~usgenweb/*. The easier and more accurate way to capture the URL is to copy it directly from the Address or Location bar in your Web browser and paste it into your HTML code for the link.

You can often add links to enhance even the offline items in your bibliography. For example, if you are including a reference to *The Source: A Guidebook of American Genealogy* by Loretto Dennis Szucs and Sandra Luebking (Salt Lake City: Ancestry, 1997), you can include a link to the catalog Web page on the Ancestry.com Web site that advertises the book *(shops.ancestry.com/product.asp?productid=1026)*. You can link other books to their appropriate pages on an online book catalog, such as Amazon.com. For references to microfilm that you've used at your local Family History Center (FHC), you can link to the Family History Library (FHL) Catalog online *(www.familysearch.org/eng/Library/FHLC/frameset_fhlc.asp)*.

Keep in mind, though, that the longer the bibliography, the more time consuming the work you must do to maintain the links. Links break easily. So if you don't want to spend much time on the upkeep, a shorter list is probably better for your site.

Figure 9.1 is an example of what a bibliography might look like on your Web page. It combines typical online and offline references for genealogical research. You can display the URLs as text within the text on the page, or you can insert them into the HTML for a hypertext link, which hides the URL behind the link text in the browser display. The HTML code for the example in Figure 9.1 is shown in Figure 9.2.

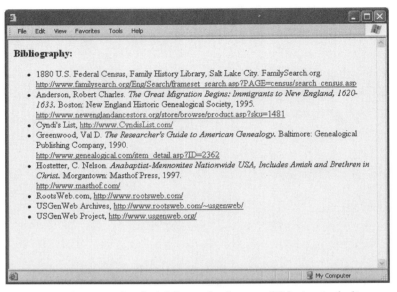

Figure 9.1 An example of a bibliography for your Web site, including both online and offline sources for your research

Photographs and Scanned Documents

You have shoeboxes full of family photographs. You can pull them out and look at them any time you like. But what about all those cousins who have never seen them? The Web is an ideal way to share photos with others—without those photos ever leaving your house.

Choose the photos you want to include on your Web site. Then use your scanner to create digital copies of them. Image-editing software generally recommends scanning the photos in one of two formats: JPG or TIFF (Tagged Image File Format). TIFF files are most commonly used for very high resolution art and photographs. Because of the high quality of TIFF graphics, the files are very large, so you must have storage space

Read your scanner's manual and the documentation for the image-editing software to learn how to put them to the best use as you scan your family's treasures.

```
<H3>Bibliography:</H3>
<UL>
    <LI>1880 U.S. Federal Census, Family History Library, Salt Lake City.
    FamilySearch.org.<BR>
    <A
    HREF="http://www.familysearch.org/Eng/Search/frameset_search.asp?PAGE=census/sear
    ch_census.asp">http://www.familysearch.org/Eng/Search/frameset_search.asp?PAGE=cen
    sus/search_census.asp</A>
    <LI>Anderson, Robert Charles. <I>The Great Migration Begins: Immigrants to New
    England, 1620-1633.</I> Boston: New England Historic Genealogical Society, 1995. <BR>
    <A HREF="http://www.newenglandancestors.org/store/browse/product.asp?sku=1481
    ">http://www.newenglandancestors.org/store/browse/product.asp?sku=1481
    </A>
    <LI>Cyndi's List, <A HREF="http://www.CyndisList.com/">http://www.CyndisList.com/</A>
    <LI>Greenwood, Val D. <I>The Researcher's Guide to American Genealogy.
    </I>Baltimore: Genealogical Publishing Company, 1990. <BR>
    <A HREF="http://www.genealogical.com/item_detail.asp?ID=2362">http://www.genealogi-
    cal.com/item_detail.asp?ID=2362</A>
    <LI>Hostetter, C. Nelson. <I>Anabaptist-Mennonites Nationwide USA, Includes Amish and
    Brethren in Christ.</I> Morgantown: Masthof Press, 1997. <BR>
    <A HREF="http://www.masthof.com/">http://www.masthof.com/</A>
    <LI>RootsWeb.com, <A HREF="http://www.rootsweb.com/">http://www.rootsweb.com/</A>
    <LI>USGenWeb Archives, <A
    HREF="http://www.rootsweb.com/~usgenweb/">http://www.rootsweb.com/~usgenweb/</A>
    <LI>USGenWeb Project, <A
    HREF="http://www.usgenweb.org/">http://www.usgenweb.org/</A>
</UL>
```

Figure 9.2 The HTML code for the bibliography found in Figure 9.1

for the file on your hard drive, a Zip disk, or a CD-ROM. Ultimately, though, for the best results on your Web page, your digitized photographs should be in JPG format.

Create TIFF (.tif) Master Copies for Posterity

Apart from including family photos on your Web site, scanning your photographs is one way to make backup copies of these prized family possessions. I highly recommend that your original scan of each photo be done in TIFF format and that you archive that copy on a Zip disk or CD-ROM for safekeeping. Having a high-quality

Your monitor's screen resolution set at 800 x 600 means that there are 800 pixels across and 600 pixels top to bottom. The more pixels you use on your monitor, the higher the resolution and the sharper the image becomes. The more pixels used to create a digitized image, the sharper and clearer that image will be displayed.

digitized copy of your photo ensures that you will be able to recreate the photo any time should something happen to the original. From the TIFF master copy, you can convert to any other image format, so converting the photo to a JPG for your Web site is an easy task that you can accomplish with your image-editing software.

Digital Cameras

If you have a digital camera, depending on its features, you can probably create the same types of files described above. To publish on the Web, you save your digital photos in JPG format. To create copies for posterity, first create a TIFF file for long-term storage. Be sure to read your camera's manual to learn how to use its specific features. For comprehensive advice on using digital cameras, read Dennis Ridenour's series of articles previously published in *UpFront with NGS*. These articles, beginning in August 2002, are archived online at *www.ngsgenealogy.org/upfront/archives/*.

640 Pixels Wide

Although your screen resolution and that of many visitors searching online may be at least 800 x 600, the lowest screen resolution that could possibly be used by a visitor to your site is 640 x 480. Therefore, digitized copies of your photos should be no wider than 640 pixels. If you make them any wider, users with 640 x 480 resolution are forced to scroll from left to right in order to see the complete width of the picture. The height of your picture may vary, depending on the dimensions of the original photo. Most people don't seem to mind scrolling up and down as much as they do from side to side, so the height isn't as important as the width.

Thumbnails

When you create a full-sized JPG version of your photograph with your image-editing software, you should also create a thumbnail version at the same time. A thumbnail is

More on Screen Resolution

Most computer users have monitors set to a screen resolution of 800 x 600 pixels or higher. Choosing a higher resolution (such as 1024 x 768) means more pixels per inch, thus finer detail and a clearer picture on the screen. Higher resolutions display images slightly smaller, but with sharper definition. To view images at a higher resolution, you must have computer hardware capable of displaying higher resolutions (monitor, video adapter, RAM, etc.). The lowest setting for screen resolution still in use is 640 x 480. To accommodate visitors using that resolution, design your Web site so that tables and graphics are no more than 640 pixels wide. The more commonly used resolutions are 800 x 600, 1024 x 768, and some at 1280 x 1024. Rectangular background graphics with a border on the left should be at least 1280 pixels wide (make it 1600 for good measure) to allow the graphic to tile properly in the browser.

a smaller version of a photograph or Web graphic (see Figure 9.3). A Webmaster uses small, fast-loading thumbnails to display multiple graphics quickly on one page. The thumbnails act as links to the larger versions of the same photos. Visitors to the site can click on a thumbnail, which is linked to a larger copy of the same graphic. Using thumbnails this way means that your Web page isn't loaded down with overly large, slow-loading photographs. But you can still entice the visitor with a small glimpse of the photograph behind the thumbnail.

Thumbnails can be whatever size you want, but as a general rule, make them between 50 and 100 pixels wide. Anything larger and you lose the advantage of using the smaller, easy-to-load thumbnail versus the larger, original-sized photo. Name the thumbnail something similar to the larger version. For example, if the larger picture is named "john_pendergrass.jpg," you might name the thumbnail "john_pendergrass_thumb.jpg." After creating the thumbnail files, you will upload them, along with the full-sized versions, to your Web host's server.

Photos in JPG format can be viewed in a Web browser on their own, without being referenced in a Web page with HTML. The thumbnail for a photo can be incorporated into one of the Web pages. In this example, you might insert the thumbnail on the Pendergrass surname index page or on a Web page that has genealogical information about John Pendergrass. When visitors click on the John Pendergrass thumbnail

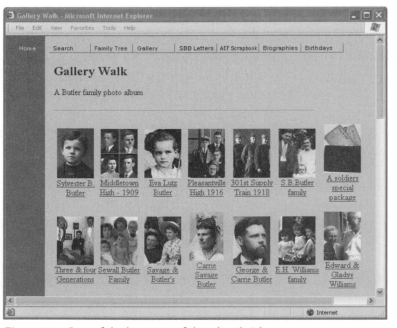

Figure 9.3 One of the best uses of thumbnails I have seen, found on the Butler Family of Cromwell CT Gallery Walk *(www.cromwellbutlers.com/gallery.htm)*

picture, the Web browser loads a copy of the larger John Pendergrass picture. The HTML code for linking your thumbnail to the larger version is this:

```
<A HREF="http://www.YourISP.com/john_pendergrass.jpg"><IMG
SRC="http://www.YourISP.com/john_pendergrass_thumb.jpg" WIDTH="50" HEIGHT="75"
BORDER="0" ALT="John Pendergrass Photo"></A>
```

After viewing the photo, the visitor can use the browser's Back button to return to the page with the thumbnails. Because the larger photo can be viewed in the browser

Use thumbnail pictures on your Web pages so that the pages load quickly. Visitors can always click on the thumbnail to load a larger picture if they want to see the full-size image.

by itself, you don't need to create a separate Web page just to display that photo. But you can create a separate Web page for the larger photograph if you have more information to accompany the picture, such as a biography or a story. Having a Web page for the larger version of the photograph ensures that you can include navigational links and contact information in the same browser window.

Clarity versus Speed

Webmasters must weigh the benefits of a clearer picture versus a larger file size and longer download time. A higher resolution on a scanned image of a handwritten document is important so that visitors can read the text. But a photograph might be easy to view at a lower resolution, which means a quicker download time for visitors, with little loss of quality.

Labeling Your Photographs

After you have scanned your photos, you need to label them. Think about all those photos in that shoebox of yours. How many have nothing written on them? How many are pictures of people you don't know? If the photos ever leave your possession, will the next person know who is in each one? This is a risk we all face as we attempt to preserve these precious family keepsakes. We all seem to be aware of this risk with paper photos. However, most Webmasters are unaware that the same problem exists with online photos.

A scanned, digitized photograph on a Web site is a stand-alone file that isn't attached to a Web page. People can view the photograph on its own by entering the photo's unique URL into their Web browser. They can make a copy of that photograph and store it on their own computer. If they do this and the photograph is not labeled, how will they be able to tell who is in the photo or from whom they obtained the digitized copy? It is not enough just to identify a photo by placing text next to the photo on the Web page. Labeling the photo itself is vital so that no matter where the photo file goes, the people and objects in the photo remain properly identified—as does the owner of the original photo.

Using your image-editing software, add a blank, white border to the bottom of a copy of your scanned photograph (never alter the original scanned version—your master copy). That bottom border is your blank canvas for the descriptive text. The size of the border depends on the amount of text you want to place there. The border becomes part of the graphic itself, so you now have a new graphic composed of the photo and the border. Using this border as your canvas, add black (or very dark) text in a plain, easy-to-read font. In Figure 9.4, I have indicated the object of the photo, and the date and place it was taken, as well as the owner of the original, the owner's contact information, and the date the picture was scanned.

The border and labels for your photos will differ, depending on the contents of the photo itself. The photo in Figure 9.4 is a four-generation family picture, but the family members aren't standing in order of birth. So labeling the photo along the side (see Figure 9.5) may clarify who is who in this picture.

Records and Documents

The Web also makes it easy to share copies of research documentation with others. You may want to share copies of records and documents in order to support the research findings that you are publishing on your site. Or you may have a rare copy of a record, such as a family Bible, letter, or diary, that you can't easily share with others. Scanning copies of documents works in the same way as photographs. You should create TIFF master copies for high-quality, high-resolution images that you can archive in order to preserve the document. Then select the TIFF images you want to publish on your site, and create JPG versions of them. You should also create JPG thumbnails as described in the previous section. Add a border to the document (as

Four-generation photo taken in Exira, Iowa, in 1909. Top to bottom: Nellie Mae Knox, Xerxes Knox, Clara Belle Frederick, Ruth LaVern Johnson. (1996 Cyndi Howells, cyndihow@oz.net)

Figure 9.4 A scanned photograph, labeled with identifying information at the bottom

Nellie Mae Knox

Xerxes Knox
(Nellie's father)

Clara Belle Frederick
(Nellie's daughter)

Ruth LaVern Johnson
(Clara's daughter)

Four-generation photo taken in Exira, Iowa, in 1909.
(1996 Cyndi Howells, cyndihow@oz.net)

Figure 9.5 A scanned photograph in which the people aren't standing in order of birth. The text on the border helps to identify each person.

Digitize and Transcribe

When publishing a digitized copy of a family document such as Great-Grandpa's handwritten diary or the family Bible, take the time to transcribe the text. A transcription is a complete, exact copy of everything in the document. You can publish the transcription on the Web page in addition to the image of the scanned document. This helps others read the text on the image, particularly when portions are illegible, faded, or otherwise difficult to read. Clearly label your transcription with your name and the date. For example, "Transcribed by Joe Genealogist, 1 January 2000."

described above) and label it to identify the type of document, the owner, and the date it was scanned. For example, "Photocopies of the Civil War diary of Isaac Spears Sanderlin, 1998, in the possession of Cyndi Howells, cyndihow@oz.net."

Depending on your experience using your computer, scanner, and image-editing software, you may have to work a bit to obtain a quality copy of some documents. If letters are faded or handwriting is illegible, try working in gray scale, rather than color. Or in color, rather than black and white. Adjusting contrast and brightness or reversing the background and text colors may also enhance the document. These online resources offer advice for making the most of your scanner:

- The Digital Album
  www.city-gallery.com/digital/index.html

- A Few Scanning Tips: Scanner Basics 101
  www.scantips.com

- SCANNERS-PHOTOS Mailing List
  lists.rootsweb.com/index/other/Internet_Help/SCANNERS-PHOTOS.html

- More online help for scanning can be found at Cyndi's List—Scanners
  www.CyndisList.com/scanners.htm

Look through your scanner's manual and the image-editing software help files for further information.

Downloadable Files

Another way to share your research data and photos, besides publishing them on individual Web pages, is in downloadable files. You can make it easy for visitors to download

Be aware of copyright issues when you scan documents to place on your Web site. Some public records may be under copyright, which means you are not allowed to scan and publish a copy on your Web site. If you obtain copies of public records, look into the rules, regulations, and guidelines for each repository to determine whether you can publish copies on your site.

copies of your research files, such as your GEDCOM files, photographs, audio files, word-processing documents, and compressed (.zip) files. For example, you may have dozens of ancestral photos already scanned and ready to share with others. But you don't want to publish all of them individually on your Web site. You can take the whole batch, incorporate it into one zipped file, and upload that file to your Web server. Zipped or compressed files are created by software such as WinZip, PKZip, Stuffit, and Windows XP. A file—or a set of files—is compressed to make the size of the file(s) smaller and quicker to upload or download. Figure 9.6 lists different types of files that can be downloaded from the Internet, along with the software programs that open them.

Perhaps you prefer to share your GEDCOM file as it is, rather than convert it to Web pages. You can upload copies of your GEDCOM (.ged) to the host server for downloading by visitors to your site. You might also want to share your research notes with others. If you keep them in a word-processing document (.doc, .txt), you can convert them to RTF (rich text format) so that they are readable in any word-

File Type	Extension	Software Program Needed
HTML	.htm, .html, .asp	Web browser (Microsoft Internet Explorer, Netscape Navigator)
Graphics	.gif, .jpg, .tif	Graphics program (Paint Shop Pro, Photoshop, Adobe Illustrator) or a Web browser (for .gif and .jpg)
Text	.txt, .doc, .rtf	Word-processing program or text editor
Compressed or encoded files	.zip, .sit, .hqx, .tar, .gz, .bin	WinZip, PKZip, Stuffit Expander, ZipIt
Audio files	.au, .wav	Audio player
Video files or movies	.mov, .mpeg	Video player (Quicktime, Real Player, Windows Media Player)
Adobe Acrobat Portable Document Format	.pdf	Adobe Acrobat Reader
GEDCOM	.ged	Genealogy software programs or GEDCOM viewers

Figure 9.6 File types you can download from the Internet, along with the names of programs you can use to open those files

processing program, and then upload those documents to the server, as well. Most text documents can also be converted to PDF files so that they can be viewed with the Adobe Acrobat Reader *(www.adobe.com)*. Some of these files will be viewable in a Web browser, but most will just be stored on the Web server so that your visitors can download them to their own computer. Another approach is for you to bundle groups of files (GEDCOM, photos, and word-processing files, for instance) together by surname and put them all into surname-specific zipped files for downloading.

Compression Software

Visitors to your site need to know how to unzip the file once they download it. Be sure to let them know that the files are compressed, and share Web site addresses, via links from your site, for some of the popular file compression software programs, such as

- PKZip
  www.pkzip.com
- StuffIt
  www.stuffit.com
- WinZip
  www.winzip.com
- ZipIt
  www.maczipit.com

Make It Easy

Create a section on your main index page for links to each of your downloadable files. Or include a section for downloadable files on each of the appropriate chapter index pages for each surname. Make it easy for your visitors to download your files: Explain that the files can be downloaded, and tell them what software programs they will need in order to use the files. Then set up links to each file. The HTML code for the links to your files is the same as for any other link. For example, a link to your Anderson surname GEDCOM file would be

<A HREF="http://www.yourisp.com/~yourdirectory/anderson.ged">Anderson GEDCOM</A>

A Word of Caution

Once you publish anything online—and once you put files online that can be easily downloaded by others—you lose all control over those files. You will not know where the files go, who uses them, or how they are used. Before you make things available to others on the Internet, be sure you are completely comfortable knowing that once the files are online, they are out of your hands.

A complete set of links to downloadable files for a specific surname from your research might be displayed on your site as in Figure 9.7. The HTML code that corresponds to that example is shown in Figure 9.8.

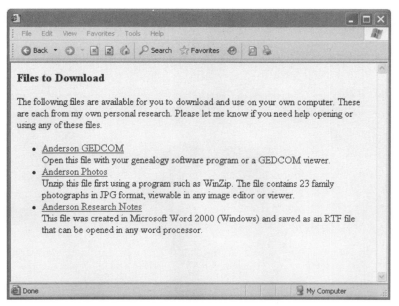

Figure 9.7 An example of a set of links to downloadable files for a specific surname or topic

```
<H3>Files to Download</H3>
The following files are available for you to download and use on your own computer. These
are each from my own personal research. Please let me know if you need help opening or
using any of these files.
<UL>
    <LI><A HREF="URL for your Anderson GEDCOM.ged">Anderson GEDCOM</A><BR>
    Open this file with your genealogy software program or a GEDCOM viewer.
    <LI><A HREF="URL for your Anderson Photos file.zip">Anderson Photos</A><BR>
    Unzip this file first using a program such as WinZip. The file contains 23 family photo-
    graphs in JPG format, viewable in any image editor or viewer.
    <LI><A HREF="URL for your Anderson Research Notes.doc">Anderson Research
    Notes</A><BR>
    This file was created in Microsoft Word 2000 (Windows) and saved as an RTF file that can
    be opened in any word processor.
</UL>
```

Figure 9.8 The HTML code used for the example in Figure 9.7

Multimedia

Multimedia takes full advantage of the power of the Web, using your computer and Web site to present interactive features, most often designed to entertain and enrich the content of your site. Multimedia features include animation, audio, and video.

Animation

Before using animation on your family history Web site, think carefully. I discourage you from using animations at all (see Chapter 10 for more discussion on this matter). Animated graphics are fun—the first few times visitors see them. After that, they quickly become annoying. So first think about the visual effect of the animation. Some graphics move quickly, some are jittery or flickering, and many are far too hyperactive and erratic. Animated graphics may distract and irritate your visitors and keep them from having a productive and enjoyable visit to your site.

Animated features also tend to use a lot of your visitor's system resources when they load in a Web browser. Everything on a Web page uses a bit of hard drive space and memory on the visitor's computer. Some animated graphics, depending on the complexity of the graphic and the animation, tend to use a lot of memory. And they are slow to load in the Web browser the first time your visitors come to your Web page. Nothing is more aggravating for visitors than waiting for a Web page to load in their browser, only to learn that they were waiting for a dozen animated graphics to appear.

If you want to use animation on your site, be sure there's a good reason to add it. Will it enhance the use of your site? Does it help to illustrate your research? If not, don't use it. In several years of indexing genealogy Web sites, I have seen only a few examples of the justifiable use of animation on a family history site, and each of those involved animation used in conjunction with family photos. One site used animation to transform a series of ancestral photographs from one person to another. But this was an exception. When it comes to animations, my best advice is don't use them.

Audio

The best audio files to incorporate into your family history Web site are taped conversations and oral interviews with your family members. Do you have any tapes with your ancestors speaking? Perhaps an interview you did with an aunt or your grandparents? If so, consider converting those tapes to digital audio files that can be played on your computer. You can either buy the appropriate audio-editing software to convert the tape yourself, or you can have it done professionally. As with your family photos and records, creating digital audio files for your archives means the data will survive long after the audiotape disintegrates. And you can upload whichever audio files you wish to your Web server, along with all the other files for your Web site.

You may be tempted to include music on your site. Think twice (and see "It Really Isn't Music to My Ears" in Chapter 10). By and large, including music on a Web site is *not* a good idea. If you want to do so, though, at least don't force your music on your poor, unsuspecting visitors—don't embed the music on the site. Embedding music on a Web site means hiding it within the HTML commands in the Web page. The music then turns on as soon as the Web page loads in the browser, and the visitor has no way to turn it off. The music turns off only after the visitor leaves that page. If you want to use music with a user-controlled console, do not set the music to start automatically when the Web page loads in a browser. Give visitors the option to turn on the music if they choose.

Audio files require a browser plug-in to work if you want your visitors to play the audio file by clicking on a console button. But you don't have to be that elaborate. You only have to supply a link to the audio file in order to make it available to your visitors. Once they click on the link, they have the option to save a copy of the file to their own computer or to play the file in the audio player already installed on their computer. If you prefer, you can provide the audio file and a link to the plug-in required to hear it, and then supply simple instructions on how to use it. These are typical audio plug-in programs:

 Apple—Quicktime
www.apple.com/quicktime/

 RealPlayer
www.real.com

 Windows Media Player
www.microsoft.com/windows/windowsmedia/download/default.asp

Video

The ideas we explored for audio apply to video, as well. Do you have movies of your grandparents or great-grandparents or special home movies that capture your family? You can convert videotape to digital files using special software, or you can hire a professional service to do this for you. Because of the complexity of this process, I recommend the latter unless you are a video expert yourself. You can upload a digitized video file to your Web server and make it available to your visitors via a link on your site. The plug-ins generally used for audio files can also be used for video.

Keep in mind that videos, like photographs and other scanned images, can be very large in file size. Visitors to your site must access, download, and play the files during their visit to your site. When accessing the Internet, we all have a limited amount of bandwidth to use. Bandwidth is the physical space available for us to transmit files and requests back and forth from our computer to the Internet via our ISP. A video file uses a considerable amount of your visitor's bandwidth. If they are connected with a slow modem and an older phone line, loading a video can take a very long time.

Automated Features and Forms

An automated feature is anything that requires visitors to interact with your site. For example, if you include a searchable database, visitors must fill in a form and press a button to search it. Other common examples are guest books, message boards, and chat rooms.

Search Engines

There are several free search engines online that you can install on your own Web site:

- Atomz.com Search
  www.atomz.com

- FreeFind.com
  www.freefind.com

- Google Free Search
  www.google.com/services/free.html

- PicoSearch
  www.picosearch.com

The search engine indexes your site and makes it easy for visitors to perform keyword searches within your pages. In exchange for the free service, some search engines include advertisements in the form of banners or sponsored links. Vendors pay to place sponsored links above search engine hits, so those links may or may not be relevant to that particular search. These free search engines are all easy to install on your site. They all work a bit differently, so you might try each of them first to find the one you like best.

How do search engines differ from one another? A search engine is really made up of two functions. The engine is the interactive form or interface that you use to search an index by keyword or phrase. The other function creates the index used in that search. Web sites are "spidered" or "crawled" by search engine indexing programs. This means that a site is visited, information is collected from the site, and the information is then included in a database. All search engines work this way whether they are used internally on your own Web site or out on the Internet as a whole.

All search engine spiders at least note the URL and title of a Web site. But search engines differ when it comes to other information gathered from each of the pages in the site. Some search engines use information found in Meta tags (see Chapter 8), but most use text found within the body of the Web page. Some use only a small bit of text, while others use a large quantity of the text to build the index. Another difference is how the engine searches the database. The exact same keyword search on four different search engines may garner four different sets of results. The only way to know how each one works is to try it.

Depending on the free search engine you use on your site, the frequency differs as

A Search Engine Is a Search Engine Is a Search Engine

Search engines that are internal to your personal Web site or external to the entire Internet work basically the same way. There is a two-part process to search engines: the indexing part and the searching part. Robot software (sometimes called a spider) visits your Web site, indexes the information it finds there (URLs, page titles, description, text) and deposits that information in a database. Search engine software searches that database by keywords entered into the search form. The database of information for each Web page or site remains static based on the data that was indexed when the robot last visited the Web pages. The database only changes if and when the robot revisits that Web page and finds new or different information to include. The database might also change if the robot indexing software is altered to create the database in a different manner.

To add more complexity to the issue, various brands of search engines work a bit differently from one another because different people, using different technologies and processes, developed them all. You can install a search engine on your personal Web site that will focus its indexing and search functions only on the pages within your site. You need to familiarize yourself with the features of various search engines to learn what options you have available to you. Some will allow you to have your site indexed on a regular basis (weekly, monthly) and others will index your site on their own timetable. Some will index only the home page and index pages, while others might scan every page on your site. Find the search engine that best suits your needs to index the pages you wish in a timely manner that fits your schedule.

to how often the search engine robots visit your site to reindex the data found there. In some cases, you have the option of requesting the specific frequency with which the engine reindexes (weekly, monthly, etc.). Some free search engines limit the number of pages that they index on a site, or they base the limit on the file size of the site. Read the Help files or FAQs for the search engines to be sure the terms or limitations are compatible with the needs of your site.

CGI

CGI stands for Common Gateway Interface. Check your Web host's FAQs or Help files to determine whether you can use CGI scripts on your Web site. CGI scripts can automate certain functions on your site through the use of forms and other Web interfaces. Typical CGI scripts are counters, guestbooks, and Mailmerge forms. Mailmerge is a script that allows visitors to fill in a form on your site, with the results being e-mailed to you. For example, RootsWeb offers Mailmerge on its site at *www.rootsweb.com/rootsweb/wizards/basicmm.html.*

CGI scripts are generally stored in a directory named /cgi-bin. Any scripts you want to use have to be placed in that directory on your server. If your ISP already has some scripts in place for your use, your HTML code must reference the cgi-bin directory in which those scripts reside. For more detailed technical help, read the Help files supplied by your Web hosting service. For online CGI scripts and information on how to use them, visit these sites:

- The CGI Resource Index
  www.cgi-resources.com

- Free-Scripts.Net
  www.free-scripts.net

- WebScripts (Perl CGI Scripts)
  awsd.com/scripts/index.shtml

JavaScript

JavaScript is interactive browser code that can be copied and pasted into your HTML, adding dynamic features to your site. JavaScript can add specialized forms, navigation, buttons, toolbars, and other useful features to your site. However, if you use a JavaScript, keep an eye on your site for a while afterward to be sure the JavaScript doesn't compromise your site's ability to run normally in other people's browsers. People may experience problems because different browsers and different versions of those browsers interpret JavaScript differently. If you get any complaints from visitors, it is better to delete the JavaScript than risk chasing away your cousins.

Don't confuse JavaScript with Java. JavaScript is code that is part of the HTML for your Web pages, whereas a Java applet is separate software that performs functions apart from the Web page. Visitors' browsers may be able to handle JavaScript easily, but may falter when they run into a Java applet that they aren't equipped to handle. In general, for browser compatibility, using JavaScript is preferred over using Java applets on your Web site to perform certain simple, special functions. To learn more about JavaScript and find some simple copy-and-paste JavaScripts to use on your site, visit the following Web sites:

- JavaScript.com
  www.javascript.com

- JavaScript Kit
  www.javascriptkit.com

- JavaScript Source
  javascript.internet.com

- Yahoo! > JavaScript
  dir.yahoo.com/Computers_and_Internet/Programming_and_Development/ Languages/JavaScript

Online Code Generators

Online you will find some really neat tools that have prewritten code or that generate code you can copy and paste into your Web pages:

- AutoScripter—Script Engines for Web Developers
  www.autoscripter.com

- Free Code Generator
  w3.discoveryvip.com

- Meta Tag Builder
  vancouver-webpages.com/META/mk-metas.html

- WebPage-Tools.com—Free Online Web Tools and Free Code Generators
  www.webpage-tools.com

Some of these generators will create entire Web pages or supply you with templates to build the pages yourself. Most of the code generators you find online will create portions of code that you can insert into your preexisting Web pages to perform certain functions. For example, if you decide to add Meta tags to your site, you can use an online Meta tag generator. Take a look at these online tools—you may find inspiration and ideas for functions to include on your site. You might also find ready-made code for a function you already have in mind, thus speeding up the process of creating it.

You can create a genealogy Web site based on your family history database, including all the names, dates, and places you have found throughout your research. These are the bare branches on your family tree. Your ancestors lived full and interesting lives, rich with historical events—both personal and public. The sights, sounds, and records of their existence bring those branches to full bloom for you and the visitors to your site.

CHAPTER 10

Guarantee Success: Common Web Site Dos and Don'ts

THE BEST WAY TO LEARN HOW TO DO THINGS RIGHT ON YOUR WEB SITE is to learn from the trials, tribulations, and mistakes that others have made with theirs. And I have seen them firsthand as I attempt on Cyndi's List to index every genealogy Web site I can find, looking at each genealogy site with the eye of an indexer and a cataloger of the virtual library that is the Internet.

In trying to establish the name of a Web site, I have learned that consistency in titles for sites is lacking. In trying to determine the purpose of a site so that I can categorize it, I have found that Webmasters don't always define their site or state what they intend their site to accomplish. In exploring genealogy Web sites, I have run up against colors, sights, sounds, and technology that have made me happy, some that have made me cry, and a few that have made me scream. In the end, I know that if I can't figure out a Web site—its title, its purpose, or how to use the site—then other visitors are having the same difficulties. And if a Web site makes me want to run away, I know that others are jumping in the getaway car with me. So if you read nothing else in this book, I hope you read this chapter!

Web Site Title Follies

The title is a vital component of your site. It is a brand you put on your work that identifies the Web site as your own. Let's return to our book analogy. When you peruse the shelves of books at the library or bookstore, you see a title on the spine of each book. Pull a book off the shelf, and you see the same title on the cover and on the title page of the book. The cover and title page may include information that doesn't fit on the spine, such as a subtitle. When you thumb through the pages, you see the same title throughout the book, usually at the top of every other page. Each chapter may have its own name and headings, but overall, the book has a single consistent title. That is the style we must all mimic on our genealogical Web, so pick *one* title and stick with it!

If your genealogy Web site has information that others are going to use or reference in some way, they will likely refer to your Web site by its title, as well as its URL. Displaying several variations of the title throughout a Web site confuses and misleads your visitors. After visiting a Web page that displays one title, then moving to another page on the same site with a different title, the average genealogical Web surfer may end up thinking she has visited two different Web sites. Moreover, the title you choose affects each of these important research tools for you and your visitors: bookmarks or favorites, search engine results, indexes and link lists, genealogy source citations written by others, and bibliographies. To ensure that visitors know they have been to *your* site and that they correctly reference your site—thus giving you credit for the hard work you have done—spend time choosing a single appropriate title for your entire genealogy site. If your site has several chapters or sections that are devoted to different surnames or topics, give each their own distinct title. That way each chapter will have a specific title and URL that will help it to stand on its own as a genealogical reference.

The <TITLE> Tag in HTML

Just as a book has a spine, so does a Web site. Its "spine" is the Title bar that appears at the top of the Web browser window. The Webmaster uses the HTML <TITLE> tag to place the appropriate title in that bar. Unfortunately, on the vast majority of Web sites I have visited, the title showing on the "spine" of the site doesn't match the "cover" or "title page" for the site. In fact, they often don't bear even a slight resemblance to one another. To make matters worse, the "spine" often changes as the visitor navigates from page to page throughout the site.

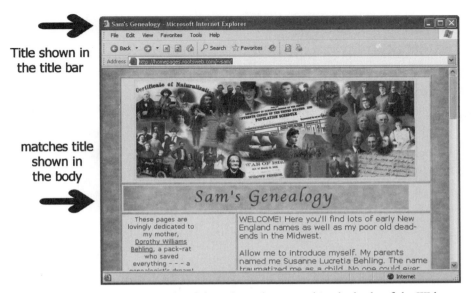

Title shown in the title bar

matches title shown in the body

Figure 10.1 A proper example of the title in the tag and in the body of the Web page, found at Sam's Genealogy *(homepages.rootsweb.com/~sam/)*

In my experience as an indexer, this <TITLE> element is the most ignored, abused, and misunderstood component in a Web site. The text contained in the <TITLE> tag should exactly match the title shown in the body of the Web page (see Figure 10.1). I see several common problems in regard to this tag, but the one I see most often is that the Webmaster has not inserted a title in the <TITLE> tag at all (see Figure 10.2), which either leaves the browser title bar blank or causes it to default to something like the following:

 "index"

"index.html"

"Home Page"

"Insert Title Here"

"Index of Surnames"

In some cases, Webmasters overload the <TITLE> tag, using it to store a zillion keywords, rather than a true title for the site—often because someone told them it would help get more search engine hits. If you do everything else correctly on the rest

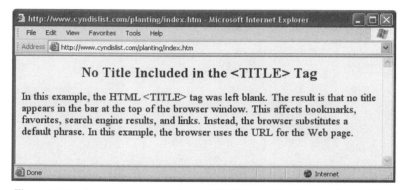

Figure 10.2 An incorrect use of the <TITLE> tag, leaving the bar to display the default URL (index.htm) rather than the title of the Web page

of the site as you develop it, this is not necessary. To learn more about getting search engines to notice your site, see the discussion at the end of Chapter 8. Similarly, I have seen some Webmasters use the <TITLE> tag for the title, plus a description, and a list of keywords—definitely overkill. Keep the title succinct in the <TITLE> tag. If you can't see the majority of your title in the title bar at the top of the browser window, the content of your <TITLE> tag is too long.

But as I mentioned earlier, one of the most common mistakes is that the title in the <TITLE> tag doesn't match the title on the home page. Most often in these instances, Webmasters refer to their own site by yet another title altogether. For example, a new link is submitted to Cyndi's List, and the Webmaster tells me that the title of the site is "Comprehensive SMITH Family Genealogy in Tennessee." Upon visiting the site, I find that the title bar shows the name of the site to be "My Family in Tennessee and Kentucky," while the body of the page displays the title as "Some

The Snodgrass, Pifflehammer, and Smith families are fictional examples, created only for the purpose of discussion in this chapter. This disclaimer is inserted here because otherwise I know all of you *real* Snodgrass, Pifflehammer, and Smith descendants will write me and ask me to send you everything I know about them. These are *not your* Snodgrass, Pifflehammer, and Smith ancestors. These people never existed.

Snodgrass and Pifflehammer Families in the Bluegrass Area." As someone who is attempting to catalog the site, I have to look at these three very different titles and try to determine what the true title is. If the Webmaster submitting the link wants me to catalog the site under the title "Comprehensive SMITH Family Genealogy in Tennessee," why doesn't she use that title on the site herself?

Search engines, bookmarks, and favorites all take advantage of the <TITLE> tag. The title you place in that tag is what appears when someone creates a bookmark to your site. Have you ever wondered why some search engine hits result in oddly named Web pages? The Webmaster for that site didn't use the <TITLE> tag correctly—make sure you do!

Chapters, Sections, and Pages

Open one of your genealogy books to any page and look at the headings. At the top of the page on the left, you see the title of the book. At the top of the page on the right, you see the name of the chapter. How can you make this work on a genealogy Web site? On each Web page, there are four places you can display the titles for your Web site and its chapters, sections, and pages:

1. The title bar at the top of the Web browser

2. The header, separated from the text and content of the page by a horizontal rule or graphic

3. The body

4. The footer, separated from the text and content of the page by a horizontal rule or graphic

The home page serves as the cover and title page for your site (see Figure 10.3). The title of your site should appear prominently on this page in all four elements outlined above. Don't rely on a banner graphic alone to display the title of your site. Search engines and text-only Web browsers cannot read the words displayed on a piece of artwork. Along with the graphic, be sure to include a line of text for the title. That ensures that the title shows up on search engine results.

Treat the main index pages for each of the chapters or sections on your Web site as mini versions of the home page—they serve as the "home page" for each section (Figure 10.4). The title for the chapter should be most prominent; put the Web site title in a slightly less prominent place or a smaller text size. Using different sizes of

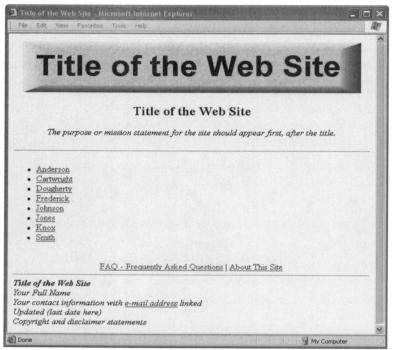

Figure 10.3 An example of a home page, or main index, with the title in both a graphic and in text in the body of the Web page

fonts and headers can help to draw attention to the chapter title. The title bar and navigational footer on each page should include both the name of the site and the name of the chapter (see Figure 10.5), mimicking the top of the pages in a book.

So use the <TITLE> tag appropriately. Put the title of your site in the <TITLE> tag, which then displays that title in the bar at the top of the browser window. The *same* title should appear in text in the body of each Web page. On the home page, put the title prominently at the top of the page. On subsequent pages, the title can be secondary to the chapter, section, or page names. Most important of all, choose one specific title and stick with it.

Purpose or Mission Statement

A purpose or mission statement defines your Web site. It communicates to other genealogists why you have published your site, what you plan to do with the site, and what they will likely find as they visit your site. You'd be amazed how many sites don't

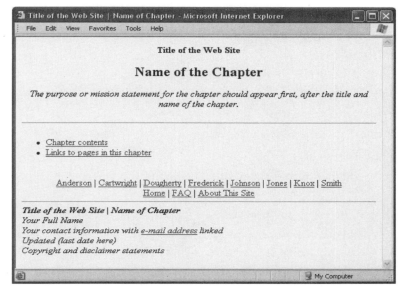

Figure 10.4 An example of an index page for a directory or chapter on the Web site, with the name of the chapter prominently displayed in the Title bar and in the body of the page

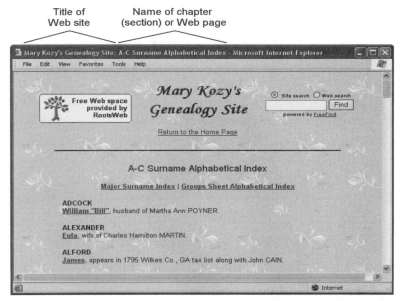

Figure 10.5 Mary Kozy's Genealogy Site *(homepages.rootsweb.com/~marykozy/grpsht_indexes/ AtoCgrp.shtml)*. This site demonstrates terrific use of the Title bar for the title of the Web site and the name of the chapter, with both duplicated in the body of the Web page.

use this simple communication tool. To illustrate this idea, let's use the example from the preceding section:

- The link is submitted as this:
  "Comprehensive SMITH Family Genealogy in Tennessee"
- The title bar displays this:
  "My Family in Tennessee and Kentucky"
- The body of the page displays this:
  "Some Snodgrass and Pifflehammer Families in the Bluegrass Area"

By reading those titles, is it clear to you what the *purpose* of the site might be? The titles suggest three different directions. The site might be an all-encompassing research project for the Smith surname in the state of Tennessee. The title bar leads us to believe that the site is only the personal research efforts for a specific family in Tennessee and Kentucky. And the body tells us that the site contains partial information for two very specific surnames in a regional area. Our first impression leaves us confused about the real purpose or mission of this particular Web site. As a Webmaster, you can easily avoid confusing your site's visitors by incorporating the purpose into the title you choose and into a brief mission statement. By stating your purpose or mission at the beginning, you make a good first impression; you ensure that visitors easily understand the purpose of your site.

The Title

The title you choose for your Web site should indicate the purpose of your site. In Chapters 3 and 4, we discussed the reasons you might be publishing your genealogy Web site. Is your site about your personal research, covering several different families and surnames? If so, you might incorporate the purpose into the title like this:

"Snodgrass, Pifflehammer, and Smith Families in Tennessee and Kentucky"

Is your site about one specific surname or the descendants of one specific individual? Then you might incorporate the purpose into the title one of these ways:

"Snodgrass Genealogy in Tennessee and Kentucky"
"Descendants of Isaiah Snodgrass, from Tennessee and Kentucky"

Does your site focus instead on a specific locality? You might state the purpose in the title one of these ways:

"Bluegrass Area Genealogy: Snodgrass, Pifflehammer, and Smith"
"Genealogy in Fayette County, Kentucky: Snodgrass and Other Families"

Short and Sweet

Whatever you choose for your title, be sure to keep it succinct. Don't waste space with unnecessary words like "Welcome to the. . ." or "Welcome to my . . ." or "Family History Research for . . ." or "My Personal Genealogy Home Page . . ." In fact, there's no need to insert the words "home page" or "Web page" or "Web site" in your title at all. Those things are redundant. Keep the title short, including names and places, with just enough descriptive wording to help state your site's purpose.

The Statement

Once you've chosen a title, write a brief statement that defines the purpose of your site. This mission or purpose statement should be the first thing your visitors see under the title. It should consist only of a few sentences that provide this information:

- What your site is about
- The information that can be found on your site
- The goals or long-term plans you have for your site

Here are some examples that you can copy and customize:

"My ancestors lived mainly in the Bluegrass area of Kentucky, as well as in Tennessee. I have spent the last six years researching the SNODGRASS, PIFFLEHAMMER, and SMITH families, as well as several others. The information on this site will continue to grow and evolve as I make further discoveries about my ancestors. I plan to focus on each of my family lines and publish on this site everything I learn from my research."

"This family history site is my online research workbook. I want to use the site as a research aid and a log of everything I learn about my SNODGRASS, PIFFLEHAM-MER, and SMITH ancestors in Kentucky and Tennessee. I plan to focus on each of my family lines and publish everything I learn from my research. I hope that my cousins will visit the site often and enjoy learning about our ancestors as much as I do."

"This site is dedicated to research about my ancestor, Isaiah Snodgrass (1827–1898), born in Tennessee. He moved with his brother's family to the Bluegrass area of Kentucky in 1848. All information found on this site about Isaiah is the result of six years of research. Sources are available throughout the site, along with photographs and scanned documents. My goal is to connect all descendants of Isaiah by sharing the details of this man's fascinating life."

Defining your site clearly from the beginning helps your visitors. Otherwise, your visitors are inclined to walk away from your site after a few clueless minutes trying to find something that holds their interest. Presented at the top with a clear, stated purpose, fellow genealogists and cousins know right away that they have found a site worth exploring.

Contact Information

A new visitor to your site is very excited. You are her long-lost cousin! She is amazed to see that you have a picture of her Great-Grandma Pifflehammer. She can't wait to write to tell you everything she knows about her. But her excitement soon turns to frustration. Who are you? How can she find you? She has looked all over the Web page with the picture on it, but she can't figure out how to contact you.

Does any of this worry you? It should. One of the main reasons we genealogists publish our family history on a Web site is to make contact with cousins. Genealogy sites make it possible for people to connect and to share what they know and what they possess. Someone, somewhere in the world, has your family photographs and other heirlooms. Someone, somewhere in the world, knows that one detail or fact crucial to helping you get past a genealogical brick wall. So make it as easy as possible for them to contact you!

Put your contact information on every page of your Web site. Keep in mind that people will enter your Web site through any one of the pages it contains. You cannot

You've Got Mail!

Your new genealogy Web site will generate new e-mail correspondence. New cousins—and possible cousins—will contact you to ask about the information they find on your site. Try a few organization tricks to help you deal with the new correspondence. Create mailboxes or folders in your e-mail program to sort the messages by surname or by research project. Write some generic e-mail messages about each of the families represented on your Web site and store them in those folders. You can copy details directly from your genealogy database and paste them into these generic messages in order to easily supply specific data for that family. You can use these prewritten messages to reply to queries that you receive from your Web site visitors. To save even more time, you can zip together a GEDCOM copy of your genealogy database, digitized copies of photos and documents, and any other files you want to share with others. Have the zipped file all ready to go and send it out with your prewritten reply.

control how or where people will begin their visit to your site. They may see the home page, or they may not. If you are counting on their visiting your home page to find your contact information, you may lose them. People learn about your site through bookmarks, favorites, links from other sites, search engine hits, and word of mouth from friends and other genealogists. In any one of those instances, visitors may enter your site on a page that is several layers deep within your site (see Figure 10.6). If that one page has no contact information, they may leave and you may never hear from them. This is especially true if your visitors aren't savvy about navigating through a new Web site. They may not know how to backtrack through your URL and reach your home page. Also, people might see a paper printout of a Web page from your site that does not display the URL, which means they have no way to tie that page to the remaining Web pages. If that one page has no contact information, you may lose them. Don't risk losing visitors—especially when some of them have just the information you've been looking for.

If you generate your Web pages with a software program, look first to see whether that program allows you to insert contact information into a footer at the bottom of every page. If the software doesn't offer you that feature, use a text editor to find and replace or copy and paste your contact information onto each Web page yourself. The

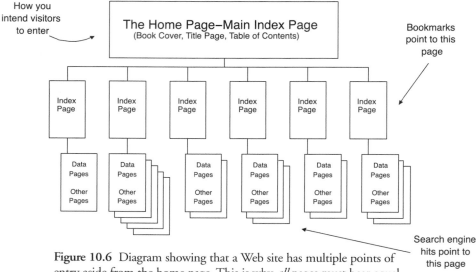

Figure 10.6 Diagram showing that a Web site has multiple points of entry aside from the home page. This is why *all* pages must bear equal responsibility to identify the name of the site and the Webmaster.

common footer is discussed in detail in Chapter 8. Don't allow limitations in the HTML software to decrease your Web site's potential to help you connect with your cousins. Customize and edit your pages whenever the HTML software you use falls short of your needs and expectations.

Your contact information should include each of these elements:

- Your full, *real* name
- Your e-mail address
- A postal mailing address (consider a post office box for privacy)

Many people avoid using their real name on the Internet in an attempt to retain some anonymity. If you want to be anonymous on the Internet, not only are you in the wrong venue for research, you are in the wrong hobby. Genealogy and family history are all about finding people—both the dead and the living. It is vital that you use your real name, rather than an online handle or nickname. This is particularly true if you want others to take you and your research seriously. If your online nickname is "FluffyHead" and that is how you choose to correspond with me, with no real names involved, I will have a very hard time taking a sincere interest in helping you with your genealogy.

Another element of anonymity comes to play when using a mailing address. People often want to retain some privacy by not publishing their physical address on the Internet. This only works if you are sure that your physical address has never been published in a phone book or similar directory. If it has, then your address may already be available somewhere else online. If not, and you want to retain some bit of privacy and security, or at least peace of mind, consider getting a post office box for your genealogical correspondence. Having a post office box also helps to keep one stable address for a long period, even if you end up moving from one residence to another. Sharing your mailing address online via your Web site is a personal decision that you must be comfortable with for the long term. If you do not feel at ease publishing your mailing address on your Web site, be sure your published e-mail address stays current.

Why publish your physical mailing address on your Web site? So that people can contact you even if you change your e-mail address or leave your ISP. A traditional, stable address can be useful for several reasons. The first is the instability (and the eventual inaccessibility) of e-mail addresses. People change their e-mail address whenever they change from one ISP to another. Sometimes ISPs change e-mail addresses for their customers due to upgrades and changes in server hardware or technology, or due to mergers with other ISPs. If you don't download your e-mail on a regular basis, your mailbox on the ISP's mail server becomes full and new incoming messages bounce back to the sender as undeliverable. E-mail addresses are simply not stable. Also, not everyone visiting your Web site has e-mail access. Some people surf the Web while using the computer at the library, an Internet café, or a friend's home and may not be able to contact you by e-mail. A traditional mailing address helps guarantee that all your visitors can correspond with you.

The next issue is the instability of Web site addresses. Again, URLs sometimes change due to ISP upgrades. Many people publish genealogy Web sites and then never look back. Their sites go completely untouched after that, with no change or update. The Webmasters lose interest in the site or in their research. Or despite best intentions, they're just too busy to maintain the site over the long term. Perhaps the Webmaster just hasn't had the time, or the technical ability, to update the Web pages. Sometimes, Webmasters abandon sites when they move to new ISPs or decide to take the site in a new direction. Even though the old site is abandoned, the information on those stale Web pages may still hold value for family historians. If so, they need to be able to find the person who published that information, no matter how long ago.

How about a Bonus?

There is also a fun reason to include your postal mailing address on your Web site: surprise packages in your mailbox! Cousins have been known to ship boxes of genealogical goodies to the family historian, especially when they don't know where else to keep these treasures.

Of course, not everyone finds your Web site on the Web itself. Perhaps a visitor prints pages from your site. Each printed page then becomes a stand-alone document that can be passed around, shared, and photocopied. Without your name and contact information, the data on that page becomes useless as a valid source. People can copy information from your Web page and paste it into their research notes, a word-processing document, their own Web pages, e-mail messages, and the notes fields in genealogy software programs. Making sure that your contact information stays with any data taken from your Web site ensures that no matter where it travels, your research material points back to you.

Don't risk missing contact with that one, long-lost cousin. Make it as simple as possible for him to find you and contact you. Supply all current, pertinent addresses on *every* page of your Web site.

Grammar, Spelling, and Punctuation

Genealogical research is about names, dates, places, and facts. We work sometimes for years to prove that a certain ancestor was in a certain place at a certain time. Even those of us who are new to genealogy know that this hobby is all about recording information and data. So why are so many genealogists so careless about grammar, spelling, and punctuation? Your Web site represents you and the efforts that you put into your genealogical research. If you care about your research enough to publish it online, you should care enough to keep it error free. If you don't know how to spell words like *genealogy* (see Figure 10.7), what kind of faith can we put in the rest of the data and information on your site?

Misspelled Versions	Correct Spelling
geneology genology geneaology	genealogy
cemetary	cemetery
sirname	surname
sight	site

Figure 10.7 Misspelled words seen frequently on genealogy Web sites

You want your cousins to take you and your research seriously. You want fellow genealogists to interact with you, share with you, and learn by your example. So pay careful attention to the text you publish on your site. Use the following check-list to make sure your text (including your titles!) is as clean and readable as possible:

- Be sure you spell *genealogy* correctly.

- Before you publish your Web pages, proofread them carefully.

- Ask a friend to proofread them for you. Having a second set of eyes look things over is always a good idea.

- Keep a dictionary by your computer for quick reference.

- Run a spell-checker on your Web pages. If the text you plan to use comes from a software program that doesn't have a spell-checker (such as some genealogy software databases), copy and paste the text into your word-processing program, spell-check it, then copy and paste the resulting text back into the Web page. Note: Be careful that the spell-checker doesn't alter any HTML code.

- Use proper punctuation (see Figure 10.8). I have seen text on Web pages with no periods, no commas, and no punctuation at all. Misplaced commas and apostrophes make it difficult for visitors to read your text.

Incorrect	Correct
They were married in the 1850's.	They were married in the 1850s.
My ancestors were the Smith's, Snodgrass's and Pifflehammer's.	My ancestors were the Smiths, Snodgrasses, and Pifflehammers.
We are the Williams'.	We are the Williamses.

Figure 10.8 Punctuation problems commonly seen online

Put as much care into your Web "book" as you would a printed book, and always put your best foot forward. Then visitors will take you—and your research—seriously.

Location, Location, Location!

Sometimes we get tunnel vision as we talk or write about our own research. We become so close to our work that we can't see something that may be obvious to others. One glaring example is when we talk about locations where our ancestors lived or where we focus our research. For example, genealogists talk about Washington County, but fail to mention which state that county is in. They get so involved in the details that they forget to communicate the bigger picture. Do you have any idea how many Washington Counties there are? Many times as I catalog sites for Cyndi's List, I see titles such as "Washington County Public Library" or "Washington County Genealogy Society"—but nowhere does the site mention which state that particular Washington County is in. And the problem isn't unique to locations in the United States. How many different cities are there in the world named "London"?

I recall one example that left me thoroughly flummoxed. I visited a Web site that published a cemetery transcription. The page had no title, and the cemetery was never named. All the Web page contained was this set of driving instructions: "Take Route 1 and turn left after 2 miles. The cemetery is on the right behind the church." In cataloging this site, I had no idea what to do. What title should I give the link? Under what locality should it be categorized? I located an e-mail address on the site and wrote to the Webmaster, asking for more details. That person never replied. Why did the Webmaster bother to transcribe the cemetery information and publish the data online, only to have it be virtually worthless to the Web site visitor? No one who visits that site is able to use the information published there.

It is the responsibility of Webmasters to communicate clearly with the visitors to their site. Webmasters should never assume that their visitors know what they know about their own material. To clearly communicate information about locations, follow these guidelines:

- Always give a complete title for the site.
- Always supply a complete physical address, including all pertinent information about a location (parish, town, city, county, province, state, region, country).
- Always identify the complete name, address, and location for libraries, societies, cemeteries, and similar places or organizations you mention in your site.
- Do not assume that your visitors know where you live or where your cemetery, library, or society is located.
- Do not abbreviate place names.
- It is better to repeat information than to assume visitors will find the information elsewhere on your site.

Never assume anything about your visitors; treat each one as though this were a first-time visit to your site. Publish complete details for each location you mention.

Broken Links

Webmasters can refer to other Web pages through hypertext links. One page can link to another page with a bit of HTML code and the URL for that page. If the URL is correct, the link works. If the URL is no longer correct, the link is broken. When visitors to a Web site click on that broken link, they receive an error message such as the one in Figure 10.9.

Most Webmasters publish links on their site as a supplement to the content or as a bibliography of sources to support the research published there. Sometimes the links are there just for fun. Whatever your reason for publishing links, you need to know that maintaining them requires some work. If you just publish them and then ignore them, your site will eventually suffer from a bad case of linkrot.

I customarily see two types of broken links—those with nonworking URLs and those

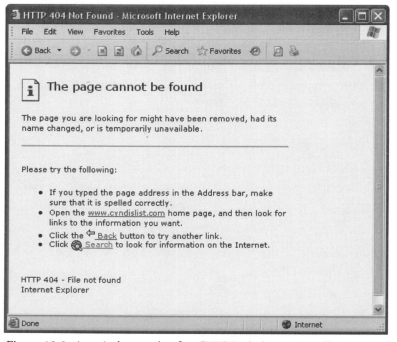

Figure 10.9 A typical example of an "HTTP 404 Not Found" error message encountered from broken links

that point to Web site content that has been altered or deleted. Check links regularly to be sure they still work and that the URL is still valid. But also regularly check the pages to which your links point. Make sure the content on those pages matches the original description of the link. If your link indicates that it will take visitors to a transcription of the "Will for John Smith," you want to be sure that the URL still works, but you also want to know that the transcription of that will is still there. For more information on checking links, see Chapter 11.

All broken links drive visitors nuts, but an internal broken link is inexcusable. If a visitor clicks on a link on your Web page to go to another page on your site, that link had better work! So test *all* links, both internal and external, to make sure they work—and test them regularly. Otherwise, why create them in the first place?

Relative Links versus Absolute Links

There are two ways to reference one of your Web pages within the HTML code for an internal link: relative links and absolute links. An absolute link includes the entire

Retain That Old URL

Once you put a Web page online with a specific file name, don't rename that file. Renaming the file creates new URLs. Any links, favorites, bookmarks, or genealogical source citations that point to the old URL become broken. Instead, either leave the file name as it is or convert the old page to a short forwarding page that points visitors to the new URL. Either way, the page with the original URL stays online and intact.

URL for a Web page, including the *http://* protocol at the beginning. An absolute link always works—as long as the URL is valid. An absolute link looks like this:

<A HREF="http://www.ngsgenealogy.org/comstandards.htm">NGS Standards</A>

A relative link includes only a portion of a URL—a file name and maybe a directory name. A relative link works only if the file referenced in the link is always located in the same directory, on the same server as the Web page that contains the relative link. A relative link looks like this:

<A HREF="comstandards.htm">NGS Standards</A>

That link works as long as that file stays in the main directory on the NGS server. Relative links tend to become broken more often than absolute links because they are so easily rearranged or shortened, which causes the URLs to be inoperable. If you change your site by inserting new directories or if you rearrange the pages on your Web site, be sure to update all relative links. To avoid such problems, use absolute links instead. Using absolute links requires Webmasters to think through the whole path for a URL. So another benefit of using absolute links is that it helps you to better visualize the directory and file structure for your Web site. And the more familiar you are with the file structure, the less likely it is that your own internal links will become broken.

Your site is useful to others only if it works. Broken links to outside Web sites or to pages within your site serve only to frustrate someone who is trying to decipher the research

Stamp Out Linkrot!

What can you do to avoid problems with broken links?

- Test all links on your site as soon as you create the Web pages.
- Test all links after you upload the pages to the host server.
- Especially test the internal links on your site after you upload the pages to your Web host's server. Many times they work on your local computer but don't work after you upload them (usually because of changes you made in directory structure or in relative links).
- Check links across your Web site regularly (monthly, bimonthly, etc.) to be sure they still work. Link-checking software makes this task easier.
- As you delete Web pages or change the file names on your Web pages, be sure to report these changes to other Webmasters who have links that point back to your site. You can find some of those sites with either Google *(www.google.com)* or AltaVista *(www.altavista.com)*. On these search engines, use this search term to find out who links back to your site: link:yourURL.
- As you delete Web pages or change their file names, be sure to announce the changes on appropriate mailing lists and in e-mail messages to friends and fellow researchers so they can update their links, bookmarks, favorites, and source citations.
- As you delete Web pages or change their file names, be sure to resubmit your site to Internet search engines so that your site can be spidered again in order to update the search engines' index files.
- If you restructure and reorganize the files on your Web site (add directories or change directory/file names), recheck your own internal navigational links.
- When you move your Web site to a new address, if possible leave behind a Web page with a forwarding address and a link to the new address.

information you have published. Regularly verify that all links work on every page of your site to ensure that your hard work is rewarding for you and your site's visitors.

Background Graphics

A background graphic is the picture that serves as the wallpaper behind the text on your Web site. It is the backdrop—the paper on which you print your Web book. Background graphics can add character, color, and flair to your Web site. However,

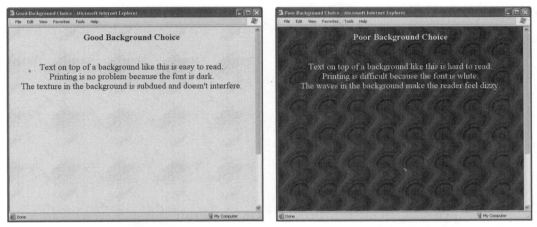

Figure 10.10 Good background choice *(left)* and poor background choice *(right)*

we don't need character or flair on a genealogical research site if it only serves to distract visitors and prohibit their use of the information on your site. I see background graphics in every color and pattern. Those in light, muted colors with nondistinct patterns are easy to handle. But others make it impossible to read the text on the site. Still others make me dizzy, especially as I scroll up and down the page (see Figure 10.10). The worst have been dark, plaid patterns and animated backgrounds that dance around behind the text. All of these make it virtually impossible to read the text or navigate a site successfully.

To guarantee that your site is easy to read, use a light background, with a dark font for the text. If you don't want to chase visitors away, avoid busy patterns and animations. If you really want to use a textured background, be sure it's a subtle, muted design that doesn't interfere with the display of the text.

Backgrounds with Borders

Background graphics "tile"—the graphic repeats itself over and over to fill the browser window. If the graphic is the type that displays a border down the left side of the window, the graphic is a rectangular shape with the border on the left, and the remaining section has another color or pattern. One problem I often notice is that bordered background graphics aren't wide enough, so they end up tiling in funny places (see Figure 10.11). If a graphic is only 800 pixels wide, anyone who uses a higher screen resolution of 1024 x 768 sees the left-hand border twice—once down

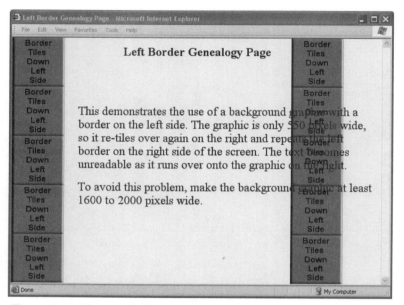

Figure 10.11 The use of a background graphic with a border on the left side

the left side and again down the middle as the graphic tiles to fill in the additional space. The text becomes unreadable as it runs over onto the repeated graphic on the right. To correct this problem, expand the width of a bordered background graphic to 1600 pixels or more.

Colors That Blind or Hypnotize

Another problem I encounter often is color clash—the text color competes with the background color for dominance. Some colors clash so much they appear to move on top of the background. Really hot, neon colors can even appear fuzzy and wavy around the edges. Some sites are completely illegible because of clashing colors (for instance, turquoise blue glowing on a dark blue background). One of the most important rules in Web design is don't rely on your monitor alone. The way your visitors see your site depends on their computer, monitor, screen resolution, color settings—and vision. Bifocals can add a whole new dimension to viewing a bright, wavy bit of neon-pink text on a lime-green background.

When choosing your colors, keep in mind that the text should stand out and be easy to read and print. A solid, dark color for the text is always best for both reading and printing. Dark text on a light background guarantees readable text. When it comes to neon or glowing colors, just don't use them. And whatever colors you choose, stay within the 216-color safe palette *(www.walrus.dircon.co.uk/wpg/safe.html)* so you can be sure the color you choose is the color your visitors see. Always test the site on a variety of monitors, under a variety of color settings, and with various screen resolutions.

Anything That Moves

If it moves, you should delete it. Just because things can jiggle, sway, fly, flash, and zoom across a Web page doesn't mean they should do so on a genealogy page. Keep in mind who your audience is. People visit your Web site to research their family history. You don't want to scare off your visitors, crash their browsers, or hypnotize them with your site's hyperactivity. If you want your genealogy Web site to be effective, helpful, and useful for everyone, *avoid* the following:

- Scrolling text on a Web page or anywhere in the browser window.
- Flashing or blinking text
- Animated graphics
- Animated cursors that follow the mouse around the Web page
- Moving letters, banners, or arrows designed to help with navigation (such as a flashing button that says "<———Click Here!")

For the most part, Web site animations exist only to entertain. But the reason we publish our family history site is to share information with fellow genealogists and cousins. It is the information on your site that interests your visitors.

It Really Isn't Music to My Ears

I am a music lover. And I'm fascinated with the multimedia capabilities of the Web. With our computers and a Web browser, we can view pictures, watch video clips, and listen to sound files and music. But just because we *can* do these things doesn't mean your visitors should be forced to endure them. Enthusiastic new Webmasters often want to include a bit of background music on their Web site. Unless there's a good reason for a genealogical Web site to include music, it should not—and I have yet to see a genealogical site enhanced by a musical accompaniment. We publish our genealogical research on Web sites in order to share with others and to further our research efforts. Mainstream genealogical surfers are looking at your Web site in order to learn about your family history. It isn't likely that they are visiting your site to be entertained. In every instance that I have witnessed where music was included on a genealogical Web site, it was clear to me that the music was only there because the Webmasters were attempting to entertain their visitors (or themselves). Music seems to be used merely as an enhancement along the lines of pretty colors, swirly fonts, and fancy graphics, rather than being used as a research tool.

I have seen one good use of sound on a genealogy Web site: audio files made from recordings of ancestors. If you have tape recordings of your ancestors being interviewed or speaking, you should definitely harness the unique multimedia abilities of the Internet and share that recording online. I have a wonderful family picture of my great-grandparents and great-great-grandfather playing violins and a mandolin. Were I lucky enough to have a recording of their music, I would convert that tape to an audio file and include it on my Web site with a scanned copy of the photograph. But I wouldn't automatically turn that music on in the background and force it on my guests. Instead, I would offer the audio file as a choice for the visitor to make.

Give Your Visitor Options

If you have ever visited a Web site that features music, you may have found that you had the option to stop, pause, or replay the music—probably using a console with buttons similar to those found on a stereo or VCR (see Figure 10.12).

It is always a relief for me to locate that console and hit the Stop button. To me, the only thing worse than having background music suddenly blast from my computer speakers is not being able to turn it off! Some Webmasters even embed music

Figure 10.12 A typical audio and video Web site control panel

in their Web pages—the music begins to play automatically, then plays constantly in the background, and cannot be turned off. It stops only when you leave the site. If you simply must have music on your Web pages, please do your visitors a favor. Do not embed the music in your pages. Give visitors the option to turn off the music. Better yet, give your visitors the option to turn it *on* in the first place. Install the console on your site, and install the audio files you want your visitors to hear. Then invite them to click the Play button if they want to hear the music. In other words, give your visitors the freedom to enjoy your site on their own terms. You are less likely to offend them, and they are more likely to come back.

Compatibility

Not all computers are created alike. Visitors to your site will arrive using a variety of hardware and software configurations. Not everyone who comes to your site will have these items, but they are all necessary for your visitors to hear your audio files online:

- Audio volume turned on
- Speakers
- A Web browser (brand or version) that supports audio files
- Web browser plug-ins for playing audio files
- The Web browser plug-in that is *specific* to the type of audio file on your site

You can't control the final output and how your visitors respond to it, so aim for the most common denominator. The easiest thing to do is avoid the music altogether. The next alternative is to offer the music, but give the visitors an easy way to turn the music off. The best decision is to give your visitors the option to turn on the music or to listen to the audio clip. The last two options give you the power to present your musical selection without impacting the compatibility issues between your computer and your visitors' computers.

Frames Are Evil

Frames are Web design features that allow you to separate the display for your Web pages into several windows that all fit side by side within the Web browser. Frames can be spiffy, if done well, and they can serve a functional purpose. The problem is that most people don't do frames well and often don't use them for a logical, functional purpose. As with many other technical gizmos and doo-dads on a Web site, people tend to create frames on their Web sites simply because they *can*, not because they *should*.

Each frame on a Web page is made up of an individual HTML file. Generally, one main frame page contains the HTML instructions for how the other frames work, where they are placed, and so on. In the example in Figure 10.13, there are four URLs—one URL for the main page with the instructions (the URL that appears in the Web browser's Address or Location bar), and one each for the three frames.

Problems with frames stem from the difficulty we have getting a framed page to behave like a nonframed page. We have experience with nonframed pages. We know how to print a Web page. We know how to set bookmarks or favorites to a regular Web page. We know how to locate the URL for a Web page and reference it in e-mail or in our research notes. But frames work differently. URLs for each frame don't appear in the Address or Location bar of the Web browser. The only URL that appears there is the one for the main page.

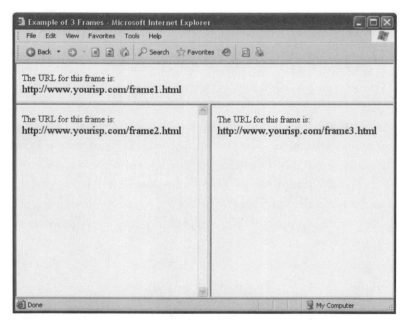

Figure 10.13 An example of frames and the URLs assigned to each framed window

Unless your visitors thoroughly understand how Web browsers work, they have problems dealing with a site in frames. For example, let's say you are viewing a framed Web page with two frames. The links in the frame on the left launch new Web pages within the frame on the right. If you decide to bookmark this page, the URL used is the one for the main frame—the frame on the left. You don't have a bookmark to the right-hand frame, even though that's the information you probably wanted.

The same problem arises when you want to print a page in frames. You first have to highlight the frame that you want to print by clicking within the body of that frame. Then all that prints is the information in that one frame. If one frame contains the contact information for the Webmaster and the other frame contains the actual data, they exist in two separate documents—and you are left to figure out how to cite the Web page as a source of information in your research. Which URL do you use? Which frame? How do you determine the URL for each separate framed page? Windows users can use the magic of the right mouse click in a framed window and look at Properties to find the URL. Macintosh users can view Properties by holding down their mouse button until the menu appears. But how many of your visitors know that?

When it comes to linking to outside Web pages, more confusion occurs. If the frames are not constructed properly, the external Web pages end up being displayed within the frames of the current site. Because it's not clear that they have actually accessed an external URL, visitors often think the content they are viewing is from the original site, not the external linked site. Moreover, framing a Web page from an external site on your own framed site—even if unintentional—is poor netiquette.

Break Out of Frames

If your site isn't using frames, and you don't want visitors to view your site within someone else's frames, include the following link on your page to help them "break out of frames" and view your site within a new Web browser window:

```
<A HREF="http://www.your Web site address.com/"
TARGET="_BLANK">Click here to break out of frames</A>
```

Each of these problems with frames makes researching on your Web site a less-than-desirable activity and adds a layer of difficulty that doesn't need to be there. The point should always be to make it easy for people to use your Web site. In the majority of Web sites using frames, the frames have no reason to be there. I can think of only a handful of sites where the frames truly served a useful, navigational purpose, but even on those sites, there were other ways to make the navigation work in much the same way without using the frames at all.

So don't use frames on your genealogy Web site. If you insist on them, be sure to insert an HTML target attribute into links that point to external Web sites. This ensures that a new browser window will open to display the next Web site. For example, the HTML code for a link to Cyndi's List looks like this:

```
<a href="http://www.CyndisList.com/" target="_blank">Cyndi's List</a>
```

If you must use frames, give your visitors another option: Create another set of plain-text Web pages, without frames or any other fancy doo-dads that might hinder their visit.

Things That Make My Browser Crash

Your visitors should always be foremost in your mind. Know your audience—who they are and what type of computers they have. Your visitors may be newbie or veteran, young or old, and their computers may be new, snazzy, and speedy or old, archaic, and slooooooooow. They may have

- High-speed connections and the latest Web browsers
- Slow modems and outdated Web browsers
- High screen resolution and large monitors
- Average screen resolution and small monitors

So how do you make all those people happy? How do you guarantee they will all be able to use your site equally successfully, with as little frustration as possible? Here's how: Design your site with the simplest of features. Anything that makes my browser crash and anything that requires me to shut down my computer and start over again is *not* a simple feature. Anything that overwhelms my senses and chases me away is *not* a simple feature. If you have taken the time to create a Web site, you must have a desire for people to view your work. So facilitate their visits. Don't include anything on your site that will hinder a visitor or keep some people from being able to access your site. The latest and greatest whiz-bang features for Web pages will not work for everyone. Keep your Web page design as simple as possible.

Memory Hogs

A Web site can become a resource hog, and that can be a big problem for you when you visit that site. Your computer has a limited amount of system resources that it can devote to the Web browser. The amount depends on the type of computer processor, the amount of hard disk space, and the amount of memory (RAM) your computer has. In general, the older the computer, the lower the amount of system resources it has, unless you have done extensive upgrading over time.

Each Web site you visit needs to use a bit of hard disk space and a bit of memory on your computer. The more elements on that site, the more memory it uses when you visit. Animated graphics, large pictures, music, and other multimedia will load very slowly and will slow down other functions on your computer. Eventually, you have to close down a browser window or shut down another software program in order to continue surfing from one overactive Web site to another. If Webmasters keep these memory-hungry elements to a minimum, their Web sites have much less impact on your computer's performance. Animated graphics are one of the worst memory hogs. That's one more reason dancing bunnies and flying monkeys have no place on a genealogy research site.

Don't risk scaring away new cousins with unnecessary, cumbersome features that may crash their browsers. Keep your Web site design and functionality simple!

Plug-ins

Another big problem is when Web sites rely on the use of specialty software plug-ins that visitors are required to download before they can use a Web site. This is a bit like saying, "Sure, you're welcome to read my book. But you can see the text only if you buy some special glasses and spend four days figuring out how to make the glasses work." Plug-ins mean extra work for your visitor, because they have to download the plug-in, install it, and figure out how to use it. And plug-ins may not work on every computer. If you plan to incorporate a special feature that requires a plug-in, give it a lot of thought first. Do you really need to use it? Will it enhance the site? Is it a commonly used plug-in such as Adobe's Acrobat reader *(www.adobe.com/products/acrobat/readstep2.html)*? A well-known plug-in is likely to have fewer compatibility problems than an obscure plug-in. If you decide to use a feature that requires visitors to use a plug-in, you must do everything you can to make it easy on them. Provide complete instructions, and warn your visitors about compatibility issues ahead of time.

Java Jive

Java is a programming language that some Web developers use to automate certain functions on Web sites. Java is used to write applets, which work in conjunction with the visitor's browser to perform some fancy tricks on a Web site—some that serve a purpose and others just for fun. But not all browsers can handle Java. And computer users can choose whether or not their browser is "Java enabled." Because Java applets are inconsistent in some browsers and can be unstable, you do everyone a favor if you don't use Java on your site at all.

JavaScript is another scripting language that you can use to automate some functions, such as toolbars, navigation, forms, and repetitive Webmaster's maintenance tasks. You can insert JavaScript code directly into your HTML. Most modern browsers support JavaScript, although some of the older browsers have problems running JavaScript code and different browsers might support different JavaScript commands. Users whose browsers can support JavaScript can benefit from the automated features you might insert. Of course, you should thoroughly test your JavaScript in a variety of browsers so you can reduce the chance of creating problems for your visitors whose browsers do not support JavaScript.

Test Various Browsers

If even one visitor finds your site hard to use, you defeat the purpose of having published it in the first place. *Always* take the time to test your site—when you first create it and every time you substantially change it. Try to test it under different Web browsers (Microsoft Internet Explorer, Netscape Navigator, America Online, Opera, Mozilla), on different platforms (Windows, Macintosh, Unix, Linux), using different versions of each software program. Ask your friends and fellow genealogists to test your Web site using their own computers, especially if they have hardware and software different from your own.

Learn More about Web Design Dos and Don'ts

In addition to the NGS "Guidelines for Publishing Web Pages on the Internet" (see page 75), there are other online sources for Web site dos and don'ts:

- Alertbox: Jakob Nielsen's Column on Web Usability
  www.useit.com/alertbox/
    - Top Ten Guidelines for Homepage Usability (12 May 2002)
      www.useit.com/alertbox/20020512.html
    - Top Ten Mistakes in Web Design (May 1996)
      www.useit.com/alertbox/9605.html
- Designing Web Usability: The Practice of Simplicity by Jakob Nielsen (Indianapolis: New Riders Publishing, 2000)
- Don't Make Me Think: A Common Sense Approach to Web Usability by Steve Krug (Indianapolis: New Riders Publishing, 2000)
- How to Make an Annoying Web Page
  www.users.nac.net/falken/annoying/
- HTML Bad Style Page
  www.earth.com/bad-style/
- The Top Fifteen Mistakes of First Time Web Design
  www.sid-ss.net/geek/g-15.htm
- Web Pages That Suck—Learn Good Web Design by Looking at Bad Design
  www.webpagesthatsuck.com
- Web Publishing for Genealogy: A Web site and book by Peter Christian
  www.spub.co.uk/wpg/index.html

Many genealogy Webmasters struggle through the process of creating their Web sites, stumbling and tripping here and there over some common mistakes. I certainly learned my lessons the hard way. Take advantage of the suggestions and cautions discussed in this chapter—they will help you create the best possible Web site and reach as many visitors as possible.

CHAPTER 11

Check Your Work and Give Your Site a Trial Run

YOU HAVE PUT A LOT OF WORK INTO CREATING YOUR WEB SITE. NOW that the Web pages are all ready to go, it's time to thoroughly review your site. In this chapter, we go step by step through the process of checking, verifying, and validating your Web site. Returning to our book analogy, this chapter covers the final editing process before the book goes to print. So open your Web browser and view your site as you walk through the next several steps.

Proofread and Review the Site

As we discussed in Chapter 10, grammar, spelling, and proper punctuation are vital to you and your Web site because they lend credibility to your research. Cousins and fellow genealogists will be viewing your Web site with a fresh set of eyes. They are sure to spot obvious errors and misspelled words. The first impression is important. Visitors who find errors the first time they visit your site aren't likely to visit again soon. And because they don't take you seriously, they are much less likely to quote your site or use the information they find there. Moreover, if they perceive your site (and therefore your research) to be sloppy, they won't be any more likely to share what they know with you.

Proofread your site. If your Web site comprises hundreds of Web pages, it may not be necessary to proof every single page, particularly those generated by a genealogy software program or GEDCOM conversion utility. Those pages are composed of names, dates, and places found in your genealogy database file. But carefully check the pages you created manually, including each section index page. Go through all those custom-made pages with a fine-tooth comb. Read aloud any text that you wrote (that's the best way to find errors in your own work). Spell-check the text. If your HTML editor doesn't have a spell-checker, use your word processor instead. Copy text from your Web browser window (not the text and HTML code in the file itself) and paste it temporarily into a blank word-processing document. Spell-check that document, then copy and paste any corrected text back into the original Web page file.

Validate Your HTML for Accuracy and Usability

A Webmaster writes HTML code with the aid of an HTML editor or from scratch with a text editor. Web browser software reads the HTML, interprets it, and displays the resulting Web page for the visitor. HTML is logical, with a series of tags that you turn on and off in order to accomplish a specific type of formatting. If you don't write some of the HTML code correctly, the Web browser may misinterpret it. If you leave out a closing tag, or if you have any typographical errors within the HTML code, the Web browser won't display the page as you intend it to appear.

Some of the newer versions of Web browser software programs are very forgiving of errors in HTML code. They allow certain mistakes to slip through without causing a display error. But older versions aren't nearly so forgiving. Many display the errors for everyone to see. Certain HTML errors even cause the page to appear blank. Keep in mind that visitors to your site will be using all types of Web browsers and every version. Be sure your HTML code can be read by everyone, whatever the browser.

How do you avoid problems with your HTML code? Validate the code to look for errors or compatibility problems. Your HTML editor may allow you to validate your code. Check its Help files. But there are also several online services you can use to check your HTML code:

- Page Valet
  valet.webthing.com/page/
- The W3C MarkUp Validation Service
  validator.w3.org

- WDG HTML Validator
  www.htmlhelp.com/tools/validator/
- Yahoo > HTML > Validation and Checkers
  dir.yahoo.com/Computers_and_Internet/Data_Formats/HTML/
  Validation_and_Checkers/

Some of these programs require that you first upload your Web pages to the host server. If so, you will need to follow the instructions for uploading in the next section *before* validating the HTML on your site.

Upload the Pages to the Web Server

Now that you have proofread the pages and verified the HTML, you can upload the Web pages to their new home on your Web host's server. You use an FTP client software program to log onto the host server. You have several FTP software programs to consider, some of which are shareware:

- CuteFTP
  www.cuteftp.com/cuteftp/
- Fetch Macintosh FTP Client
  www.fetchsoftworks.com
- FTP Explorer
  www.ftpx.com
- Ipswitch Software—WS_FTP
  www.ipswitch.com/Products/file-transfer.html

When you opened your account, your ISP or Web hosting service supplied you with the following pieces of information, all necessary to successfully log onto the server via FTP. Enter these pieces of data into the software program to set up your regular FTP user profile:

- Your user ID
- Your password

🍃 The host or server address

🍃 The path or directory name where your site's files will be stored

Create Directories

If you haven't already done so during the Web page creation process, the first thing to do now is create folders or directories on the host server for your site. In Chapter 4, we discussed organizing your files and your Web site. Depending on the FTP program (and possibly the HTML editor) you are using, you may need to create a series of directories (and perhaps subdirectories) on the Web server that mimics the organization scheme you created for the site. Directory names and file names on the Web are case-sensitive. The names you give the directories must match exactly in order to ensure that all URLs are valid. If you make the directory names on the server match the folder names on your own computer, you will make very few errors as you transfer files back and forth between the two.

If you have used a genealogy software program or GEDCOM conversion utility to create your Web pages, a directory structure has already been built into the page setup. At this point you have created a home page and index pages for the site, as well. With most FTP programs, during the uploading process you can manually create new directories on the host server, or the FTP software can duplicate the directories from your computer's hard drive during the transfer process itself. Let's say you created your genealogy Web site in a directory on your C drive called "Genealogy Web Site" and in that directory you have one directory for each of the eight surnames. Additionally, your software program inserted more directories and subdirectories for each surname. Your hard drive folders would then be labeled as shown:

C:\Genealogy Web Site\Anderson\docs\pages
C:\Genealogy Web Site\Cartwright\docs\pages
C:\Genealogy Web Site\Dougherty\docs\pages
C:\Genealogy Web Site\Frederick\docs\pages
C:\Genealogy Web Site\Johnson\docs\pages
C:\Genealogy Web Site\Jones\docs\pages
C:\Genealogy Web Site\Knox\docs\pages
C:\Genealogy Web Site\Smith\docs\pages

When you are ready to upload all the Web pages that are contained in those directories and subdirectories, your FTP software may allow you to choose the top-level directory in that structure: \Genealogy Web Site. Most FTP programs then ask you to confirm that you want to transfer all folders and files contained within that top-level directory and whether you want them to be duplicated in the same structure on the server. The answer to both questions is "yes!" This saves you a lot of work. Here is the duplicated directory structure on the host server after the FTP process:

http://www.genealogywebhost.com/~mydirectory/Anderson/docs/pages
http://www.genealogywebhost.com/~mydirectory/Cartwright/docs/pages
http://www.genealogywebhost.com/~mydirectory/Dougherty/docs/pages
http://www.genealogywebhost.com/~mydirectory/Frederick/docs/pages
http://www.genealogywebhost.com/~mydirectory/Johnson/docs/pages
http://www.genealogywebhost.com/~mydirectory/Jones/docs/pages
http://www.genealogywebhost.com/~mydirectory/Knox/docs/pages
http://www.genealogywebhost.com/~mydirectory/Smith/docs/pages

Some HTML editors, like FrontPage, also have FTP capabilities built into the program. Once your Web pages are ready, you can use the editor to transfer the files. Again, the software will have created a set of directories and subdirectories during the Web page creation process. During the FTP upload, the editor will create the directories on the host server and transfer the files to duplicate what it did on your computer's hard drive.

Mirroring your Web site's organization of files and directories on your computer's hard drive makes it easy to avoid errors when you upload files onto the host server.

Upload Your Files
Once the directories are created, you can start uploading your Web site files. During the upload process, you are transferring copies of files from your computer to the

server, rather than moving them. So copies remain in both places. The FTP client tells you the date, time, and file size for each file on the server. Use these facts to compare the files between your computer and the server whenever you are attempting to move or delete files from one place or another. If your Web site host server is located in another time zone, keep in mind that there may be a time difference displayed between the files on your computer and the corresponding files on the server.

Pay careful attention to the directories you are working in when you use FTP. If you have several directories, they each have their own index file (index.htm, .html, or .asp). Be sure you upload the correct index page to the right directory.

These are typically the types of files you will transfer from your computer to the Web server:

- Your Web pages (files ending with .htm or .html)
- A main index page—the home page (usually named index.html)
- An index page for each directory you create (usually named index.html)
- The graphics for your site (files ending with .jpg or .gif)
- Scanned copies of documents (files ending with .jpg or .gif)
- Scanned copies of photographs (files ending with .jpg or .gif)
- GEDCOM files (files ending with .ged)
- Compressed files (files ending with .zip or .sit)
- Word-processing documents (files ending with .doc, .txt, or .rtf)
- Adobe Acrobat files (files ending with .pdf)

Check Navigation, Verify Links, and Confirm Accessibility

Some people are tempted to check all links and navigation before uploading their Web site and making it "live" online. But be sure to also check the site thoroughly once it is online—and check your site on a computer other than your own. You may find more errors on a live site than the one housed safely on your own computer. For example, relative links (see complete discussion in Chapter 10) behave inconsistently. As you create your Web pages, the relative links always work on your own computer. And they may still work in your own Web browser once you upload your pages to the Web host's server because the relative link might reference a page or graphic on your local hard drive. But relative links may not work from another computer or browser. For example, if a relative link references the file /backgroundgraphic.gif, your browser will look for that file in the same directory on the same server as the Web page. That link will only work if you uploaded that graphic file to that place. If the graphic file wasn't uploaded, or if you uploaded to a different directory, your relative link may not work for others. Absolute links are a better alternative to ensure reliable links. Using absolute links throughout all your Web pages instills discipline in the format for your site. As noted in the previous chapter, it also means that you will be able to visualize the file structure for your Web site and place the proper files in the proper directories. Doing so ensures that you will have fewer broken links and broken graphics on your Web site.

Navigation

Navigation refers to the internal links and structure on your site. To test the navigation on your site, start with your home page and scroll up and down.

- Can you easily find the links that will take visitors to other areas within the site?
- Are your internal links labeled correctly?
- Follow some of your internal links several layers deep into your site. Once there, can you find links or a path that easily leads you back to the home page (without having to use the Back button on the Web browser toolbar)?
- Can you easily move between each section on your site?
- Is anything blocking you from moving quickly around your site? If you have problems moving from one page to another, it is time to add more navigational links.

Check Your Links

Broken links are a never-ending problem for Webmasters. A link becomes broken when the URL in the link is no longer valid. See Chapter 10 for more about broken links. If you have a long list of links that will take a while to check, consider using link-checking software, which can check a whole page on your site at one time—or your entire Web site, if necessary. Give some of these a try and use them often in the regular maintenance of your site:

- CyberSpyder Link Test
  www.cyberspyder.com/cslnkts1.html
- Link Alarm
  linkalarm.com
- W3C Link Checker
  validator.w3.org/checklink

Accessibility for Everyone

Is your site accessible to absolutely everyone, including visitors with disabilities? To test your site's accessibility, use the best-known accessibility validation tool online: Bobby *(bobby.watchfire.com/bobby/html/en/index.jsp)*.

Test Your Site in Various Web Browsers

Keep in mind that your site may work great on your own browser, but not all computers or browsers are the same. Genealogical surfers, both PC and Mac users, have several different versions of the two popular Web browsers: Microsoft Internet Explorer (IE) and Netscape Navigator. America Online users have a version of the IE browser built into the program, and several different versions of AOL software are currently used online. A few lesser-known browser programs are also available. The following sites help you test your site's compatibility with different browsers:

- Microsoft Internet Explorer
  www.microsoft.com/windows/ie/default.asp
- Netscape Navigator
  download.netscape.com/

🍃 Opera
    www.opera.com/

🍃 Webmaster@AOL
    webmaster.info.aol.com/

About Browsers

To learn more about Web browsers, visit the following sites. You'll find lists of their features, as well as statistics and information about how the general public uses browsers.

- Viewable with Any Browser: Campaign
  www.anybrowser.org/campaign/

- Webmonkey | Reference: Browser Chart
  hotwired.lycos.com/webmonkey/webmonkey/browserkit/

- W3Schools.com—Browser Statistics
  www.w3schools.com/browsers/browsers_stats.asp

Begin testing your site with the browser or browsers that you already have installed on your own computer. Then download different versions or other browsers whenever you can locate them online. Install them on your computer—in a different directory or location than other versions, if possible, so you don't overwrite one with the other. Microsoft Internet Explorer gives you no choice where the program is installed and definitely overwrites older versions. But Netscape allows you to install several different versions in different places on your computer. This gives you the advantage of having more than one version with which to test your site.

Ask Your Friends

Once you've exhausted all the versions you can find and installed them on your computer, it is time to impose on your friends and fellow online genealogists. Ask them to visit your site and inspect it for you. To keep track of what type of testing is done for your site, ask them these questions:

- What browser and version are you using?
- PC or Macintosh?
- What is your screen resolution?
- Can you read the site easily?
- Can you print a page from the site and read it easily?
- Are there any broken graphics?
- Are there any broken links?
- Is the site easy to navigate?
- Is there consistency from page to page?
- Is there clear communication, including proper spelling and punctuation?
- Do you understand the purpose of the site?
- Did you experience any problems with the site that you didn't anticipate?

Back Up and Archive Your Web Site

Back up or archive—what is the difference? You should make backup copies of your Web site to use in case something happens to the pages and other files on your computer or on the Web host's server. The backup files can be overwritten with fresh backups each time you change your Web pages. Just before you make a change to your pages, though, you should archive copies of your site. Archived copies serve as a record of how your site appeared before the changes were made. If research discrepancies ever arise regarding genealogical information you published on your site before and after changes you make, having archived copies will help you resolve them. Keep archived copies permanently—never overwrite them. Keep them on a Zip disk or burn them on a CD.

This first time you back up your new Web site, create both a backup set and an archived set of all files contained on your family history Web site. Include copies of the graphics files and digitized images that your site contains. Be sure to label each set appropriately, including the date you made the copies. For security, you might even make two sets of each and store one somewhere outside your home—at the office, at a friend's home, or in your safe deposit box. Having an additional set of backups in "off-site storage" ensures that you won't lose all your hard work in case something happens—theft, fire, or flood—to the backup copies that are left at home.

After creating a beautiful site to pay tribute to your ancestors, you must be sure it works well and that everyone can access the information you so painstakingly researched and published. Otherwise, why plant your family tree online? Checking your site for usability and accessibility, as well as spelling and punctuation, shows that you care about your research—from start to finish.

CHAPTER 12

Make It Official:
Publicize Your New Web Site

YOU DREAMED ABOUT A GENEALOGY WEB SITE. YOU PLANNED, CREATED, personalized, and tested your site. Finally, you put your genealogical Web masterpiece online. Now what? Don't just rest on your laurels. After all that work, don't just assume that because you built it, they will come. It's time to publicize your site to others online.

Strategies for Making Your Site Known to Other Genealogists

Once your Web pages have been uploaded to the Web host's server, they are accessible to anyone on the Internet. Eventually, people will stumble across your Web pages and may share their new find with others. As search engines spider your Web neighborhood, they may index your site and add it to their database for others to use. But you don't know when that might happen. To ensure that the online genealogical community knows about your new Web site, you must spend time telling them about it.

Where Should You Advertise?

You can promote your new family history Web site in many places, both online and offline. In this chapter, we primarily discuss online venues for announcing your Web site. Most visitors will learn about your site through online sources, but that doesn't mean you should ignore the traditional offline publications and points of contact. At the end of this chapter, you'll find a list of offline sources where you can announce your Web site, including family/surname associations, family/surname newsletters, genealogical or historical societies, regional archives or libraries, and genealogical periodicals and newsletters.

For both the offline and online sources, you need to consider which are most appropriate based on the content of your Web site. If your site focuses on a specific family or surname, then search for Web sites, mailing lists, newsletters, and other publications associated with that family or surname. If your site has subject matter that relates to a specific locality, look for sources that pertain to that place. No matter what type of genealogical content your site has, always announce it to Webmasters, list-owners, editors, and columnists with publications of general genealogical interest to everyone.

How Often?

When you first publish your site online, announce it to as many people, in as many places, as you can imagine—as long as they are appropriate, of course. After that initial announcement, think about the particular venue to determine how often you should reintroduce your site to your fellow genealogists. Expense may determine how often you announce your site. If you use free services to announce your site, be sure not to repeat your announcement too often—don't abuse the privilege of complimentary services such as mailing lists and message boards. Instead, come up with a plan to use these support systems in a responsible manner so that you don't wear out your welcome. Consider making your announcements to mailing lists, message boards, and other free resources bimonthly, quarterly, or just a few times a year, but never more than once each month. Check with the owner or administrator of the forum for advice or rules on how often you may post messages. You might also find a FAQ for the forum that outlines the rules and regulations.

Tell people about your genealogy Web site each time you substantially change or update it. If you add a new family name, a new chapter, or a new section, let people know. Announce your finds whenever you have completed a major research project or made progress on a specific research problem. Tell others whenever you change the site in a way that alters the data; that altered data may impact the cousins and fellow researchers who rely on your site as a source of information or inspiration for their own research. If you don't change your site often, be sure to reintroduce the site to the online community at least twice a year—just to remind them you're there. Such an announcement also tells online newcomers about your site—perhaps connecting you with that long-lost cousin who has finally joined the Internet community.

Genealogy Mailing Lists and Message Boards

The places your site gets the most online exposure to the genealogical community is on interactive discussion forums. Spend time exploring all the options available for you to announce your new family history Web site. The instructions and samples in the following sections help make these tasks as trouble free as possible.

Genealogy Mailing Lists

Mailing lists are interactive discussion groups via e-mail. There are more than twenty-eight thousand mailing lists for genealogical research. RootsWeb is home to most of them. You'll find a mailing list for just about every topic in genealogical research, thousands for particular surnames, and many for specific individuals or couples. There are mailing lists for ethnic groups, religious denominations, historical topics, and almost every locality. Best of all, mailing lists are free and open to everyone online.

Mailing lists are automated; each list is run by special software that distributes messages to everyone who subscribes to that list. To participate in a mailing list whose subject matter applies to your research and the contents of your Web site, find the subscription instructions for that list. Most mailing lists require that you subscribe to them before you post any messages for other subscribers to read. When you subscribe to a mailing list, you can post a message about your new genealogy Web site. And you can follow the conversations that take place on the list, answer questions from other subscribers, and post your replies for the rest of the mailing list to read. Because the mailing list on which you post your message is topically relevant to your Web site, you will obviously have a research interest in the conversations that take place on the list.

Even though mailing lists are automated, each list has a listowner or list administrator—the person who saw the need for a mailing list on a particular genealogical topic, then created the list, and continues to maintain the list. Listowners help people subscribe, unsubscribe, and post messages. They deal with bounced messages and other behind-the-scenes administrative issues.

Each mailing list has two versions, especially those at RootsWeb. Mail mode allows subscribers to receive a copy of each message as it is posted to the list. Digest mode accumulates individual messages for the list that day and sends them out in one large message, usually once or twice a day. Each version of the mailing list has its own address to be used for subscribing and unsubscribing, and a separate address to be used for posting messages.

Quick Mailing List Instructions

1. Send an e-mail message to the mailing list software to join or "subscribe" to the list.

2. Receive a welcome message that outlines the purpose of the list and supplies instructions on how to participate.

3. Post your own message to the list for the other subscribers to read.

4. Continue to participate in the list as long as you like.

5. Unsubscribe from the list when you no longer want to participate in the discussions.

6. Resubscribe to the list for a short period each time you wish to post an update or a reminder about your genealogy Web site.

7. Whenever you use a mailing list, be sure to follow the rules and adhere to the wishes of the listowner.

Finding Mailing Lists

RootsWeb *(lists.rootsweb.com)* hosts the vast majority of all genealogy mailing lists online, processing millions of mailing list messages and maintaining the computers and equipment on which they run. All the mailing lists are archived so that visitors can search messages previously posted by others, without having to subscribe to the lists. RootsWeb also has a Web page for each of the mailing lists it hosts. The Web page for each list provides

- A description of the topic for the list

- An e-mail address for contacting the listowner

🌿 Instructions for how to subscribe to the list

🌿 Instructions for how to unsubscribe

🌿 Links to the online archives for the list (if applicable)

One of the oldest genealogy Web sites is Genealogy Resources on the Internet, run by John Fuller and Christine Gaunt *(www.rootsweb.com/~jfuller/internet.html)*. Fuller maintains the part of the site that is devoted to genealogy mailing lists *(www.rootsweb.com/~jfuller/gen_mail.html)*. While RootsWeb's Web pages have details for the lists they host, you will find John Fuller's site is more comprehensive because he keeps track of *all* lists for genealogy—at RootsWeb and elsewhere online. His list is always current because he updates the site several times each week. On his Web pages, Fuller sorts the mailing lists by categories, describes the topic for each list, gives instructions for how to subscribe, and provides links to corresponding Web pages when they're available.

Use either Fuller's site or the RootsWeb index to locate the mailing lists that best fit the purpose(s) and topic(s) for your Web site. Create a section in your research notes to keep track of the mailing lists on which you promote your Web site. Log the details for each list, so you'll have the information you need to post updates and reminders about your site as it grows and evolves.

Some mailing lists are "gatewayed" with either newsgroups or message boards. For newsgroups, this means that messages posted on the mailing list or the newsgroup will be duplicated on the other. For message boards, the gateway allows messages to be automatically duplicated on the mailing lists.

Genealogy Message Boards

Message boards are similar to mailing lists in how they are arranged and in the purpose they serve. But while messages on mailing lists are delivered to the subscribers by e-mail, those on message boards are posted live via a form on a Web site. Mailing list users can be force-fed your e-mail, making it easier for you to get the word to them.

With message boards, you must rely on the users to visit the message board Web site and seek out your post. Usually message boards can be searched by keyword or browsed by topic and "thread." A thread is a series of messages in a conversation, beginning with the initial message and followed by each successive reply.

You can find genealogy message boards several places online. The two most often used are the Ancestry.com Genealogy Message Boards *(www.ancestry.com/share/main.htm)* and the message boards at Genealogy.com *(www.genealogy.com)*. RootsWeb also has a series of message boards that mirror the messages found on the Ancestry.com boards.

Whenever you include a URL in an e-mail message, be sure to use the full URL, including the beginning *http://* protocol. This ensures that most e-mail programs will display the URL as a clickable link in your message. And that makes it easy for people who read your messages to get to your Web site.

Writing Your Announcement

The announcement you post, whether to mailing lists or message boards, or both, can be substantially the same. By the time you are ready to post a message to a mailing list or message board, you may find that you have several appropriate forums on which to make your announcements. Posting numerous announcements, on two different types of forums, does not entail that much extra work. To do this easily, write one generic message suitable to any mailing list or message board. Then copy and paste the text into new e-mail messages or into message board forms online. In this initial, generic message, don't include specific details that apply only to the topic for a specific list. Keep a copy of your announcement to use as boilerplate for future messages. You can customize the message for specific venues and use it over and over on several different mailing lists or message boards.

When writing your message, be sure to

🍃 Use a clear and concise subject line with surnames, dates, and place names.

🍃 Introduce yourself or your reason for writing your message.

- Describe your Web site, its purpose, and your goals for the site.

- Provide the complete, proper title for your site.

- Supply the complete URL for the Web site (including the leading protocol: *http://*). Check the URL to be sure it's accurate—or even better, copy and paste your URL to be sure it's error free.

- Sign your full, real name to the message.

- Include your e-mail address in the body of the message, following your signature.

- Keep in mind that once you post your message, you can't get it back. Proofread and spell-check it before you send it.

- Keep in mind that messages will be forwarded and shared with others. In most cases, they will also be archived. Don't include any information or make any promises that you may not be willing to have known to the general public.

You can use the example in Figure 12.1 to create your own Web site announcement. Keep your message short; use only the most important bits of information to

```
SUBJECT LINE:   New "Title of Your Site" Web site

Dear Cousins (Hello All; Greetings Everyone),

I'm very pleased to announce that I have published a new genealogy Web site. The
site is dedicated to research for descendants of (fill in the name of your ancestor). This
site reflects my personal research efforts from the past (insert number) years.

    Descendants of (your ancestor's name—or whatever the complete title might be)
    http://www.yourisp.com/~your_directory/filename.html

I'm proud of my site, and I hope it helps my cousins and fellow family historians. Please
e-mail me if you find anything on the site that you want to discuss. I have included on
the site a short list of the sources used in my research. Full sources are available upon
request.

Sincerely,
Your Full Name
YourE-MailAddress@YourISP.com
```

Figure 12.1 A generic e-mail template

convey what your visitors need to know. Retain a copy of the message in your e-mail files so you can quickly and easily send it again. Also keep a copy in your research notes as a record of what you have done.

General Announcement with Details

You can edit and alter the example in Figure 12.1 to accommodate any list to which you might post your message. For example, if your Web site represents your research for eight different surnames, you might announce your site on eight different surname mailing lists, as well as the locality mailing lists for each county and state in which your ancestors lived. Using our eight-surname model, the example in Figure 12.2 shows the type of generic message you might send to general-interest mailing lists.

SUBJECT LINE: New "SMITH & KNOX Genealogy" Web site

Hello all:

I'm very pleased to announce that I have published a new genealogy Web site. The site is dedicated to my personal family history research from the past 18 years.

Smith & Knox Genealogy
http://www.yourisp.com/~your_directory/filename.html

The surnames and locations found on my Web site are:
SMITH: Audubon County, Iowa, 1870
FREDERICK: Audubon County, Iowa, 1850 to present
ANDERSON: Sweden to Illinois
KNOX: Morgan County, Ohio, 1834 to present
JONES: England to Pennsylvania
DOUGHERTY: Ohio to Indiana
JOHNSON: Sweden to Illinois, to Audubon County, Iowa
CARTWRIGHT: Indiana to Towner County, North Dakota

I'm proud of my site, and I hope it helps my cousins and fellow family historians. Please e-mail me if you find anything on the site that you want to discuss. I have included on the site a short list of the sources I have used in my research. Full sources are available upon request.

Sincerely,
Your Full Name
YourE-MailAddress@YourISP.com

Figure 12.2 A generic e-mail template, which features such details as surnames, dates, and places

The following general-interest mailing lists can be found on the Genealogy Resources on the Internet Web site at *www.rootsweb.com/~jfuller/gen_mail.html.*

- ALT-GENEALOGY: Gatewayed with the alt.genealogy newsgroup for general genealogical discussions. To subscribe, send a new e-mail message with only the word "subscribe" to alt-genealogy-l-request@rootsweb.com.

- NEW-GEN-URL: A mailing list for the posting of information on genealogy-related Web sites. Postings should contain your title, full name and e-mail address, the URL (address) of your site, and a brief description of your site's contents. You may also include a surname list if your site is a personal Web site. To subscribe, send a new e-mail message with only the word "subscribe" to new-gen-url-l-request@rootsweb.com.

- ROOTS-L: The best-known genealogy mailing list, with over nine thousand subscribers from around the world. To subscribe, send a new e-mail message with only the word "subscribe" to roots-l-request@rootsweb.com.

SUBJECT LINE: George SMITH, Audubon County, Iowa

Hello all:

I'm very pleased to announce that I have published a new genealogy Web site. The site is dedicated to my personal family history research from the past 18 years.

   Smith & Knox Genealogy
   http://www.yourisp.com/~your_directory/filename.html

One section on my site is devoted to George SMITH, of Audubon County, Iowa. He and his wife, Kesiah, are buried in the Exira Cemetery. They are the parents of Nancy Catherine SMITH, who married Xerxes KNOX. George appears on the 1870 census in Audubon County, Iowa.

Collateral families on the site are:
   FREDERICK, Albert: Audubon County, Iowa, 1850 to present
   KNOX, Xerxes: Morgan County, Ohio, 1834 to present

I'm proud of my site, and I hope it helps my cousins and fellow family historians. Please e-mail me if you find anything on the site that you want to discuss. I have included on the site a short list of the sources I have used in my research. Full sources are available upon request.

Sincerely,
Your Full Name
YourE-MailAddress@YourISP.com

Figure 12.3 A generic e-mail template, which features details for a specific surname

Surname-Specific Announcement

Subsequent messages to surname-specific mailing lists or message boards might be written like the example shown in Figure 12.3, adding more details as necessary. This particular example could be posted on FREDERICK-L@rootsweb.com, KNOX-L@rootsweb.com, and SMITH-L@rootsweb.com—all likely venues for this surname-specific announcement.

Locality-Specific Announcement

If you decide to post a message to a mailing list or message board for a particular location, your message might look like the example in Figure 12.4. Likely venues on which to post this locality-specific example are IOWA-L@rootsweb.com and IAAUDUBO-L@rootsweb.com.

SUBJECT LINE: Audubon County, Iowa: SMITH, KNOX, FREDERICK

Hello all:

I'm very pleased to announce that I have published a new genealogy Web site. The site is dedicated to my personal family history research from the past 18 years.

Smith & Knox Genealogy
http://www.yourisp.com/~your_directory/filename.html

Several branches of my family resided in Audubon County, Iowa, for several generations. The earliest known ancestors in Audubon County, particularly in Exira, are:
George and Kesiah SMITH
Xerxes and Nancy (Smith) KNOX
Albert and Nellie Mae (Knox) FREDERICK

Each of these couples is now buried in the Exira Cemetery.

I'm proud of my site, and I hope it helps my cousins and fellow family historians. Please e-mail me if you find anything on the site that you want to discuss. I have included on the site a short list of the sources I have used in my research. Full sources are available upon request.

Sincerely,
Your Full Name
YourE-MailAddress@YourISP.com

Figure 12.4 A generic e-mail template, which features details for a specific locality

E-mailing Other Family Historians

As you spend time online, you'll find other genealogists who are researching the same families and surnames, locations, or topics that you are researching. You'll find them through their Web sites, mailing list posts and archives, search engines, and mutual acquaintances. As you find them, let them know about your common surname or research interests. Use the samples of e-mail messages in the previous section to first contact those new people you come across online.

When you encounter genealogists with Web sites of their own, ask to exchange links. This means that you set up a link to their Web site from your own and they provide a reciprocal link from their site to yours. Exchanging links with other Webmasters who share a common bond with you is a natural way to help one another. For example, you can direct researchers their way, and they can do the same for you. Figure 12.5 shows a sample e-mail requesting such an exchange.

SUBJECT LINE: SMITH & KNOX Genealogy Web site

Hello ——:

I visited your Web site online. I believe we may have some ancestors in common. My family history is online at:
  Smith & Knox Genealogy
  http://www.yourisp.com/~your_directory/filename.html

The surnames and locations found on my Web site are:
  SMITH: Audubon County, Iowa, 1870
  FREDERICK: Audubon County, Iowa, 1850 to present
  ANDERSON: Sweden to Illinois
  KNOX: Morgan County, Ohio, 1834 to present
  JONES: England to Pennsylvania
  DOUGHERTY: Ohio to Indiana
  JOHNSON: Sweden to Illinois, to Audubon County, Iowa
  CARTWRIGHT: Indiana to Towner County, North Dakota

Please take a look at my site when you have a chance. I will be creating a link from my site to yours later today. Would you also be willing to set up a reciprocal link back to my site?

Sincerely,
Your Full Name
YourE-MailAddress@YourISP.com

Figure 12.5 A generic e-mail template, which you can use to correspond with individual fellow genealogists who have Web sites

E-mail Signatures and Taglines

Use the signature file feature in your e-mail software program to create custom "sig files" for the genealogy research that you e-mail to others. Signature files, sometimes called taglines, are small text files that are automatically added to e-mail messages that you send out. Create one general sig file that lists your surnames and your genealogy Web site address. You can also create a separate sig file for each surname and chapter in your Web site, supplying the individual URLs for each chapter. Using signature files in e-mail will help get the word out to others online that your Web site exists.

Online Genealogy Columnists and Editors

After you post your own announcements on genealogy mailing lists, your next best bet to get the word out quickly is through online genealogy columnists. There are several popular e-mail newsletters (also known as "e-zines") with regular issues sent to a large number of readers. Some of these newsletters feature notices of new Web sites. To take advantage of this opportunity, take time to write a clear, concise, and polite e-mail request to the editor or columnist of each publication. Your message should contain the announcement that you request they publish in their newsletter. Write that portion as you would a classified ad or a short blurb in a newspaper or magazine. In the mailing list announcements, you are "talking" informally to individuals who subscribe to the lists. But the e-zine announcement should be more formal, though short and to the point. Alter the example in Figure 12.6 to fit your own needs and personal style.

The following are a few popular online newsletters, along with their columnists or editors:

- *Eastman's Online Genealogy Newsletter*
  www.eogn.com/home/
  Richard Eastman, richard@eastman.net
- *MISSING LINKS: A Magazine for Genealogists*
  www.petuniapress.com
  Julia M. Case, juliecase@prodigy.net

RootsWeb Review (only for sites hosted by RootsWeb)
e-zine.rootsweb.com/
Myra Vanderpool Gormley, CG, Editor-RWR@rootsweb.com

UpFront with NGS
www.ngsgenealogy.org/upfront.htm
Carla and Dennis Ridenour, UpFront@ngsgenealogy.org

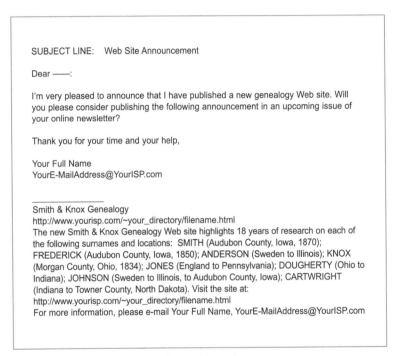

SUBJECT LINE: Web Site Announcement

Dear ——:

I'm very pleased to announce that I have published a new genealogy Web site. Will you please consider publishing the following announcement in an upcoming issue of your online newsletter?

Thank you for your time and your help,

Your Full Name
YourE-MailAddress@YourISP.com

———————————
Smith & Knox Genealogy
http://www.yourisp.com/~your_directory/filename.html
The new Smith & Knox Genealogy Web site highlights 18 years of research on each of the following surnames and locations: SMITH (Audubon County, Iowa, 1870); FREDERICK (Audubon County, Iowa, 1850); ANDERSON (Sweden to Illinois); KNOX (Morgan County, Ohio, 1834); JONES (England to Pennsylvania); DOUGHERTY (Ohio to Indiana); JOHNSON (Sweden to Illinois, to Audubon County, Iowa); CARTWRIGHT (Indiana to Towner County, North Dakota). Visit the site at: http://www.yourisp.com/~your_directory/filename.html
For more information, please e-mail Your Full Name, YourE-MailAddress@YourISP.com

Figure 12.6 A generic e-mail template, which you can use to announce your Web site to columnists

Genealogy Web Indexes and Search Engines

One of the most daunting tasks on the Internet is indexing the Web sites published there. But for family history research to succeed online, genealogy Web indexes and search engines are essential. Genealogists thrive on indexes and bibliographies because they are vital to our finding sources (both new and old) for family history research. Books and other material published on paper can be indexed once. That index can then be published in a book, microform, or CD-ROM for the future use of genealogists. Indexing on the Internet differs quite a bit. You might index a Web site today and publish the URL (electronically or in print) only to find a few weeks later that the URL doesn't work. Maintaining an index of Web sites is an ongoing process that never produces a final product. New genealogists publish new Web sites each day, which adds new resources to the index. Old genealogy Web sites change as information is updated, sometimes altering the purpose and description of an existing Web site. And some people lose interest in their genealogy site and decide to take it offline. Therefore, an index of genealogy Web sites continually grows and evolves, just as the Web itself does.

Most often, there is a human being behind a genealogy Web index. This person seeks out new genealogy Web sites to index, learning about them by word of mouth or finding them by using Internet search engines. Genealogy search engines usually build their indexes with software through a process of automation. Either way, the technology is basically the same—and imperfect. This means you need to use all the genealogy Web indexes and search engines you can find in order to advertise your new Web site, including these:

- Cyndi's List of Genealogy Sites on the Internet
  www.CyndisList.com

- FamilySearch
  www.familysearch.org/Eng/Share/Add/frameset_add.asp

- The Genealogy Home Page
  www.genhomepage.com

- Genealogy Resources on the Internet
  www.rootsweb.com/~jfuller/Internet.html

- RootsWeb.com—RootsLinks
  resources.rootsweb.com/~rootslink/search.html

- Cyndi's List—Handy Online Starting Points (links to more genealogy Web indexes)
  www.CyndisList.com/handy.htm

Each index or search engine has a Web form for you to fill out in order to announce your site. Since you will be repeatedly submitting the same information, simplify the process and save some time: Copy and paste your answers from form to form. To begin with, prepare the information you need to complete each form, particularly these five items:

- Title of your Web site

- Complete URL for your Web site (including the protocol: *http://*)

- A clear and concise description for your site—four sentences at most

- A set of keywords that best describe the highlights of your Web site. These keywords help the indexer or search engine categorize your site appropriately. (Also see Chapter 8, "Meta Tags" section.)

- Your name and e-mail address

As you use genealogy search engines and Web indexes, be sure to read all the instructions and follow the guidelines supplied by the administrator of the site. Because these are free services, take care to provide everything required the first time you submit your link so that you don't create any extra work for yourself or for the index administrator.

In your research workbook, keep track of all the Web indexes and genealogy search engines to which you have submitted your new Web site. That way, if you update your site and make any major changes, or if you move your Web site to a new address, you can easily revisit those sites to change the description or the URL.

Surname Registry Sites

Some genealogy index sites are devoted to cataloging surnames found on personal home pages or within GEDCOM files found on personal sites. Most people who research their family history begin with a surname hunt. So keeping track of surnames found on specific Web sites makes a lot of sense in order to connect new genealogists with those who have been around long enough to have already published their research findings on a Web site.

You may find that some surname registries record your Web site several times, usually once for each of the surnames highlighted on your site. As you submit your URL to the registries, be sure to emphasize each surname that is most important to you and your research. And read all the instructions on the sites before you submit your URL to them for cataloging. Don't forget to make research notes of which sites you submit to so you can visit them again in the future. Here are a few you should try:

- Connect with Surnames
  www.connectwithsurnames.com

- *GENDEX*—WWW Genealogical Index
  www.gendex.com/gendex/

- Surname Resources at RootsWeb
  resources.rootsweb.com/surnames/

- Surname Springboard
  www.geocities.com/Heartland/2154/spring.htm

- SurnameWeb
  www.surnameweb.org

- Cyndi's List—General Surname Sites (links to more surname indexes)
  www.CyndisList.com/surn-gen.htm

Internet Search Engines

As we saw in Chapter 9, search engines use automated software to index the Internet by sending out "spiders" to crawl the Web and bring back information about Web sites. If you wait long enough, search engines will eventually find your site and index it for you. But why wait? With a simple form, you can submit your Web site to the indexes of your favorite search engines. By submitting your URL to the search engine, you help draw attention to your site sooner. The search engine adds your request to its list of sites to crawl. Most search engines make no guarantees about how soon your site will be indexed.

At many search engines, you can submit your Web site for free. The only expense is your own time and the energy it takes to visit each search engine and enter the information about your genealogy Web site. Some search engines have both free and fee-based submission services. By paying the fee, your site should appear more quickly within the search engine's index. There are also several fee-based link-submission services online. They offer you convenience because you submit your information to their service once and they do the rest of the work for you by submitting your site to numerous engines. But it's really not necessary to use such a service unless you want to avoid visiting individual search engine sites yourself. Overall, you will have great success submitting your URL to search engines yourself without paying any fees to the search engines or to other services.

Here are some search engines to which you can submit your Web site, without paying a fee:

- AlltheWeb.com
  addurl.alltheweb.com/add_url

- AltaVista
  addurl.altavista.com/

- Google
  www.google.com/addurl.html

- Yahoo!
  docs.yahoo.com/info/suggest/

As you submit your site to search engines, copy and paste from the same five pieces of information you prepared in the "Genealogy Web Indexes and Search Engines" section (pages 214–215).

Offline Announcements

After you have exhausted all online sources for promoting your Web site, it is time to turn to traditional, offline sources. Use the examples we drafted earlier for mailing lists and for newsletter editors to come up with a generic letter that you can send to genealogy magazines, family association newsletter editors, newspaper columnists, genealogical society editors, and other institutions that have genealogical publications. Your letter to them should provide the same information we've discussed above, along with your full mailing address. The following is a list of sources for finding offline publications and their editors:

- *Directory of Family Associations* by Elizabeth Petty Bentley and Deborah Ann Carl (Baltimore: Genealogical Publishing Company, 2001)

- Family History—Society Hall—Genealogical Society Directory
  www.familyhistory.com/societyhall

- Family Newsletter Registry and Surname Search
  familynewsletterregistry.homestead.com/index.html

- *The Genealogist's Address Book* by Elizabeth Petty Bentley (Baltimore: Genealogical Publishing Company, 1998)

- International Society of Family History Writers and Editors, Inc. (ISFHWE)
  www.rootsweb.com/~cgc/index.htm

- Cyndi's List—Magazines, Journals, Columns & Newsletters (locate more genealogy publications)
  www.CyndisList.com/magazine.htm

- Cyndi's List—Societies & Groups (locate more society newsletters)
  www.CyndisList.com/society.htm

Last, but Not Least: Stationery

Whatever you do, don't forget the obvious, ongoing opportunity to promote your genealogy Web site. Each day you generate e-mail messages or old-fashioned snail mail correspondence. Every piece of stationery you use, both electronic and pulp based, should have your name and contact information clearly printed in plain sight. Contact information includes your physical mailing address, as well as your e-mail address. *And be sure to include your Web site URL in all your correspondence.* Make it as easy as possible for those elusive cousins to track you down. By supplying them with the URL for your family history site, you guarantee that they can find you. You also give them the opportunity to see what you have accomplished in your research. By giving them something tangible to visit, read, and absorb, you might even inspire them to contact you and share information, memories, photos, or artifacts.

Your local office supply store has all sorts of paper products that you can buy to create custom stationery. A quick letterhead template created with your word-processing software ensures that your Web site URL is not left behind. You can also pick up blank business cards on which to print your name and address (physical, e-mail, and Web), as well as a short list of surnames in your research. Include your new genealogy "hobby cards" in each letter you send out, and keep a handy supply in your wallet for those trips to the library or your local Family History Center. You never know when you will make contact with someone whom you don't want to forget.

You can build your family history Web site, but it won't do you any good if people don't know about it and can't find it. Actively publicizing your new site is a sure way to get visitors to come see what you have done. Don't rely on word of mouth from cousin to cousin. Take time to announce to the world that your ancestors are on the Internet.

CHAPTER 13

Keep Your Web Site Alive and Kicking: Give It a Checkup

A BOOK IS A STATIC PUBLICATION. ONCE YOU WRITE IT AND IT IS published on paper, it stays that way forever. Not so with a Web site. Web sites are dynamic, living publications. Your Web site can change every day, in small ways or big. As time passes and you progress in your research of your family's history, you will update your site with new information and current data. Your genealogy Web site grows as your research project grows.

Why You Should Check and Update Your Site

The Web itself is a living and dynamic thing—it changes and evolves. As we saw in Chapter 10, one of a Webmaster's prime tasks is to maintain links. If you refer to other Web sites on your own site, you will need to check those references periodically to make sure that they are still valid. If you have links from your site to another, you will need to verify that the links still work. If a link doesn't work, you will have to track down a new URL in order to repair the broken link. If you are unsuccessful in finding a replacement URL, you should delete the broken link. If you want your site to be visited more than once by cousins and family members, you must change and improve your site every once in a while. Of course, the frequency with which you update depends on the time you have available and how much new or different material you have. Even something as simple as adding new photographs or scanned documents to your site, at least on the home page, encourages visitors to return to your site. It takes little time or energy to add one new photo each month. And that change alone can be enough to keep the site growing and bring back visitors.

An active Web site stays actively listed on search engines. If your Web site languishes, it eventually falls further down the ranks in search engine indexes. Some search engines have systems that rank placement of links within their databases. The ranking systems are different for each search engine, but in some cases, search engines rank a site's popularity by the number of relevant hits the site gets. Other search engines rank sites based on the number of links from other sites that point to that site. Either way, the ranking is based on how popular your site is and how often people refer to it. So keeping your site updated and active in the genealogical community online helps keep your site current in the search engine databases—and that brings new visitors.

Unnecessary Updates

You don't have to update your site or make changes to your Web pages if there is no reason to do so. If you have no new content or new purpose for your site, there's probably no reason to change your site. Some people like to change and redecorate their Web site as if they were rearranging furniture in their home. These types of changes tend to be merely cosmetic and not really functional. But decorative changes can create new interest in your site when you have nothing new to add to it. Before you redecorate, make sure that the changes you intend to make won't have a negative impact on the decisions you made earlier as you planned your site and made it accessible to everyone. Evaluate the reasons for making changes, and weigh the pros and cons. Will the changes enhance the site and make it easier to use? Or will the changes make the site more difficult to view, print, or navigate?

Create a Maintenance Routine

Once your site is online, determine how often you should update it. The time you spend on maintenance is up to you. It depends on how large your site is, how active you are in your genealogical research, and how much value you put in the usefulness of your site to others. Regular maintenance consists of these types of activities:

- Make backup copies of the files (Web pages, documents, graphics, photos, etc.) that make up your Web site. Back up your files monthly, quarterly, or after each major revision to a section or to the site as a whole.

- Archive copies of your site before making any changes. Archived copies can be saved for posterity and referenced should discrepancies appear during later research.

- Add new research material to your site: data, notes, photographs, digitized documents, etc.

- Edit material already on your site to incorporate any new breakthroughs in your research.

- Correct inaccurate data as you find it.

- Remove outdated material.

- Reevaluate the purpose, size, and scope of your site to determine whether you should change the original layout or concept you had for the site.

- Verify links and update any that are broken.

- Test navigational links and special features (plug-ins, forms, search boxes) unique to your site.

- Examine your home page and the rest of the site, looking at them as if for the first time.

- Promote your site on new mailing lists and other forums.

- Reintroduce your site in old venues.

- Submit your site to new search engines, or request old search engines to reindex your site to update the description and ranking.

Your Research Workbook

As you research your family's history, you generate a lot of paper—and that means a lot of filing. One way to keep track of everything you do in your research is to maintain a research workbook. You can create a paper workbook that travels with you to each library and courthouse as you research. Or a virtual workbook on your laptop computer to take with you as you research online and with electronic sources. Ideally, you can combine your offline research notes with your online research notes.

Your research workbook should be divided into sections, with one section for each surname or family you're researching. Publishing your family history Web site is part of your research activities. With the publication of your new site, you should create another section in your research workbook for notes about the site. There you can maintain a log with the following notes:

- An outline of the basic structure for your site that shows how many chapters or sections it contains and how many index pages it has (this helps you update the pages more easily)

- A timeline for the events in your Web site: planning, creation, updates, etc.

- A record of each time you back up and archive the site

- Search engines and link lists to which you have submitted your site

- Mailing lists and message boards on which you have advertised your site (name, date, and type of message)

- Messages and correspondence between you and visitors to your site

- Hard-copy printouts of the Web page source code, just in case electronic backup copies fail. This alternative backup is especially important for any specialty bits of code unique to your site or pages.

- A list of goals and aspirations you have for the site—a to-do list to which you can refer as you become more comfortable in your new role as a genealogical Webmaster

Leave Your Site Online!

One of the oddest occurrences I have witnessed on the Web has to do with site maintenance and upgrades. Some Webmasters take their entire Web site offline, leaving behind a message like "This site has been taken down for maintenance. New pages are coming soon." There is absolutely no need to take the site offline. It is quite easy to update a Web site behind the scenes, while the old version remains available to others on the Web. Visitors continue to use your site even while you change or update it. If you take your site offline, you give the impression that your site has no stability or that it has been taken offline permanently. When you update your site—whether you make slight changes or give it a complete overhaul—leave the old pages online until you are ready to launch the new version of your site.

Each time you do any work relating to your site, take a minute or two to update the notes in your research workbook. Keeping track of what you are doing as you do it saves you time and energy in the long run.

What's New

Many Webmasters have found that a great way to tell visitors about changes to their site is with a Web page dedicated to that purpose—a "What's New" page with a timeline of the changes, updates, and improvements you make to your site. For example, if you publish new information about one of your family lines, add a note to your What's New page indicating the date you updated the site, what the new information is, and where that information can be found on your site. Set up a link to the appropriate page so that visitors can go from your What's New page directly to the updated page. Figure 13.1 has an example of a What's New page from a genealogy site with frequent updates.

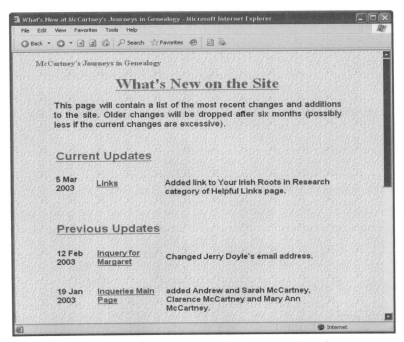

Figure 13.1 What's New at McCartney's Journeys in Genealogy (*www.geomacc.com/whats_new.html*). In this terrific example, George McCartney tells visitors what updates he has done on his site and includes links to those updates.

Annual Maintenance

Some maintenance activities and updates must be made at least annually. Whatever maintenance schedule you set up for yourself, at least once a year, be sure to make a few certain changes, such as updating your copyright statement and checking into software upgrades. These routine activities help keep your site current and on track.

Copyright

A basic copyright statement looks like this:

Copyright © 1996 Your Name Here. All rights reserved.

If your site never differs, the year in the copyright statement is always the same. But if you regularly change and update any of the pages on your site, the copyright statement should show a range of years from the first year it was published to the current year:

Copyright © 1996–2003 Your Name Here. All rights reserved.

Each year, consider what changes you have made to the site (you can use the notes in your research notebook), and then determine whether you should update your copyright statement. When you change the date, you can use your text editor's find-and-replace function to quickly update that field across all the pages on your Web site at once.

Review Policies for the Host Server

Your Web hosting service has an Acceptable Usage Policy (AUP)—the rules you must follow for your site to remain on its servers. When you first set up your account, you were notified about the AUP. Over time, your hosting service might change its policies. So at least once a year, review the latest AUP on the Web host's site to be sure your site doesn't violate any rules.

Software Upgrades

At least once a year, investigate possible software upgrades for programs you use in conjunction with your genealogy Web site. Upgrades may offer new features for your site or more flexibility for maintaining your site. Particularly, check for updates to your genealogy database software, GEDCOM-to-HTML conversion utilities, HTML editors, text-replacement editors, FTP software, Web browsers, and plug-ins.

Your genealogy software serves many purposes. You use it to keep track of all the people in your family history, and all the names, dates, places, and information about those people. From that program, you can generate a variety of reports, charts, and forms to help you research and to illustrate what you have learned to date. Another feature that most genealogy software programs now have is the ability to create genealogy Web pages from your family history database. In most programs, that feature is relatively new, so each updated version of that software is likely to improve that feature. Look into an upgrade to see whether you might gain more flexibility in your Web site by using a newer version to generate the Web pages.

Perhaps you used a GEDCOM-to-HTML conversion utility to create your Web pages. Revisit the Web site for the utility to see whether there's a new version available or an upgrade with bug fixes. Again, you may find new features or improved flexibility in an upgrade. As Web page standards rise and as GEDCOM conversion standards improve, the performance of those utilities will advance.

Software programs for HTML editors and text-replacement editors are updated frequently. Most of the updates tend to be patches and fixes for problems and bugs, but periodically larger improvements are made that will greatly improve your Web pages. Especially watch for upgrades that allow you to make mass-replacements to HTML code and text across numerous Web pages all at once.

Share New Things You Have Learned

Once you publish your site, you have more time to devote to your research. Your Web site becomes a tool you can use in your daily routine. Inevitably, as your family history research advances, new questions arise. Now you can use your site to broadcast those questions. We genealogists enjoy a good family history puzzle. One way to bring visitors back to your site is to post new requests for advice and guidance.

Advice works both ways. You, too, have expertise in certain areas that you can share with your visitors—you likely know about a type of record that you have used extensively in your own research. You can use your knowledge and experience to help others online. Write a set of instructions on how to obtain specific records or how to research in a specific locality. Post details and addresses for record repositories that you frequently use so that others can more easily find them.

Share your success stories, as well as your failures. Help others learn from your mistakes. For example, explain how you first learned the importance of taking only what you truly need to the library, rather than half your research filing cabinet. One way to bring visitors to your site is to provide them with just such helpful information. Each time you learn something new, share it with the world! Your visitors will learn by your example and through your generosity.

Reevaluate Your Research and the Purpose of Your Site

Genealogical research involves assessing data and interpreting information about your ancestors' lives. During the course of your family history project, you will evaluate and reevaluate bits and pieces of facts and records as you find them. The longer you research your ancestry, the more you realize that you are in a constant state of assessment. Just as you evaluate each piece of data, you should periodically evaluate your genealogical research project overall and the impact your Web site has had on that project. Consider these questions:

- Since you first published your Web site, have you had a chance to look through your research workbook and think about the various paths that each line of research follows?

- Does your site accurately reflect the research you have done?

- Does your site layout and presentation mimic the way you organize and process your research project?

- After your site has been online a while, and after you've had a chance to receive some feedback from visitors, are you able to view your research through fresh eyes?

- Are there any new revelations or ideas inspired by your site now that it is online?

Apply what you learn from publishing your site to your research methodology. Use your Web site as a research tool. Your site not only helps you connect with family members and other researchers, but it also helps you improve your communication and genealogical research skills.

After you create your site, don't just ignore it and let it languish. Your online family tree needs care and maintenance so that it continues to develop and flourish as a live, active, fundamental part of your everyday research activities.

Plant your family history online. You might be surprised to see what grows.

National Genealogical Society Standards and Guidelines

THE NATIONAL GENEALOGICAL SOCIETY HAS WRITTEN A SERIES OF genealogical standards and guidelines, designed to help you in your family history research. NGS developed these as a concise way to evaluate resources and skills, and to serve as a reminder of the importance of reliable methods of gathering information and sharing it with others.

All of the NGS Standards and Guidelines appear in this book. They also appear online at *www.ngsgenealogy.org/comstandards.htm.*

Standards for Sound Genealogical Research
Recommended by the National Genealogical Society

Remembering always that they are engaged in a quest for truth, family-history researchers consistently

- Record the source for each item of information they collect
- Test every hypothesis or theory against credible evidence, and reject those that are not supported by the evidence
- Seek original records, or reproduced images of them when there is reasonable assurance they have not been altered, as the basis for their research conclusions
- Use compilations, communications, and published works, whether paper or electronic, primarily for their value as guides to locating the original records or as contributions to the critical analysis of the evidence discussed in them
- State something as a fact only when it is supported by convincing evidence, and identify the evidence when communicating the fact to others
- Limit with words like "probable" or "possible" any statement that is based on less than convincing evidence, and state the reasons for concluding that it is probable or possible
- Avoid misleading other researchers by either intentionally or carelessly distributing or publishing inaccurate information
- State carefully and honestly the results of their own research, and acknowledge all use of other researchers' work
- Recognize the collegial nature of genealogical research by making their work available to others through publication, or by placing copies in appropriate libraries or repositories, and by welcoming critical comment
- Consider with open minds new evidence or the comments of others on their work and the conclusions they have reached

Guidelines for Using Records, Repositories, and Libraries
Recommended by the National Genealogical Society

Recognizing that how they use unique original records and fragile publications will affect other users, both current and future, family history researchers habitually

- Are courteous to research facility personnel and other researchers, and respect the staff's other daily tasks, not expecting the records custodian to listen to their family histories nor provide constant or immediate attention
- Dress appropriately, converse with others in a low voice, and supervise children appropriately
- Do their homework in advance, know what is available and what they need, and avoid ever asking for "everything" on their ancestors
- Use only designated workspace areas and equipment, like readers and computers intended for patron use; respect off-limits areas; and ask for assistance if needed
- Treat original records at all times with great respect and work with only a few records at a time, recognizing that they are irreplaceable and that each user must help preserve them for future use
- Treat books with care, never forcing their spines, and handle photographs properly, preferably wearing archival gloves
- Never mark, mutilate, rearrange, relocate, or remove from the repository any original, printed, microform, or electronic document or artifact
- Use only procedures prescribed by the repository for noting corrections to any errors or omissions found in published works, never marking the work itself
- Keep note-taking paper or other objects from covering records or books, and avoid placing any pressure upon them, particularly with a pencil or pen
- Use only the method specifically designated for identifying records for duplication, avoiding use of paper clips, adhesive notes, or other means not approved by the facility
- Return volumes and files only to locations designated for that purpose
- Before departure, thank the records custodians for their courtesy in making the materials available
- Follow the rules of the records repository without protest, even if they have changed since a previous visit or differ from those of another facility

Standards for Use of Technology in Genealogical Research
Recommended by the National Genealogical Society

Mindful that computers are tools, genealogists take full responsibility for their work, and therefore they

- Learn the capabilities and limits of their equipment and software, and use them only when they are the most appropriate tools for a purpose

- Do not accept uncritically the ability of software to format, number, import, modify, check, chart or report their data, and therefore carefully evaluate any resulting product

- Treat compiled information from online sources or digital databases in the same way as other published sources—useful primarily as a guide to locating original records, but not as evidence for a conclusion or assertion

- Accept digital images or enhancements of an original record as a satisfactory substitute for the original only when there is reasonable assurance that the image accurately reproduces the unaltered original

- Cite sources for data obtained online or from digital media with the same care that is appropriate for sources on paper and other traditional media, and enter data into a digital database only when its source can remain associated with it

- Always cite the sources for information or data posted online or sent to others, naming the author of a digital file as its immediate source, while crediting original sources cited within the file

- Preserve the integrity of their own databases by evaluating the reliability of downloaded data before incorporating it into their own files

- Provide, whenever they alter data received in digital form, a description of the change that will accompany the altered data whenever it is shared with others

- Actively oppose the proliferation of error, rumor, and fraud by personally verifying or correcting information, or noting it as unverified, before passing it on to others

- Treat people online as courteously and civilly as they would treat them face-to-face, not separated by networks and anonymity

- Accept that technology has not changed the principles of genealogical research, only some of the procedures

Guidelines for Genealogical Self-Improvement and Growth
Recommended by the National Genealogical Society

Faced with ever-growing expectations for genealogical accuracy and reliability, family historians concerned with improving their abilities will on a regular basis

- Study comprehensive texts and narrower-focus articles and recordings covering genealogical methods in general and the historical background and sources available for areas of particular research interest, or to which their research findings have led them

- Interact with other genealogists and historians in person or electronically, mentoring or learning as appropriate to their relative experience levels, and through the shared experience contributing to the genealogical growth of all concerned

- Subscribe to and read regularly at least two genealogical journals that list a number of contributing or consulting editors, or editorial board or committee members, and that require their authors to respond to a critical review of each article before it is published

- Participate in workshops, discussion groups, institutes, conferences and other structured learning opportunities whenever possible

- Recognize their limitations, undertaking research in new areas or using new technology only after they master any additional knowledge and skill needed and understand how to apply it to the new subject matter or technology

- Analyze critically at least quarterly the reported research findings of another family historian, for whatever lessons may be gleaned through the process

- Join and participate actively in genealogical societies covering countries, localities, and topics where they have research interests, as well as the localities where they reside, increasing the resources available both to themselves and to future researchers

- Review recently published basic texts to renew their understanding of genealogical fundamentals as currently expressed and applied

- Examine and revise their own earlier research in the light of what they have learned through self-improvement activities, as a means for applying their new-found knowledge and for improving the quality of their work-product

Glossary

THE TERMS BELOW ARE DEFINED IN RELATION TO GENEALOGY AND family history Web page creation. The definitions are neither all-encompassing nor definitive technical descriptions. For more complex and detailed definitions, see the following:

- NetLingo
  www.netlingo.com
- W3Schools.com Web Glossary
  www.w3schools.com/site/site_glossary.asp
- Whatis.com IT-Specific Encyclopedia
  whatis.techtarget.com/definitionsSearch/

Absolute link: Contains the entire URL for a Web page, including the *http://* protocol at the beginning. An absolute link always works as long as the URL is valid. See also Relative link.

Abstract or abstraction: A synopsis of names, dates, places, and other information taken from a genealogical record. For example, abstracts of wills are commonly used in genealogical research. See also Extract; Transcription.

Acceptable Usage Policy: See AUP.

Active Server Pages: See ASP.

Adobe Acrobat Reader: A free software program from Adobe Systems Incorporated that reads and displays PDF files. The Acrobat Reader acts as a plug-in with your Web browser software. When you click on a link to a .pdf file on the Internet, your Web browser launches the Acrobat program and opens the file. You can download a free copy of Acrobat at *www.adobe.com/products/acrobat/readstep2.html.* See also PDF; Plug-in(s).

Ahnentafel report: A German word meaning "ancestor table." An ahnentafel numbering system assigns a number to each ancestor in your database, beginning with the number 1 for you, 2 for your father, 3 for your mother, and so on for each generation thereafter. Many genealogy software programs generate ahnentafel reports that display information in a paragraph, which includes the names, dates, places, and notes for each person in your database.

Ancestor chart: Commonly known as a *pedigree chart;* a standard genealogical chart used to display the ancestry of one person, generation by generation. Most display four generations on one page (you, your parents, grandparents, and great-grandparents).

Archive: A permanent copy kept in storage. To archive your Web site is to make permanent copies of all the files and retain them as a record of your online publication. Archived copies are printed or kept on a floppy disk, a Zip disk, a CD-ROM, or other digital media.

ASCII: American Standard Code for Information Interchange; a document in plain text format that has no formatting—no bold, italics, centering, etc.—and no extraneous junk attached to the file. Web pages are written in HTML and saved as ASCII text files.

ASP: Active Server Pages; a script developed by Microsoft that generates HTML Web pages dynamically, as they are requested by a browser. ASP scripts implement ActiveX and Visual Basic programming. To use ASP technology, the Web server must be able to serve ASP executable scripts. See ASP tutorial at *www.w3schools.com/asp/.*

AUP: Acceptable Usage Policy; the rules and policies published on a Web hosting service that Webmasters must follow in order to keep their Web site on that server. For example, see RootsWeb's AUP at *www.rootsweb.com/rootsweb/aup.html.*

Back up: To copy all files (Web pages and graphics) and keep them safe in case of emergency. Each new backup copy replaces the last. If necessary, you can use your backup to recreate part or all of your site. Backups can be printed or kept on a floppy disk, a Zip disk, a CD-ROM, or other digital media.

Banner ads: Advertisements that often appear on Web sites hosted by free Web hosting services. Banners are commonly 468 x 60 pixels and appear at the top of the page.

Bookmarks: A Web browser feature that helps you keep track of Web sites you have visited. You can create a bookmark when you visit a site that interests you and to which you intend to return. Bookmarks are also known as *favorites*.

Broken link: A link that no longer works due to a change in the URL, directory structure, or file name. A Webmaster can use link-checking software to locate and repair broken links. See also Link(s); Linkrot.

Browser: See Web browser.

Byte: A unit of measure for the capacity of computer files that is roughly equal to one character. See also KB (kilobyte); MB (megabyte).

Cascading Style Sheet (.css): Used to apply a specific style and set of formatting options to a Web site. With your text editor or Web design software program, you can create one set of color and style instructions for your Web site and store that information in a Cascading Style Sheet. Each Web page on your site then has code that refers to that one style sheet. See *www.w3.org/Style/CSS/*.

CD-ROM: Compact Disc-Read Only Memory; an optical storage disc used for large-capacity computer files such as software programs.

CGI: Common Gateway Interface Programs; an automated script that runs on a Web Server. CGI scripts can automate certain functions on a Web site, such as mail forms. CGI scripts are generally stored in a directory named /cgi-bin.

Chat room: An online meeting place for people to "chat" via text messages. Genealogy chat rooms have scheduled times and dates for chats on specific topics. See Cyndi's List—Chat & IRC at *www.CyndisList.com/chat.htm*.

Citation: A specifically formatted and arranged record of the source of data used in genealogical research to reach a specific conclusion. See Cyndi's List—Citing Sources at *www.CyndisList.com/citing.htm*. See also Source.

Copyright: An author's right to reproduce the work, to permit copies to be made by others, to prepare derivative works, and to display the work publicly. See "10 Big Myths about Copyright Explained" at *www.templetons.com/brad/copymyths.html*; the U.S. Copyright Office at *lcweb.loc.gov/copyright/*.

Cyndi's List: Cyndi's List of Genealogy Sites on the Internet *(www.CyndisList.com);* a categorized and cross-referenced list of links to genealogical resources on the Internet. If the Internet is a library, Cyndi's List is the card catalog to its genealogy collection. You can browse the site with several different indexes or use the site's search engines by keyword. There are categories for specific localities, ethnic groups, religions, record types, and other genealogical topics.

Database: A compilation of information. An electronic database is made up of fields for specific bits of data; the fields can be organized, sorted, and searched. Genealogy software programs help you maintain a database of information about your ancestors, with fields for names, dates, places, sources, and other information.

Descendant report: Displays the descendants of one individual in a simple, outline format. Genealogy software programs produce descendant reports, and many of them generate similar reports for Web pages. A descendant report makes a good visual aid on the index page for the section on your Web site devoted to a specific ancestor.

Digitize: To convert something to a digital format with your computer. Digitized documents or photographs are computer images created using a scanner. Digitized images can be edited, altered, and enhanced in order to incorporate them into your Web site.

Directory: A designated file storage area on a Web server or file server. In a Web site's URL, directory names follow the slash (/) after the domain name. The terms *directory* and *folder* are used interchangeably.

Domain name: The main portion of a URL that denotes the host or the owner of the Web site. A domain name is registered for a small yearly fee so that only one Web site can use it. In a URL, the domain name usually follows the protocol *(http://www).*

Download: The process of transferring files from a server on the Internet to your own computer. You use FTP (File Transfer Protocol) software to download your Web pages and other files from the host server. See also FTP; Upload.

DSL: Digital Subscriber Line; a high-speed Internet connection that uses your existing phone line (but not the analog, voice part of the line). With DSL, you have a constant Internet connection that doesn't interrupt your use of the phone.

Editor: A software program used to create and edit a file. Use a text editor for plain text files, an HTML editor to create Web pages, and a graphics editor, image editor, or photo editor for scanned photographs and images.

E-mail: Electronic mail.

eXtensible Markup Language: See XML.

Extract or extraction: A portion of information, generally the highlights, copied from a source and inserted—exactly as written—into another document. Genealogists who incorporate names, dates, and places from a record into their research notes are creating one type of extraction. There are forms for specific types of extractions (such as census records) that genealogists frequently use. See also Abstract; Transcription.

E-zine: Electronic magazine; sometimes a magazine on a Web site, but most often a newsletter delivered by e-mail. Genealogy e-zines include *Eastman's Online Genealogy Newsletter* and *UpFront with NGS*.

FAQ: Frequently Asked Questions (pronounced *fack*); a list of answers to common questions that are asked about a Web site or a service. Your ISP's FAQ should help answer all the basic questions you have about hosting your Web site on their servers.

Family group sheets: Standard genealogical forms used to maintain data for each family in your research. You create a family group sheet for each couple in your family; your genealogy software program generates family group sheets from the information you put in the database. Some genealogy software programs generate Web pages in this format.

Family history: The study of a person's lineage—names, dates, and places. The terms *family history* and *genealogy* are often used interchangeably, but a family history tends to be more personal, going beyond the facts to incorporate pictures, stories, and multimedia into the research process, thus adding flesh to the bones of ancestors.

Family History Center (FHC): Branches of the Family History Library in Salt Lake City, Utah. The more than thirty-seven hundred Family History Centers around the world are all run by volunteers. Everyone is welcome to use the resources of the Family History Library through their local FHC. To find a Family History Center near you, see *www.familysearch.org/Eng/Library/FHC/frameset_fhc.asp*.

Family History Library (FHL): The largest genealogical library in the world, founded in Salt Lake City, Utah, in 1894 by the Church of Jesus Christ of Latter-day Saints. Everyone may use the FHL, including its searchable online catalog at *www.familysearch.org/Eng/Library/FHLC/frameset_fhlc.asp*.

FamilySearch: The genealogy Web site from the Church of Jesus Christ of Latter-day Saints. FamilySearch hosts the comprehensive catalog to the holdings of the Family History Library in Salt Lake City, Utah—the world's largest family history library. FamilySearch also hosts the IGI, Ancestral File, Pedigree Resource File, the 1880 U.S. census, and much more. See *www.familysearch.org*.

Favorites: See Bookmarks.

FHC: See Family History Center.

FHL: See Family History Library.

File: Each document, e-mail, Web page, graphic, and scanned image stored on a computer. Each file has a unique name that ends with a specific extension denoting the type of software used to open and operate it.

File Transfer Protocol: See FTP.

Folder: A designated file storage area on a computer's hard drive or other computer media (floppy disk, Zip disk, CD-ROM). Though the terms *folder* and *directory* are used interchangeably, a *folder* usually refers to file storage on a personal computer, while a *directory* generally denotes a file storage structure on a Web site or file server.

Freeware: A type of software program that can be downloaded and used without paying a fee. Fellow genealogists and computer enthusiasts develop freeware software programs—often to perform a specific function they cannot find elsewhere. Several freeware programs generate specific reports or genealogy Web pages from GEDCOM files. Find freeware programs online at *www.tucows.com* and *www.download.com*. See also Shareware.

Frequently Asked Questions: See FAQ.

FTP: File Transfer Protocol; used to upload files to or download files from a server. You use FTP client software to move copies of your Web pages, scanned photos, and other graphics from your computer to the Web host for your site. And you use FTP software to access the files on the Web server and to delete files, rename files, or create directories on the server in which to store the files you are uploading.

GEDCOM: GEnealogical Data COMmunications; a generic, database format designed to allow users to share their family history database files between differing genealogy software programs. See Cyndi's List—GEDCOM at *www.CyndisList.com/gedcom.htm*.

Genealogy: The study of one's ancestry—the process of researching names, dates, and places in records. See also Family history.

GIF: Graphics Interchange Format (.gif); a common image format for Web graphics, particularly buttons, bars, and banners.

Google: One of the most popular search engines on the Internet, located at *www.google.com*. Webmasters can submit their links to the search engine at *www.google.com/addurl.html*. Google offers a free search engine form to use on your site so that visitors can search your site by keyword or surname.

Graphic: An image displayed on a Web site. The two most common Web graphic formats are JPG and GIF. JPG files work best for photographs and scanned images. GIF files work best as buttons, bars, and other line art.

Hex or hexadecimal: A numeric value used to specify colors for fonts and backgrounds on a Web page.

Home page: The front page and main entry point of a Web site, and often its index. The file name for the home page almost always defaults to index.htm or index.html.

Host: The service or computer that provides Web server space for your Web site. See also Web server; Web host.

HTML: Hypertext Markup Language; the programming language of the Web. Using an HTML editor or a text editor, the Webmaster writes the HTML code for a Web page. When opened in a Web browser, the browser interprets the HTML code and displays the results as a finished Web page.

HTML editor: A software program used to create and edit Web pages. Most HTML editors are similar to word-processing software, with toolbars for formatting and layout options. See also WYSIWYG.

Hypertext link: See Link(s).

IE: See Internet Explorer.

Hypertext Markup Language: See HTML.

Index page: The default starting Web page in each directory on a Web site. Most often the file name defaults to "index.html" or "index.htm." See Home page.

Internet: The vast global network of computer networks. Also known as the *Information Superhighway*, the Internet comprises several components, including the Web, e-mail, and FTP.

Internet Explorer (IE): Microsoft's Web browser program, which is resident on most computers. See *www.microsoft.com/windows/ie/default.asp.*

Internet Protocol Address: See IP address.

Internet Service Provider: See ISP.

IP address: Internet Protocol address; a unique number assigned to every computer on the Internet. Each Web server has a static IP address associated with a domain name. Web surfers have either a static or dynamic IP address assigned to their connection by their ISP. See also ISP.

ISP: Internet Service Provider; the company that provides your connection to the Internet.

Java: A programming language for writing interactive programs used on Web sites. Java applets can be added to a Web site for animated features, chat rooms, password protection for certain pages or areas on a site, and so on. See *java.sun.com/applets/.*

JavaScript: Interactive browser code that can be copied and pasted into your HTML, adding such dynamic features to your site as forms, navigation, buttons, and toolbars. See *javascript.com, javascript.internet.com.*

JPG or JPEG (.jpg): A common image format for Web graphics. JPG files are compressed so they are suitable for large images such as photographs and digitized documents.

KB: Kilobyte; a unit of measure for the capacity of computer files that is equal to one thousand bytes. See also Byte; MB.

Keyword(s): The words or terms you use to perform searches in databases and search engines. Webmasters determine a list of relevant keywords that apply to the content of their Web site. The keywords can be used in Meta tags, link descriptions, and in the advertisements Webmasters use to promote their Web site.

Kilobyte: See KB.

Linkrot: Broken links on a Web site. A site may suffer from linkrot if links aren't verified and updated regularly, a task that can be performed with link-checking software, which helps you locate and repair broken links. See also Broken links; Link(s).

Link(s): A connection from one Web page to another or from one section of a Web page to another section on that page. A text link is usually underlined and a separate color from the rest of the text on the page. It is made up of HTML code, a URL, a title, and descriptive text for the link. Graphics can also have links.

Listowner: A volunteer who creates a mailing list for a specific topic, then maintains subscribers' daily use of the list. Listowners determine the need for the list and set the rules and guidelines for it. They are sometimes known as *list administrators*.

Mailing lists: Free interactive discussion forums by e-mail. Mailing lists are run by automated software programs that distribute messages to each subscriber. Many mailing list discussions are archived and can be searched. RootsWeb hosts most of the more than twenty-eight thousand mailing lists for genealogy. See Genealogy Resources on the Internet—Mailing Lists at *www.rootsweb.com/~jfuller/gen_mail.html*.

MB: Megabyte; a unit of measure for the capacity of computer files that is equal to one million bytes or one thousand kilobytes (KB). See also Byte; KB.

Megabyte: See MB.

Message boards: A Web site feature that hosts interactive discussions, browsable and searchable by topic or keyword. The messages form a thread of ongoing conversation.

Meta tags: Special HTML tags used to provide information about a Web page. Meta tags are located at the top of a Web page within the <HEAD> tag. Some search engines use information from Meta tags when building their databases. See Chapter 8 for examples.

Multimedia: Interactive features on a Web site, such as animation, audio, and video.

National Genealogical Society (NGS): Founded in 1903, NGS is the premier national membership society for individuals, families, genealogical societies, family associations, libraries, and other groups that share a common interest in the field of genealogy. Contact the society for more information at *www.ngsgenealogy.org*.

Nav bar or navigation bar: A toolbar, either a graphic or a line of text, that supplies links and navigational direction to visitors using a Web site.

Navigation: The functionality of a Web site; the links, buttons, and toolbars that enable visitors to easily find their way from page to page and section to section.

Netiquette: The etiquette of the Net—a set of commonly understood rules and guidelines by which we should all behave when online. For example, using all UPPERCASE letters in an e-mail message is considered to be shouting and therefore rude. See also Netiquette Home Page at *www.fau.edu/netiquette/netiquette.html*.

Netscape: A brand of Web browser. See *channels.netscape.com/ns/browsers/default.jsp*.

Newbie: A person who is new to the Internet, to computers, or to family history. Veterans should keep in mind that a newbie to the Internet isn't always a newbie to genealogy, and vice versa.

NGS: See National Genealogical Society.

PDF (.pdf): Portable Document Format; PDF files are created by and viewed with Adobe Acrobat software. A PDF file is a standardized file that can be generated from documents created by all types of software programs, across all platforms. This makes it simple to share and transfer files on the Internet. PDF format also allows the author to control the final output and appearance of a file. See also Adobe Acrobat Reader.

Pedigree chart: See Ancestor chart.

Pixels: Small units on your computer's monitor that use light and color to display an image on the screen. A monitor's screen resolution set at 800 x 600 means there are 800 pixels across and 600 pixels top to bottom. The more pixels, the higher the resolution and the sharper the image.

Plug-in(s): Specialty software programs that run certain small applications within a Web browser. Webmasters who incorporate special features (such as music, video, and interactive functions) into their Web pages often rely on plug-ins to perform those functions. Visitors must already have or must download the plug-in software program to make the features work while they visit the site. Commonly used plug-ins are found at these sites:

- Adobe Acrobat Reader
  www.adobe.com/products/acrobat/readstep2.html

- Macromedia Flash Player
  www.macromedia.com/software/flashplayer/

- QuickTime
  www.apple.com/quicktime/download/

- RealPlayer
  www.real.com/realone/index.html

- Shockwave by Macromedia
  www.macromedia.com/software/shockwaveplayer/

Pop-unders: Small windows containing advertisements that appear under the current Web browser window. Visitors are forced to view the ad and close the pop-under before they can close their browser entirely at the end of a session. See also Pop-ups.

Pop-ups: Small windows, generally for advertisements, which float over the top of a Web page. Visitors to a Web site are forced to view the ad and close the pop-up before they can see a Web page. See also Pop-unders.

Privacy: The right of individuals to keep personal information to themselves, a particularly hot topic on the Internet. Genealogy Web sites generally include personal information such as names, birth dates and places, spouse's information, children's information, and a mother's maiden name. Family history Webmasters should not publish any information about any living person on their genealogy Web site. For more on privacy, see Chapter 5.

Reciprocal links: Links that Webmasters exchange with each other so that each site can be accessed from the other site.

Relative link: A link with only part of a URL—a file name and maybe a directory name. A relative link works only if the file referenced in the link is located in the same directory, on the same server as the Web page that contains the relative link. See Chapter 10; see also Absolute link.

Resolution: The detail, quality, and clarity of an image as denoted in pixels. The more pixels a graphic uses, the higher the resolution—thus the crisper and more detailed the image. But the more pixels, the larger the file size for the graphic. See also Screen resolution.

RGB: Red-Green-Blue; the colors combined to create colors on computers.

Rich Text Format: See RTF.

Robot: Automated software programs used by search engines to travel the Internet and gather information from Web sites. The information is added to a central database for the search engine to use. Also known as a *bot*. See also Search engines; Spiders.

Rollover: A feature that makes a link perform a specific trick—pop out, change color, change formatting—when visitors move their mouse over it. The feature is created with JavaScript or inserted into a Cascading Style Sheet. Also called a *mouseover*.

RootsWeb: The home to free, genealogical research services such as personal genealogy Web sites, mailing lists, and message boards. Originally known as the RootsWeb Genealogical Data Cooperative, it was founded on the principle of volunteerism and sharing. RootsWeb is the home to the oldest genealogy mailing list, Roots-L, as well as many major online genealogy projects. See *www.rootsweb.com*.

RTF (.rtf): Rich Text Format; a basic text document that includes formatting. RTF is a common, generic alternative to use when exchanging word-processing documents with others across different platforms and different software programs. For example, if you want to share your PC word-processing document with a Mac user, or vice versa, converting it to RTF first ensures it can be opened and read by the recipient.

Scanner: Peripheral hardware connected to your computer. Scanners make digitized copies of photographs, genealogical records, and other family history mementos and heirlooms. Most scanners come with software that helps you edit and enhance the digitized images.

Screen resolution: The settings used to determine the quality of the display for an image on a computer monitor. Screen resolution is measured in pixels. See also Resolution.

Search engine: A Web site service used to perform keyword searches on the Internet. Services such as Google *(www.google.com)* send out spiders or robots to gather data from Web sites. That information is added to their database, which users can then search by keyword.

Server: See Web server.

Shareware: A software program that can be downloaded and used for a small registration fee. Fellow genealogists and computer enthusiasts develop shareware programs. Find shareware online at *www.tucows.com* and *www.download.com*. See also Freeware.

Society: An organization or association of members with a common interest and purpose. Genealogical societies, often nonprofit groups run by volunteers, promote the study of genealogy and the preservation of records.

Source (as in genealogical source citation): Any means by which you obtain genealogical information about your ancestors. A source might be a person, Bible, book, microfilm, database, vital record, census record, or anything else that records the events in a person's life. Genealogists cite sources to record where they found particular data used in their research; others can then go to the source to verify that information and confirm how a specific conclusion was reached. See also Citation.

Source code: The programming code used to create software programs. HTML source code, as referenced in a Web browser, is the HTML language for a Web page.

Spider: Automated software programs used by search engines to travel the Internet and gather information from Web sites. See also Robots; Search engines.

Style sheet: See Cascading Style Sheet.

Surf: To click on link after link, traveling from site to site on the Internet.

Surname: A name shared by a family. In Western cultures, the surname is generally a person's last name.

Tag: In HTML, the piece of programming code that defines how text, graphics, and other objects behave when displayed in a Web page. Each item has an opening tag and a closing tag: <B>text here appears boldfaced</B>. Some tags apply certain attributes to the behavior of the text; for example, in the <FONT> tag you can specify a font name and color: <FONT Name="Arial" Color="#000000">.

Text editor: A software program used to create and edit text files. In Windows, Notepad and WordPad are two common text editors used for plain text. Word processors are also text editors, with many extra features. You can use a text editor to write HTML in Web pages.

Thread: On a mailing list or message board, a series of messages posted for a single conversation. The original message, followed by each successive reply, including replies to some of the replies, all compose a thread.

Thumbnail: A smaller version of a Web graphic. Webmasters use thumbnails on Web pages so that the graphics load quickly. Visitors can click on a thumbnail, which is linked to a larger copy of the same graphic.

TIFF (.tif): Tagged Image File Format; a graphic file format most often used for high-resolution art and photographs.

Transcription: A *complete, exact copy* of the text in a genealogical record or document. When you transcribe a document, you copy everything in the document exactly as you find it, including errors, misspelled words, odd characters, and other items that you might normally feel inclined to "correct." A transcription should appear exactly the same as the original. See also Abstract; Extract.

Upload: The process of transferring files from your computer to a server on the Internet. You use FTP (File Transfer Protocol) software to upload your Web pages and other files to the host server. See also Download; FTP.

URL: Uniform Resource Locator; the address for a Web site or a file stored on a Web server.

Visited link: A link to a site the visitor has already been to. In order to indicate that the link has already been visited, the visited link should be a different color than the other links and text, as designated in the <BODY> tag. See Chapter 7.

Web: World Wide Web; the part of the Internet composed of documents written in the HTML language. The pages are connected by hypertext links. The series of interconnecting links across each of the pages creates a Web of documents, strung together by common topic or interest.

Web browser: A software program that displays Web pages. The browser reads and interprets the HTML language in a Web page and displays the results. The most common Web browsers are Microsoft Internet Explorer (IE) and Netscape Navigator. America Online users have a version of IE that is built into the AOL program. See Microsoft at *www.microsoft.com/windows/ie/default.asp;* Netscape at *channels.netscape.com/ns/browsers/default.jsp.*

Web host or Web hosting service: The service that provides Web server space for your Web site. See also Host; Web server.

Webmaster: The person who maintains a Web site. A Webmaster is responsible for generating the Web pages, uploading them to a Web server, and managing the Web site and all its functions. The Webmaster may or may not be the author of the material published on the Web site. If you publish a Web site yourself, you are the author and the Webmaster. If you hire someone else to create your Web pages, that person is the Webmaster for your site and you are the author because you supply the content for the site.

Web page: A plain text document written in HTML code. Each Web page on the Internet has its own, unique address (URL) that begins with the *http://* protocol. Web browsers read HTML and display Web pages.

Web server: A computer that hosts the files that make up Web sites. Someone who clicks on a link or types a URL into a Web browser is requesting to see a particular Web page. The Web server then "serves up" that page.

Web site: A collection of information usually composed of one or more Web pages. Web sites are usually maintained by one Webmaster or designed to deal with one topic.

Whois: A service used to determine who administers a domain name on the Internet. You can use the information you find in a Whois database to contact a domain name registrant or the technical contact for a specific domain name. See *www.networksolutions.com/en_US/whois/index.jhtml* and *www.uwhois.com.*

World Wide Web: See Web.

WYSIWYG: What You See Is What You Get (pronounced *whiz-ee-wig*); rather than writing the HTML code and then viewing the results in your Web browser, a WYSIWYG HTML editor lets you see the Web page display as you create it. WYSIWYG editors are good choices for new Webmasters.

XML: eXtensible Markup Language; the next generation of programming developed to follow HTML. XML allows Webmasters to create their own customized tags. See also Tags; *www.w3.org/XML/*.

Yahoo!: A popular Web search engine *(www.yahoo.com)* with a categorized link index and other Internet services, including domain name registration and mailing lists.

Zip disk: A high-capacity disk used to store data. Zip disks are read with Zip drives, a product of Iomega. A Zip disk easily stores backup copies of entire Web sites. See *www.iomega.com*.

Index

National
Genealogical
Society

. . . . the national society for generations past, present, and future

What Is the National Genealogical Society?

FOUNDED IN 1903, THE NATIONAL GENEALOGICAL SOCIETY IS A dynamic and growing association of individuals and other groups from all over the country—and the world—that share a love of genealogy. Whether you're a beginner, a professional, or somewhere in between, NGS can assist you in your research into the past.

The United States is a rich melting pot of ethnic diversity that includes countless personal histories just waiting to be discovered. NGS can be your portal to this pursuit with its premier annual conference and its ever-growing selection of how-to materials, books and publications, educational offerings, and member services.

NGS has something for everyone—we invite you to join us. Your membership in NGS will help you gain more enjoyment from your hobby or professional pursuits, and will place you within a long-established group of genealogists that came together a hundred years ago to promote excellence in genealogy.

To learn more about the society, visit us online at *www.ngsgenealogy.org*.

Other Books
in the NGS Series

Genealogy 101
How to Trace Your Family's History and Heritage
Barbara Renick

A guide to basic principles of family research, this is a book the uninitiated can understand and the experienced will appreciate.

$19.99
ISBN 1-4016-0019-0

Online Roots
How to Discover Your Family's History and Heritage with the Power of the Internet
Pamela Boyer Porter, CGRS, CGL
Amy Johnson Crow, CG

A practical guide to making your online search more effective and creative. Includes how to know if what you find is accurate and the best way to make full use of the Internet.

$19.99
ISBN 1-4016-0021-2

A Family Affair
How to Plan and Direct the Best Family Reunion Ever
Sandra MacLean Clunies, CG

Family reunions can create memories and celebrate a common heritage. Here's how to do it with a minimum of fuss and maximum of good times.

$19.99
ISBN 1-4016-0020-4

The Organized Family Historian
How to File, Manage, and Protect Your Genealogical Research and Heirlooms
Ann Carter Fleming, CG, CGL

A guide to the best way to file, label, and catalog the wide variety of material and information related to a family history.

$19.99
ISBN 1-4016-0129-4
Coming Soon

Unlocking Your Genetic History
A Step-by-Step Guide to Discovering Your Family's Medical and Genetic Heritage
Thomas H. Shawker, M.D.

An informative guide to completing a meaningful family health and genetic history. Includes the basics of genetics for the non-scientist.

$19.99
ISBN 1-4016-0144-8
Coming Soon